Marcus Andrew Hislop Clarke

Stories of Australia in the Early Days

Marcus Andrew Hislop Clarke

**Stories of Australia in the Early Days**

ISBN/EAN: 9783337005146

Printed in Europe, USA, Canada, Australia, Japan

Cover: Foto ©Andreas Hilbeck / pixelio.de

More available books at **www.hansebooks.com**

STORIES OF AUSTRALIA

THIRD EDITION.

*BY THE SAME AUTHOR.*

## "HEAVY ODDS."

In crown 8vo, cloth gilt, 6s.

---

### A FEW PRESS OPINIONS.

**Scotsman.**

"From the powerful pen of the Australian novelist, Marcus Clarke, comes another work of distinguished merit. Depicted with literary art that never fails to command admiration. The book is intensely interesting."

**Glasgow Herald.**

"A vigorous piece of writing, showing the author's power in handling strong situations and delineating sombre figures. Not the least able, and certainly the most agreeable, pages are those wherein two horse-races are described, with the enthusiastic animation which seems to be excited in all Australians by the turf."

**Literary World.**

"'Heavy Odds' is a capital story."

**Sheffield Independent.**

"The book is intensely interesting from start to finish."

**Sheffield Daily Telegraph.**

"'Heavy Odds' shows Mr. Marcus Clarke at his best."

**Dundee Courier.**

"An exceedingly readable story, smartly written, and with a good deal of originality about it."

**Manchester Courier.**

"The tale is a good one, and exciting to a degree. The 'odds' are not 'heavy' against the book being a great success."

**Lady's Pictorial.**

"If there is nothing very original in 'Heavy Odds,' there is enough of dash and startling incident in the story to attract readers who love a novel which keeps up the interest from start to finish."

**Dundee Advertiser.**

"'Heavy Odds' is a powerfully written story."

---

LONDON: HUTCHINSON & CO., 34, PATERNOSTER ROW.

# STORIES OF AUSTRALIA

IN THE

# EARLY DAYS

BY

## MARCUS CLARKE

*Author of "For the Term of his Natural Life," "Heavy Odds," etc.*

LONDON:

HUTCHINSON & CO.,

34, PATERNOSTER ROW.

1897.

# CONTENTS.

|  | PAGE |
|---|---|
| BIOGRAPHY . . . . . . . . . | i |
| A MONOGRAPH . . . . . . . . | xix |
| WILLIAM DAMPIER: NAVIGATOR . . . | 1 |
| ABEL JANSEN TASMAN: EXPLORER . . . . | 6 |
| THE SETTLEMENT OF PORT JACKSON (N.S.W.) . . | 12 |
| THE SCOTCH MARTYR CONVICTS . . . . | 18 |
| BARRINGTON: PRINCE OF PICKPOCKETS . . . . | 24 |
| GOVERNOR BLIGH AND THE "RUM" REVOLT . . . | 31 |
| GOVERNOR RALPH DARLING'S "IRON COLLAR" . . | 4 |
| A LEAF FROM AN OLD NEWSPAPER . . . . | 5 |
| A SETTLER'S LIFE IN CONVICT DAYS . . . | 58 |
| JORGENSON: KING OF ADVENTURERS . . . | 71 |
| MICHAEL HOWE, THE DEMON BUSHRANGER . . | 102 |
| THE SEIZURE OF THE "CYPRUS" . . . | 112 |
| THE LAST OF MACQUARIE HARBOUR . . | 118 |
| BUCKLEY, THE ESCAPED CONVICT . . . . | 131 |
| THE SOUTH AUSTRALIAN LAND BUBBLE . . . | 141 |
| THE FIRST QUEENSLAND EXPLORER . . . . | 149 |
| AN AUSTRALIAN CRUSOE . . . . . . | 158 |
| THE IRISH PATRIOT-CONVICT'S ESCAPE . . . | 172 |
| THE "NELSON" GOLD ROBBERY . . . | 184 |
| PORT ARTHUR VISITED, 1870 . . . . | 190 |

# BIOGRAPHY.

MARCUS ANDREW HISLOP CLARKE was born at Kensington—the Old Court suburb of London—on the 24th April, 1846. His father, William Hislop Clarke, a barrister-at-law, was recognised as a man of ability, both professionally and as a *littérateur*, albeit eccentric to a degree. Of his mother little is known beyond that she was a beautiful woman, of whom her husband was so devotedly fond that when her death occurred some months after the birth of the subject of this biography, he isolated himself from the world, living afterwards the life of a recluse, holding of the world an opinion of cynical contempt. Besides his father, there were among other brothers of his two whose names belong to the history of the Australian colonies; the one is that of James Langton Clarke, once a County Court Judge in Victoria, and the other, Andrew Clarke, Governor of Western Australia, who died and was buried at Perth in 1849. The latter was the father of General Sir Andrew Clarke, K.C.M.G., formerly Minister of Public Works in India, and Governor of the Straits Settlements. To the colonists of Victoria he will be better known as Captain Clarke, the first Surveyor-General of the colony, the author of the Existing Municipal Act, and one of the few lucky drawers of a questionable pension from this colony.

The late Marcus Clarke claimed a distinguished genealogy for his family, which, though hailing as regards his immediate ancestors from the Green Isle, were English, having only betaken themselves to Ireland in the Cromwellian period. And among his papers were found the following notes referring to this matter:—

> In 1612 William Clarke was made a burgess of Mountjoie, Co. Tyrone, and in 1658 Thurloe wrote to Henry Cromwell, desiring him to give Colonel Clarke land in Ireland for pay.

With an inherited delicate constitution, and without the love-watching care of a mother, or the attention of sisters, he passed his childhood. And that the absence of this supervision and guidance was felt by him in after years, we have but to read this pathetic passage from a sketch of his:—

> To most men the golden time comes when the cares of a mother or the attention of sister aid to shield the young and eager soul from the blighting influences of wordly debaucheries. Truly fortunate is he among us who can look back on a youth spent in the innocent enjoyments of the country, or who possesses a mind moulded in its adolescence by the gentle fingers of well-mannered and pious women.

When considered old enough to leave home the boy was sent to the private school of Dr. Dyne in Highgate, another suburb of London, hallowed by having been at one time associated with such illustrious names in literature as Coleridge, Charles Lamb, Keats, and De Quincey. Here he obtained whatever scholastic lore he possessed, and was, according to the opinion of a schoolfellow, known as a humorously eccentric boy, with a most tenacious memory and an insatiable desire to read everything he could lay hands on. Owing to his physical inability to indulge in the usual boyish sports, he was in the habit of wandering about in search of knowledge wherever it was to be gleaned, and not infrequently this restless curiosity, which remained with him to the last, led him into quarters which it had been better for his yet unformed mind he had never entered. Here especially was felt the absence of a mother's guidance, which was unfortunately replaced by the carelessness of an indulgent father. Of his schooldays little is known, save what can be gathered from a note-book kept by him at that period; and even in this the information is but fragmentary. According to this book he seems to have had only two friends with whom he was upon terms of great intimacy. They were brothers, Cyril and Gerald Hopkins, who appear, judging from jottings and sketches of theirs in his scrap album, to have been talented beyond the average schoolboy. Among the jottings to be found in this school record is one bearing the initials G. H., and referring to one "Marcus Scrivener" as a "Kaleidoscopic, Parti-colored, Harlequinesque Thaumatropic" being. Another item which may not be uninteresting to read, as indicating the turn for humorous satire, which, even at so early a period of his life the author had begun to develop, is an epitaph written on himself, and runs thus:—

*Hic Jacet*
*MARCUS CLERICUS,*
*Qui non malus, 'Coonius*
*Consideretus fuit*
*Sed amor bibendi*
*Combinatus cum pecuniæ deficione*
*Mentem ejus oppugnabat—*
*Mortuus est*
*Et nihil ad vitam restorare*
*Posset.*

To his schoolmaster, the Reverend Doctor Dyne, the following dedication to a novel *(Chatteris)* commenced by his former pupil shortly after his arrival in Australia was written. From this it is apparent that the master had not failed to recognise the talents of his gifted pupil, nor yet be blind to his weaknesses. It reads—

To
T. B. DYNE, D.D.,
Head Master of Chomley School, Highgate.
This Work
Is respectfully dedicated in memory of the advice so tenderly
given, the good wishes so often expressed, and the
success so confidently predicted for the author.

But whatever good influences might have been at work during his residence at Dr. Dyne's school, they were, unfortunately for their subject, more than counter-balanced by others of a very dissimilar character met with by him at his father's house. It seems scarcely credible that so young a boy was allowed to grow up without any restraining influences except those of a foolishly-indulgent father, as we are led to believe was the case from the following extract, which the writer knows was intended by the subject of the biography as a reference to his boyish days when away from school. Doubtless the picture is somewhat over-coloured, but substantially it is true:—

My first intimation into the business of "living" took place under these auspices. The only son of a rich widower, who lived, under sorrow, but for the gratification of a literary and political ambition, I was thrown when still a boy into the society of men twice my age, and was tolerated as a clever impertinent in all those witty and wicked circles in which virtuous women are conspicuous by their absence. I was suffered at sixteen to ape the vices of sixty. You can guess the result of such a training. The admirer of men whose successes in love and play were the theme of common talk for six months; the worshipper of artists, whose genius was to revolutionise Europe, only they died of late hours and tobacco; the pet of women whose daring beauty made their names famous for three years. I discovered at twenty years of age that the pleasurable path I had trodden so gaily led to a hospital or a debtors' prison, that love meant money, friendship an endorsement on a bill, and that the rigid exercise of a profound and calculating selfishness alone rendered tolerable a life at once deceitful and barren. In this view of the world I was supported by those middle-aged Mephistopheles (survivors of the storms which had wrecked so many Argosies), those cynical, well-bred worshippers of self, who realise in the nineteenth century that notion of the Devil which was invented by early Christians. With these good gentlemen I lived, emulating their cynicism, rivalling their sarcasm, and neutralising the superiority which their existence gave them by the exercise of that potentiality for present enjoyment, which is the privilege of youth.

Again, in another sketch he wrote, referring to this period of his life:—

Let me take an instant to explain how it came about that a pupil of the Rev. Gammons, up in town for his holidays, should have owned such an acquaintance. My holidays, passed in my father's widowed house, were enlivened by the coming and going of my cousin Tom from Woolwich, of cousin Dick from Sandhurst, of cousin Harry from Aldershot. With Tom, Dick, and Harry came a host of friends—for as long as he was not disturbed, the head of the house rather liked to see his rooms occupied by the relatives of people with whom he was intimate, and a succession of young men of the Cingbars, Ringwood, and Algernon Deuceacre sort made my home a temporary roosting-place. I cannot explain how such a curious *ménage* came to be instituted, for, indeed, I do not know myself, but such was the fact, and "little Master," instead of being trained in the way he should morally go, became the impertinent companion of some very wild-bloods indeed. "I took Horace to the opera last night, sir," or "I am going to show Horatius Cocles the wonders of Cremorne this evening," would be all that Tom, or Dick, or Harry, would deign to observe, and my father would but lift his eyebrows in indifferent deprecation. So, a wild-eyed and eager school-boy, I strayed into Bohemia, and acquired in that strange land an assurance and experience ill suited to my age and temperament. Remembering the wicked, good-hearted inhabitants of that curious country, I have often wondered since "what they thought of it," and have interpreted, perhaps not unjustly, many of the homely tenderness which seemed to me be a so strangely out of place and time.

In the midst of this peculiar and doubtful state of existence for a youth his father died suddenly, leaving his affairs in an unsatisfactory state. This unexpected change brought matters to a climax, and at seventeen years of age Marcus Clarke found that instead of inheriting, as expected, a considerable sum of money, he was successor to only a few hundred pounds, the net result of the realisation of his late father's estate. With this it was arranged by his guardian relatives that he should seek a fresh field for his future career, and accordingly in 1864 he was shipped off to Melbourne by Green's well-known old liner, "The Wellesley," consigned to his uncle, Judge Clarke, above mentioned. Referring to this episode of his life, he has written in the following sarcastic and injured strain :—

My father died suddenly in London, and to the astonishment of the world left me nothing. His expenditure had been large, but as he left no debts, his income must have been proportionate to his expenditure. The source of this income, however, it was impossible to discover. An examination of his bankers' book showed only that large sums (always in notes or gold) had been lodged and drawn out, but no record of speculations or investments could be found among his papers. My relatives stared, shook their heads, and insulted me with their pity. The sale of furniture, books, plate, and horses, brought enough to pay the necessary funeral expenses and leave me heir to some £800. My friends of the smoking-room and of the supper-table philosophised on Monday, cashed my I O U's on Tuesday, were satirical on Wednesday, and cut me on Thursday. My relatives said "Something must be done," and invited me to stop at their houses until that vague substantiality should be realised, and offers of employment were generously made; but to all proposals I replied with sudden disdain, and, desirous only of avoiding those who had known me in my prosperity, I avowed my resolution of going to Australia.

After one of those lengthy voyages for which the good old ship " The Wellesley" was renowned, the youth of bright fancies and disappointed fortune set foot in Melbourne ; and, after the manner of most "new chums" with some cash at command and no direct restraining power at hand, he set himself readily to work, fathoming the social and other depths of his new home. The natural consequence of this was that one who had prematurely seen so much "life" in London, soon made his way into quarters not highly calculated to improve his morals or check his extravagantly-formed habits. In other words, he began his Bohemian career in Australia with a zest not altogether surprising in one who had been negligently allowed to drift into London Bohemianism. And naturally, a youth with such exceptional powers of quaint humour, playful satire, and *bonhomie* became a universal favourite wherever he went, much, unfortunately, to his own future detriment. But, in due course, a change came of necessity o'er this Bohemian dream, when the ready cash was no longer procurable without work. It was then, through the influence of his uncle the Judge, that the impecunious youth was relegated to a high stool in the Bank of Australasia. As might have been expected of one who spent most of his time in drawing caricatures and writing satirical verses and sketches he was a *lusus naturæ* to the authorities of the bank, and this is not to be wondered at when one learns that his mode of adding up long columns of figures was by guesswork, to wit, he would run his eye over the pence column, making a guess at the aggregate amount, and so on with the shillings and pounds columns.

After a patient trial of some months it was considered, in the interests of all concerned, that he should seek his livelihood at a more congenial avocation, and thereupon he left the bank. But here must be mentioned the manner in which the severance took place, as being characteristic of him. Clarke applied for a short leave of absence. The letter containing this request not having been immediately answered he sought the presence of the manager for an explanation, when the following scene took place :—Clarke : "I have come to ask, sir, whether you received my application for a few weeks' leave of absence." The Manager : "I have." Clarke : "Will you grant it to me, sir?" The Manager : "Certainly, and a longer leave, if you desire it." Clarke: "I feel very much obliged. How long may I extend it to, sir?" The Manager: "Indefinitely, if you do not object!" Clarke: "Oh! I perceive, sir; you consider it best for us to part; and perhaps it is best so, sir?" And Mr. Clarke ceased to be a banker. Here it will not be inopportune to quote from an article on "Business Men," written by him subsequently, referring to this banking experience:—

> It has always been my misfortune through life not to be a Business Man. When I went into a bank—The Polynesian, Antarctic and Torrid Zone—I suffered. I was correspondence clerk, and got through my work with immense rapidity. The other clerks used to stare when they saw me strolling homewards punctually at four. I felt quite proud of my accomplishments. But in less than no time a change took place. Letters came down from up-country branches. "I have received cheques to the amount of £1 1s. 6d., of two of which *no* mention is made in your letter of advice." "Sir! how is it that my note of hand for £97 4s. 1¾d., to meet which I forwarded Messrs. Blowhard and Co.'s acceptance, has been dishonoured by your branch at Warrnambool?" "*Private.*—Dear Cashup: Is your correspondent a hopeless idiot? I can't make head or tail of his letter of advice. As far as I can make out, he seems to have sent out the remittances to the wrong places.—Yours, T. TOTTLE." I am afraid that it was all true. The manager sent for me, said that he loved me as his own brother, and that I wore the neatest waistcoats he had ever seen, but that my genius was evidently fettered in a bank. Here was a quarter's salary in advance, he had no fault, quite the reverse; but, but, well—in short—I was not a Business Man.

In addition to this the following remark, bearing on the same subject, written in one of the "Noah's Ark" papers in the *Australasian*, may also here be quoted:

> A Man of Business, said Marston, oracularly, is one who becomes possessed of other people's money without bringing himself under the power of the law.

Finding commercial pursuits were not his *forte*, the youthful ex-banker bethought him of turning his attention to the free and out-door existence of a bushman. Accordingly he, shortly after leaving the bank in 1865, obtained, through his uncle, Judge Clarke, a "billet" on Swinton Station, near Glenorchy, belonging to Mr. John Holt, and in which the Judge had a pecuniary interest. Here he remained for some two years mastering the mysteries of bushmanship in the manner described in the sketch in this volume, styled "Learning Colonial Experience." It was during his sojourn in this wild and mountainous region that our author imbibed that love for the weird, lonely Australian Bush, which he so graphically and pathetically describes in so many of his tales—notably in "Pretty Dick," a perfect bush idyll to those who know the full meaning of the words Australian Bush. Although sent up to learn the ways and means of working a station, it is to be feared that the results of the lessons were not over fruitful. Indeed, beyond roving about the unfrequented portions of the run in meditation wrapped, pipe in mouth and book in pocket, in case of thoughts becoming wearisome, the sucking squatter did little else till night set in, and then the change of programme simply meant his retiring after the evening meal to his own room and spending the time well into midnight writing or reading. From one who was a companion of his on the station at the time, viz., the popular sportsman—genial, generous—Donald Wallace, I have learned that though Clarke wrote almost every night he kept the product of his labour to himself. But we now know that the work of his pen appeared in several sketches in the *Australian Magazine*, then published by Mr. W. H. Williams. These were written under the *nom de plume* of Marcus Scrivener. It was while residing in this district that he took stock of the characters which he subsequently utilised in all his tales relating to bush life. For instance, "Bullocktown," is well known to be Glenorchy, the post-town of the Swinton Station, and all the characters in it are recognisable as life portraits presented with that peculiar glamor which his genius cast over all his literary work. And to one of the characters in it—Rapersole—the then local postmaster, Mr. J. Wallace, I am under an obligation for supplying me with some incidents in our author's bush career. According to Mr. Wallace young Clarke was a great favourite with everybody, and was the life and soul of local entertainments such as concerts, balls, &c., in which he took part with great zest. He was also at that time a regular attendant at church, and a frequent visitor to the local State-school, in which he evinced a lively interest, giving prizes to the boys. He was, moreover, an omnivorous reader, getting all the best English magazines and endless French novels from Melbourne regularly. But whatever progress he may have been making in his literary pursuits, it was found by Mr. Holt that as a "hand" on the station he was not of countless price. Indeed, it was discovered after he had been there some months, that not only did the gifted youth pay little heed to his unintellectual work, but that he had to a great extent imbued others engaged on the station, with such a love for reading—more particularly the novels of Honoré Balzac—that the routine duty of their daily existence became so irksome that they sought consolation by taking shelter from the noonday sun under some umbrageous gum-tree, listening to their instructor as he translated some of the delicate passages from the works of the Prince of French novelists.

Accordingly it was mutually agreed by the employer and employé that the best course to pursue under the circumstances was to part company. But, fortunately for the literary bushman, it was just at this time, when he had tried two modes of making a living and had hopelessly failed in both, that a person appeared on the scene who was destined to direct his brilliant talents to their proper groove. There came as a visitor to Mr. Holt, in the beginning of 1867, Dr. Robert Lewins. As Dr. Lewins had no small share in shaping the after career of Marcus Clarke, it behoves me to briefly refer here to him and his theories. Dr. Lewins, who had been staff-surgeon-major to General Chute during the New Zealand war, had shortly before this arrived in Melbourne with the British troops, *en route* to England; and, being a friend of Mr. Holt's, went on a visit to him to Ledcourt, on which station Clarke was then employed. Learning while there of the peculiar youth whom Mr. Holt had as assistant, Dr. Lewins, who was like most thinking men of his class, always on the look-out for discoveries, whether human or otherwise, sought an introduction to the boy, whom practical Mr. Holt considered a "ne'er do weel." And no sooner was the introduction brought about than the learned medico discovered that, buried within view of the Victorian Grampians, lay hidden an intellectual gem of great worth. Rapidly a mutual feeling of admiration and regard sprang up between the young literary enthusiast of twenty and the learned medico of sixty—an attachment which lasted through life. The *savant* admired the rare talents of his *protegé* with the love of a father; while the fanciful boy looked up to the learned man who had discerned his abilities, and placed him on the road to that goal for which he was destined. But the influence of the elder on the younger man did not cease here, as without doubt the former converted the latter to his views regarding existence. What these views were the Doctor explained in more than one pamphlet addressed to eminent men in England and Europe. As regards his pet theory, which he affirmed he had proved beyond doubt by experiments, extending over forty years, in all parts of the world, it may be, for the curious, briefly explained in his own words, as follows:—

"1. That there is no distinct vital principle apart from ordinary inorganic matter or force,

"2. That oxygen is capable of assuming an imponderable form, and that it is identical with the Cosmic '*primum mobile*,' the basis of light, heat, chemical affinity, attraction, and electric force.

"3. That the theory of materialism is, in fact, the only tenable theory."

The result of this tuition as regards Clarke was a remarkably able article on "Positivism," which he wrote some months afterwards, and which, I believe, saw light in one of the Liberal English reviews. But I am forestalling the order of the biography. Having satisfied himself upon the merits of the newly-found intellect, the doctor, on his return to Melbourne, told the proprietor of the *Argus*, with whom he was acquainted, of his discovery, advising him to secure the unknown genius for his journal, and so, in the course of a few weeks after meeting Dr. Lewins, Marcus Clarke appeared in Melbourne, and in February, 1867, became a member of the literary staff of the *Argus*. After an initiation into the mysteries of a newspaper office the young journalist was allotted the task of theatrical reporter, which routine drudgery he performed satisfactorily till one night he took upon himself to criticise an entertainment, which, unfortunately, through the indisposition of the chief performer, did not come off. This carelessness on the part of the imaginative critic led to his withdrawal from the *Argus* reporting staff, but his relations with that paper and the *Australasian* were, however, continued as a contributor. It was during this period that Marcus Clarke contributed to the *Australasian* the two masterly reviews on Doré and Balzac, published in these pages, besides writing weekly for the same journal those sparkling and humorous papers, "The Peripatetic Philosopher," which brought his name prominently before the public and placed him at once in the front rank of Australian journalists—and here it may be mentioned that the letter "Q.," under which he wrote the weekly contributions, was the stock brand of the station on which he had attempted to learn "colonial experience." Apart, however, from his contributions to the *Australasian*, he supplied special articles to the *Argus*, and acted as the theatrical critic of that paper for some time, during which he wrote some admirable critiques on the late Walter Montgomery's performances—critiques which gained for him the admiration and regard of that talented actor, though unhappily they fell out afterwards for some foolish reason or another.

But the active brain of the sparkling *littérateur* was not satisfied with journalistic work merely. With the pecuniary assistance of a friend and admirer, the late Mr. Drummond, police-magistrate—whose death shortly afterwards by poison received from one of the snakes kept by the snake-exhibitor Shires, whom he held to be an impostor as regarded his antidote, caused so much excitement—he purchased from Mr. Williams the *Australian Magazine*, the journal in which had appeared his earliest literary attempts. The name of this he altered to the *Colonial Monthly*; and with praiseworthy enthusiasm set about encouraging Australian literary talent by gathering around him as contributors all the best local literary ability available. But, despite his laudable efforts to create an Australian literature, racy of the soil, he was doomed to disappointment and loss. The primary cause of this unfortunate result may be ascribed to the sneers which any attempt made by an Australian received at the hands of a few self-sufficient, narrow-minded individuals, who, sad to say, had the ear of the then reading public, because they unfortunately happened to be in a position to dictate on literary matters.

It was in the *Colonial Monthly* that Clarke's first novel, *Long Odds*, appeared in serial form. Of this, however, he only wrote a few of the first chapters, as shortly after its commencement he met with a serious accident through his horse throwing him and fracturing his skull—an accident from the effects of which he never totally recovered.

Some months prior to this mishap—about May, 1868—Clarke, in conjunction with some dozen literary friends, started a modest club for men known in the fields of Literature, Art, and Science—THE YORICK. This has developed in the course of the past fifteen years into one in which the three elements predominating originally are lost in the multifarious folds of "Professionalism."

The Yorick Club was the outcome of the literary and Bohemian—analogous terms in those days—spirits who used then to assemble nightly at the Café of the Theatre Royal to discuss coffee and intellectual subjects. These gatherings grew so large in the course of time that it was found necessary, in order to keep the communion up, to secure accommodation where the flow of genius, if nothing else, might have full play without interruption and intrusion from those deemed outside the particular and shining pale. Accordingly a room was rented and furnished in Bohemian fashion, with some cane chairs, a deal table, a cocoa-nut matting and spittoons. In this the first meeting was held in order to baptise the club. The meeting in question debated, with the assistance of sundry pewters and pipes—not empty, gentle reader—the subject warmly from the first proposition made by Clarke, that the club should be called "Golgotha," or the place of skulls, to the last, "alas, poor Yorick!" This brief name was accepted as appropriate, and the somewhat excited company adjourned to a Saturday night's supper at a jovial Eating-House, too well known to fame. The first office-bearers of the club were:—*Secretary*, Marcus Clarke; *Treasurer*, R. F. Kane; *Librarian*, J. E. Neild; *Committee*, J. Blackburn, G. C. Levey, A. Semple, A. Telo, J. Towers. The first published list of members gives a total of sixty-four, but Time has made many changes in that list, and Death has been busy too. Of the sixty-four original members there have passed away the following well-known intellectuals:—B. C. Aspinall, Marcus Clarke, Lindsay Gordon, Henry Kendall, T. Drummond, J. C. Patterson, Jardine Smith, A. Telo, Father Bleardale, etc.

It was at the "Yorick" that Marcus Clarke first met one of whose abilities he entertained a very high opinion, and towards whose eccentric and mournful genius he was drawn by a feeling of sympathetic affection, namely, Adam Lindsay Gordon, poet, and the once king of gentleman Jocks. Nothing could have shown more assuredly the deep feeling and regard felt by Marcus Clarke for Lindsay Gordon than the pathetic preface he wrote for the posthumous edition of the poet's works (an extract from which preface is given in this volume under the title of "The Australian Bush") when the poet himself put an end to his life, to the horror of the community, which did not learn till after the heartbroken poet's death that it was only the want of the wherewith to live upon which drove one of the brightest geniuses Australia has seen into a suicide's grave. To those who knew Gordon and Clarke intimately, the keen sympathy of genius existing between them was easily understood, for there was, despite many outward differences of manner, a wonderful similarity in their natures. Both were morbidly sensitive; both broodingly pathetic; both sarcastically humorous; both socially reckless; both literary Bohemians of the purest water—sons of genius and children of impulse. That the deep feeling for the dead poet and friend lasted till death with Marcus Clarke was evidenced by his frequently repeating when in dejected spirits those pathetically regretful lines of the "Sick Stockrider"—

> I have had my share of pastime and I've done my share of toil,
> And life is short—the longest life a span;
> I care not now to tarry for the corn or for the oil,
> Or for the wine that maketh glad the heart of man.
> For goods undone and gifts misspent and resolutions vain
> 'Tis somewhat late to trouble. This I know—
> I should live the same life over if I had to live again;
> And the chances are I go where most men go.

And to see him seated at the piano humming these lines to his own accompaniment, while the tears kept rolling down his cheeks, was proof enough that the tender chords of a beloved memory were being struck, and that the living son of genius mourned for his dead brother as only genius can mourn.

Turning to a more lively memento of Lindsay Gordon, characteristic of him when the spirit of fun possessed him, the following note, written to Clarke and kept by him sacredly, will interest his many admirers:—

Yorick Club.

Dear Clarke,- Scott's Hotel, not later than 9.30 sharp. Moore will be there. Riddock and Lyon, Baker and the Powers, beside us; so if 'the Old One' were to cast a net—eh?—Yours,

A. LINDSAY GORDON.

It was shortly after Gordon's untimely and sad death that Clarke became acquainted with another erratic though differently constituted son of genius—Henry Kendall, the foremost of Australian-born poets. Kendall met with warm sympathy from the friend of Gordon, and, moreover, with a helping hand in the hard life-struggle—which the poet feelingly referred to in the following memorial verses written on the death of his friend and benefactor:—

> The night wind sobs on cliffs austere,
>   Where gleams by fits the wintry star;
> And in the wild dumb woods I hear
>   A moaning harbour bar.
>
> The branch and leaf are very still;
>   But now the great grave dark has grown,
> The torrent in the harsh sea-hill
>   Sends forth a deeper tone.
>
> Here sitting by a dying flame
>   I cannot choose but think in grief
> Of Harpur, whose unhappy name
>   Is as an autumn leaf.
>
> And domed by purer breadths of blue,
>   Afar from folds of forest dark,
> I see the eyes that once I knew—
>   The eyes of Marcus Clarke.
>
> Their clear, bright beauty shines apace;
>   But sunny dreams in shadow end.
> The sods have hid the faded face
>   Of my heroic friend.
>
> He sleeps where winds of evening pass—
>   Where water songs are soft and low,
> Upon his grave the tender grass
>   Has not had time to grow.

> Few knew the cross he had to bear
> And moan beneath from day to day.
> His were the bitter hours that wear
> The human heart away.
>
> The laurels in the pit were won ;
> He had to take the lot austere
> That ever seemed to wait upon
> The man of letters here.
>
> He toiled for love, unwatched, unseen,
> And fought his troubles hand by hand ;
> Till, like a friend of gentle mien,
> Death took him by the hand.
>
> He rests in peace. No grasping thief
> Of hope and health can steal away
> The beauty of the flower and leaf
> Upon his tomb to-day.
>
> So let him sleep, whose life was hard !
> And may they place beyond the wave
> This tender rose of my regard
> Upon his tranquil grave.

The idiosyncrasies of the two men were in many respects widely dissimilar—Clarke's belonging to the polished school of the Old World while Kendall's were akin to those of his own native land, in the New World, but the acquaintanceship ripened into mutual admiration and friendship ; and together they worked on *Humbug*, the brilliant weekly comic journal, started about this time by Clarson, Massina & Co., under the editorship of Clarke. Probably one factor which exercised an influence over Clarke in the interests of Kendall was the poem written to Lindsay Gordon's memory by Kendall, of which the following few lines may here be given :—

> The bard, the scholar, and the man who lived
> That frank, that open-hearted life which keeps
> The splendid fire of English chivalry
> From dying out ; the one who never wronged
> Fellowman ; the faithful friend who judged
> The many, anxious to be loved of him,
> By what he saw, and not by what he heard,
> As lesser spirits do ; the brave, great soul
> That never told a lie, or turned aside
> To fly from danger ; he, I say, was one
> Of that bright company this sin-stained world
> Can ill afford to loose.

During this period, 1868-69, Clarke was a regular contributor to the *Argus* and *Australasian*, writing leaders for the former journal, and, besides the "Peripatetic Philosopher" papers for the latter, a series of remarkably able sketches on "Lower Bohemia." These articles, as their name implies, were descriptive of the life then existing in the lowest social grades of Melbourne, composed to a great extent of broken-down men of a once higher position in life, drawn hither by the gold discovery. They made a great impression upon the public, being full of brilliantly realistic writing, reminding one greatly of Balzac's ruthless style of exposing without squeamishness the social cancers to be found among the vagrant section of a community. Apart from his connection with the two journals named, the prolific and sparkling journalist contributed at this time to *Punch* some of the best trifles in verse and prose that ever adorned its pages. This connection, however, he severed about the middle of 1869, on undertaking the editorship of *Humbug*, a remarkably clever publication. In *Humbug* appeared, perhaps, the best fugitive work Marcus Clarke ever threw off. Besides his own racy pen, those of such well-known writers as Dr. Neild, Mr. Charles Bright, Mr. A. L. Windsor and Henry Kendall were busy on the pages of the new spirited, satirical organ, which was ably illustrated by Mr. Cousins. Notwithstanding, however, all this array of talent the venture was not financially a success, as at that time the taste for journalistic literature was very much more limited than now, and a writer, however gifted, had then a poor chance of earning a livelihood by the efforts of his pen.

## BIOGRAPHY. ix.

While thus rapidly rising in the rank of Australia's *littérateurs*, Clarke was unfortunately induced, by the foolish advice of friends, who felt flattered by his company, to live at a rate far exceeding his income, naturally becoming involved in debt. From this there was no recourse but to borrow, and so the presence of the usurer was sought. Thus commenced that course of life which, after a few years of ceaseless worry, brought, long ere his time, the brilliant man of genius, with the brightest of prospects before him, to the grave broken-hearted. Surely those who led him into the extravagances, men his seniors in years and experience, must bear their share of responsibility for the dark end to so bright a beginning. And yet some of these were his bitterest enemies afterwards.

Undeterred, however, by the pecuniary difficulties in which he found himself, he, with characteristic thoughtlessness, plunged into matrimony by espousing Miss Marian Dunn, the actress-daughter of genial John Dunn, Prince of Comedians. This young lady was at the time of her engagement to Clarke playing with great success a series of characters with the late Walter Montgomery, who entertained so high an opinion of her histrionic abilities, as to urge her to visit England and America with him. But the little lady preferred to remain in Australia as the wife of the rising *littérateur*, and so they were married on the 22nd of July, 1869, the only witnesses of the marriage being the bride's parents and the best man, the late Mr. B. F. Kane, Secretary of the Education Department. And the strangest—but characteristic of him—part of the ceremony was that the bridegroom, after the connubial knot was tied, left his bride in charge of her parents, while he went in search of lodgings wherein to take his "better half."

Having settled down as a Benedict, so far as it was possible for him to do so, our author, doubtless inspired by the society he had married into, set himself to work for the first time as a playwright, the result being the production of a drama styled *Foul Play*, a dramatisation of Charles Reade's and Dion Boucicault's novel of that name. It met with but partial success. But not discouraged by this comparative failure, the newly-fledged dramatist wrote, or rather adapted from other sources, for the Christmas season of 1870 at the Theatre Royal, a clever burlesque on the old nursery story of *Goody Two Shoes*, which met with considerable success both from the Press and the public. But even in this, his almost initial piece, he betrayed that weakness, theatrically speaking, which, more or less, marred all his dramatic efforts, namely, writing above the intelligence of the average audience.

Soon after this overwork had told its tale upon the restless brain, and the doctors ordered change of air to the more salubrious climate of Tasmania. But as funds were, as usual with him, decidedly low, how was the change to be effected? Eureka! He would ask the publishers of the now defunct *Humbug* to bring out a tale of his in their *Australian Journal*. The tale should be full of thrilling incidents relating to the old convict days in Tasmania. Brimming over with the idea he sought the presence of the publishers in question—Clarson, Massina & Co.—and made his suggestions. The offer was at once accepted, and the needy writer received the necessary aid to take him over to Van Diemen's Land, in order to improve his health and enable him to pore over prison records. Thus was the now deservedly celebrated novel, *His Natural Life*, initiated. But as to how it was completed is another matter. Let the unfortunate publisher testify his experience. And in such manner was produced *His Natural Life*. But the reader must remember that the work, as now published by Messrs. Bentley in London, is very different, as regards the construction and ending, to that which appeared in serial form in the *Australian Journal*.

As without doubt this is the best and most sustained effort of Marcus Clarke's genius, and the one upon which will chiefly rest his fame in literature, it is only right to publish here some extracts from the various reviews written of the novel in English, American and German papers.

*The Daily Telegraph*, London :—"And who," some thousands of readers may ask, "is Mr. Marcus Clarke? Until a recent period we should have confessed the very haziest knowledge of Mr. Marcus Clarke's existence, save that in the columns of Melbourne newspapers his name has appeared. Mr. Marcus Clarke has hardly entered into the ken of perhaps more than a hundred persons in England; but, having read the forcible and impressive novel entitled *His Natural Life*, we have not only come to an acquaintance as admiring as it is sudden with the author's name, but esteem it by no means a venturesome or hazardous act to predict for it a fame as great as that achieved by any living novelist. Indeed this wonderful narrative, which, despite the thrilling incident, bears on every page the honest impress of unexaggerated truth, has the material of a whole circulating library of tragic romance within itself. The only fault is the over-abundance which necessitates hurry in its disposal. But if Mr. Clarke's future has been embarrassed in some measure by its own riches, the author may well be satisfied with the result, for he has furnished readers in the old and new countries with matter for grave and earnest reflection; he has re-opened a discussion that has too soon been abandoned to torpor, and he has, in short, rendered better service than the State of Letters is wont to receive at the hands of a mere novel writer.

We have by no means over-praised this novel. The temptation to run into superlatives is great, and it has been resisted here for the one reason, if for no other, that, highly meritorious as Mr. Marcus Clarke's first English publication seems in our eyes, we are yet of belief, after its perusal, that he is destined to give the world yet greater and more effective because more concentrated work."

*Boston Gazette*, America:—"One of the most powerfully written and most absorbingly interesting novels that has lately attracted our notice is *His Natural Life*, by Marcus Clarke. It is a story dealing with convict life in Australia, and has been written 'for a purpose.' The plot is constructed with remarkable skill, and in the depicting of character the author manifests a talent we have rarely seen surpassed in any modern writer of fiction. A similar high degree of praise may be awarded him for his description of scenery. The book is intensely dramatic both in subject and treatment, but it is quite free from 'sensationalism' in the objectionable sense of the word. The style is healthy, manly and vigorous, and shows a surprising facility in word-painting. Mr. Clarke professes to have drawn his characters, localities and incidents directly from nature, and his work bears internal evidence that he has. It is the most stirring story of its class that has appeared since Victor Hugo's *Les Misérables*, of which it has all the fire and artistic feeling, minus the affectation. This novel cannot fail to make its mark."

*The Spectator*, London:—"It is something to write a book so powerful, especially as all the power is directed to the noblest end."

*Saturday Review*, London:—"There is undeniable strength in what Mr. Clarke has written."

*Morning Post*, London: "This novel appals while it fascinates, by reason of the terrible reality which marks the individual characters living and breathing in it. The tragic power of its situations, the knowledge of the sombre life which the author shows so vividly in the able handling of its subject, the pathos which here and there crops up like an oasis in a sandy desert, lead the reader from the beaten track of fiction."

*The Graphic*, London:—"It is, of course, possible that Mr. Marcus Clarke may turn out to be a man of one book, and out of his element in any atmosphere but that of convict and penal settlements. He shows, however, too much knowledge of human nature generally to make us think this at all likely, and if so, he must be hailed as a valuable recruit to the ranks of novelists of the day."

*Vanity Fair*, London:—"There is an immensity of power in this most extraordinary book."

*The World*, London:—"Few persons will read his remarkable descriptions of convict life and antipodean scenery without recognising an author of commanding originality and strength."

*The Reform*, Hamburg (translated from the German.)—"This novel treats of a terrible subject. The life of the prisoners in Van Diemen's land is set before us in a panorama painted by a master hand. Ladies of a sentimental turn had better abstain from reading this story, unless they choose to risk a nervous fever. The romance is full of power. The writer illuminates the lowest depths of human nature in a manner which holds us spell-bound, despite ourselves. Marcus Clarke is a master of psychology, and his descriptions of nature are as effective as his style is pure."

And from no less a giant in literature than Oliver Wendell Holmes, of Boston, America, the following complimentary letter was received by Clarke in acknowledgment of a copy of the novel sent to the author of the *Autocrat of the Breakfast Table*:—"The pictures of life under the dreadful conditions to which the convicts were submitted are very painful, no doubt, but we cannot question the fact that they were only copied from realities as bad as their darkest shadows. The only experiences at all resembling these horrors which our people have had were the cruelties to which our prisoners were subjected in some of the southern pens for human creatures during the late war. I do not think they were driven to cannibalism, but the most shocking stories were told of the condition to which they were reduced by want of food and crowding together. There are some Robinson Crusoe touches in your story, which add greatly to its interest, and I should think that the colonists, and thousands at home in the mother country, would find it full of attraction in spite of its painful revelations. This work cannot fail to draw attention, and make your name widely known and appreciated as an author throughout the world."

Besides contributing this historical romance to the columns of the *Australian Journal* Clarke was busy writing in the *Australasian* those sketches of the early days of Australia, which were afterwards published in book form under the title of *Old Tales of a Young Country*. These sketches, like his great novel, though highly interesting as historical records of the colonies, were for the most part worked up from governmental pamphlets and old journals. But in the casting they were stamped by the genius of the master-hand, which could appropriate and improve upon the appropriation as only men of original *calibre* are able to do. In the meantime the "Peripatetic Philosopher" ceased to adorn the pages of the *Australasian* with his caustic and eccentric dissertations, because, through the influence of one of the noblest patrons of letters in Victoria—the late Sir Redmond Barry—the Philosopher had been found a congenial post as Secretary to the Trustees of the Public Library, of whom Sir Redmond himself was the respected President. This appointment was made in June, 1870, and from that time Clarke ceased to be connected with the staff of any journal, though remaining a brilliant and valued contributor all his life to newspapers, magazines, reviews, &c., instead of, unfortunately, concentrating his exceptional powers on the production of works of a class with *His Natural Life*. Among other articles contributed by him about this time were the "Buncle Letters," which appeared in the *Argus* and attracted much attention, being running comments of a satirically humorous character, on the social and political events of the day, supposed to be written by one brother resident in town to his less sophisticated brother in the country. In the same journal, Clarke wrote a descriptive sketch of the mining mania which had seized upon Sandhurst at the time; and for piquancy the sketch was among his best in descriptive journalism. At this period, also, he once more tried his hand at the drama, and adapted for John Dunn, his father-in-law, Molière's celebrated comedy, *Le Bourgeois Gentilhomme*, into English, under the title of *Peacock's Feathers*, which was produced with great success at the Theatre Royal.

Mention has been made of the interest Sir Redmond Barry evinced in the rising *littérateur*, whom he took under his parental wing when obtaining for him the post in the Public Library. And this interest and regard the respected judge retained for his *protégé*, despite his oft-repeated thoughtless acts, to the end of his life, which end arrived, strange to say, only some few months before that of the much younger man, who, on hearing of Sir Redmond's death, expressed himself as having lost his best and truest friend. But with all the warm regard existing between the venerable judge and the youthful author, there was always a certain characteristic *hauteur* on the one hand, and a reverential respect on the other, in their official and social relationships. In proof of this a couple of examples may be related.

It was a hot summer's day, and, as was his style in such weather, the librarian was dressed dandily in unspotted white flannel, a cabbage-tree hat shadowing his face. So clothed he was leisurely wending his way up the steps of the library when he met the President, looking more starched, if possible, than ever, and wearing the well-known, flat-rimmed, tapering, belltopper, which shone sleekily in the glare of the noonday sun. The following brief dialogue then ensued:— President: "Good morning, Mr. Clarke." Librarian: "Good morning, sir." President: "I scarcely think your hat is exactly suited to the position you occupy in connection with this establishment, Mr. Clarke—Good morning," and with a stiff bend of the erect body the President took his departure with just a glimmer of a smile playing round the firmly-closed lips. Again, not long before Sir Redmond's death, and when the librarian had got himself into "hot water" among the "unco guid" section of the Trustees, through writing his clever though caustic reply to the Anglican Bishop, Dr. Moorhouse's criticism on Clarke's article, "Civilisation without Delusion," the President appeared one evening in the librarian's office with a clouded countenance, and said, "Good evening, Mr. Clarke." The librarian, with an intuitive feeling that something was wrong, returned the salutation, when the President remarked: "Mr. Clarke, you would oblige me greatly if you were to leave *some* things *undone*. For instance, that unfortunate article of yours—attacking so estimable a man as the bishop. Very indiscreet, Mr. Clarke. I—think—I—should require—to—have—some—thousands a year of a private income before *I* would—venture—upon writing such an—article on—such a subject, and among so punctillious a community as exists here. Good evening, Mr. Clarke:" and the librarian was left dazed and speechless at the solemnity of the rebuke, and the dignified departure of his President.

Recurring back to the literary work being done by our author, we find that it was during the next two years—namely, in 1872-73—that his prolific pen was in its busiest mood, for within the space of those twenty-four months he wrote the psychological dialogues styled "Noah's Ark," in the *Australasian*; these were interspersed with those exquisitely told stories, subsequently published in book form, under the names of *Holiday Peak* and *Four Stories High*. The former was dedicated to Oliver Wendell Holmes upon whom he looked as one of the brightest gems in the literary firmament, and from whom he had received much literary encouragement; the latter was dedicated to an appreciative friend, the late kind-hearted though explosive William Saurin Lyster, the man to whom Australian lovers of music owe a deep debt of gratitude as the first introducer of high-class opera and oratorio to these shores. Of these stories, *Pretty Dick* is perhaps the finest piece of work as regards execution done by Australia's greatest literary artist. And in this opinion I am not alone, as the following letter, from one who stands very high in the world's estimate as a master of true pathos and humour will show:—

BOSTON, 23rd December, 1872.

DEAR MR. CLARKE,—

I received your letter and MS., with the newspaper extract, some two or three days ago, and sat down almost at once and read the story. It interested me deeply, and I felt as much like crying over the fate of "Pretty Dick" as I did when I was a child and read the *Babes in the Wood*. I *did* cry then—I will *not* say whether I cried over "Pretty Dick" or not. But *I* will say it is a *very* touching story, *very* well told.

I am, Dear Mr. Clarke,
Most sincerely yours,
O. W. HOLMES.

Apart from these tales, there appeared among the "Noah's Ark" papers some excellent original verse, at times approximating to poetry and several metrical translations from Greek, Latin, German and French poets. He also composed in this year—1872—his most effectively written drama, *Plot*, which was produced at the Princess' Theatre with success. Following on *Plot*, he wrote, or rather adapted, the pantomime of *Twinkle Little Star*, which was played at the Theatre Royal during the Christmas season making quite "a hit."

It was about this time that the relations between Marcus Clarke and the journals with which he had from the commencement of his journalistic career been connected became strained, as is said in diplomatic jargon, and shortly afterwards all connection between them ceased for ever.

As a good deal of misconception exists about the breach that took place between the subject of this biography and the representatives out here of the proprietors of the *Argus* and *Australasian*, it is advisable in the interest of the author to explain the cause of the breach. It was in this year that Mr. Bagot, the "indefatigable" Secretary of the Victoria Racing Club, declined while under some peculiar influence to issue free tickets to the press, as had been the universal custom from time immemorial. The very natural reply of the press to this uncalled-for and blundering affront was simply not to report the races. This was agreed to by the morning journals then published in Melbourne. But in the *Evening Herald*, which was not, through questionable motives, consulted in the matter, there appeared the night the Cup was run, a remarkably clever report of the event—perhaps the cleverest description of the Cup meeting which has been seen in the pages of any Melbourne journal. Naturally the sparkling report caused no small consternation in the ranks of journalism in the city; more especially among the authorities of the *Argus*, who did not fail to recognise it to be the ingenious brainwork of their own contributor—Marcus Clarke. When questioned on the subject the erratic journalist denied having been at the races, but admitted writing the sketch, claiming his right to do so on the ground that, as the *Argus* did not choose to employ him because of a disagreement with Mr. Bagot he had every moral right to earn an honest penny from the proprietors of another journal who afforded him the opportunity of so doing. This, however, did not satisfy the ruling power of the *Argus* (Mr. Gowen Evans), who was probably chagrined to read in another journal the work of one whom he looked upon as that paper's property. The result of this attempt at autocratic interference and dictation was the loss to the journals in question of the writer whose work above that of all others had adorned their columns, and increased their popularity.

Having parted from the journals which he had so greatly aided by his rare abilities, Clarke became attached as a contributor to the *Herald* and *Daily Telegraph* and subsequently to the *Age* and *Leader*.

The next, most important and unfortunate, event which overtook him about this period was his insolvency. Though long expected, and known to be inevitable, the victim of untoward circumstances put off the evil day by every means in his power, thereby sinking deeper and deeper in the mire, till at last his doom had to be met, and his name appeared in the bankruptcy list. What those who had helped to lead him into this position felt when the disagreeable fact became known can only be conjectured, but, at any rate, their foolish dupe felt the position more acutely than any acquaintance of his could possibly imagine, judging by the light-hearted manner in which he discussed the subject with one and all. Only those who knew Marcus Clarke intimately—and they were few—realised how keenly he suffered from the thought that one, like himself, with a name and a fame, who had had every chance of being independent, should become what he, poor, generous, thoughtless fellow, had become. Still, it was unavoidable, and his fate was sealed. Would that the first mistake had acted as a warning, but it was not to be, for no sooner was one difficulty overcome than another commenced, ending only when life was no more—that life which was driven to its death by the merciless snares of the crafty usurer, against whom, at the last, he fought as desperately as man does against the remorseless python, who knows his prey is safe in the fatal embrace.

Yet despite all these monetary troubles, the inherently strong sense of humour in him would trifle with the seriousness of the position, for it was about this time that he penned the following remarks as the real excuse for his chronically impecunious condition :—

> I have made a scientific discovery. I have found out the reason why I have so long been afflicted with a pecuniary flux. For many years past I have tried to find out why I am always in debt, and have consulted all sorts of financial physicians, but grew no better, but rather the worse. The temporary relief afforded by a mild loan or an overdraft at the bank soon vanished. I once thought that by the judicious application of a series of bills at three months I could check the ravages of disease ; but, alas ! my complaint was aggravated, while I had not courage for the certain but painful remedy of the actual cautery, as recommended by Dr. Insolvent Commissioner Noel. My friends said I had "got into bad hands," that I had been deceived by advertising quacks, whose only object was to depress the financial system, and keep me an invalid as long as possible. I applied for admission into the Great Polynesian Loan Company's Hospital, and pawned myself there, in fact, at the ridiculously low rate of 350 per cent. I was insured in the Shylock Alliance Company (which afterwards, to my great disgust, amalgamated with the Polynesian), and there I sold the reversionary interest in my immortal soul, I believe, to a bland gentleman who calculated the amount of blood in my body and flesh on my bones by the aid of a printed money-table. Yet my financial health did not seem to improve. I grew anxious, and began to reason. I resolved to write a book. I wrote one, and called it *A Theory for the Causation, and Suggestions for the Prevention of Impecuniosity ; together with Hypotheses on the Causation, and Views as to the Prevention of Composition-with-creditors, Bankruptcy, Fraudulent Insolvency, and other Pecuniary Diseases.* In the course of examination of Bills of Sale, Acceptances, Liens on Wool, and other matters, I discovered by accident the cause of my disease. It was the simplest thing in the world. The idiots of doctors had been treating me for extravagance, whereas the fact was that *I was cursed with so powerful and innate a passion for economy that I never could bring myself to the expenditure of ready money.*

But turning to a pleasanter and more interesting subject, the Cave of Adullam has to be mentioned. The Cave of Adullam ! " What is that ? " may ask the uninitiated reader. Well, the particular cave alluded to was a club house, once situated in Flinders Lane, behind the *Argus* office, where stands now some softgoods palatial structure. To this only a very select body of members was admitted, the selectness in this case necessitating that a member should be happily impecunious, and, if possible, be hunted by the myrmidons of the law. From this brief description it will be seen that the Adullamites were a family *sui generis*. The entrance to the modest building was not easy of access, being only reached by a tortuous lane of ominous appearance, guarded by an animal who boasted the bluest of blue bulldog blood. The pass-words were—" Honor ! No Frills ! " The members were mostly composed of literary Bohemians, whose wordly paths were not strewn with roses, and between whom and the trader there existed a mutual disrespect. Chief among the members of this exclusive brotherhood was the subject of this biography, who, having discarded the more conventional surroundings of the Yorick Club, became a shining light within the shades of the Cave of Adullam. And to commemorate the genius of the members of the Cave was written a Christmas tale, yclept '*Twixt Shadow and Shine,* which contains fanciful portraitures of the leading Adullamites. But, alas ! the destroyer of all things, Time, has one by one scattered its members, till now the place that knew the members of that eccentric Bohemian band knows them no more. *Sic transit gloria,* &c. And with Hamlet we may say, addressing that once coruscating group—" Where be your gibes now ? Your gambols ? Your songs ? Your flashes of merriment that were wont to set the table in a roar ? Not one now to mock your own jeering ? Quite chap-fallen ! "

Notwithstanding, however, all the merry goings on at the Cave, Clarke was, perhaps, harder at work in those years than at any other time, although certainly the work was thrown off without much effort, and with as little care for a future reputation. It was at this time he first became a contributor to the *Age* and *Leader,* with which his connection lasted up to his death, having gone through the trying ordeal incident upon the *Age cum* Berry Reform Agitation of 1877, '78, '79, into which he threw himself with all the zest of a thorough hater of Shoddocracy, writing some of the most telling articles which illumined the pages of these journals at that time. And he fought the more zealously in the fray, because he wrote under the editorial guidance of one upon whom he looked as, at once, the best read and the ablest journalist on the Australian press—Mr. A. L. Windsor. It was during this period he enjoyed the friendship and confidence of the then Governor of Victoria, Sir George Bowen, and was offered by Mr. Graham Berry (now Sir) the Librarianship of the Parliament Library, which he declined, relying upon securing that of the Public Library, in which, however, he was doomed to disappointment a year or two later.

Clarke, apart from Melbourne journals, contributed largely to the *Queenslander* as also to the *Sydney Mail*, through the introduction of the late Mr. Hugh George, the gentleman who as general manager of the *Argus* raised that paper to a high position, and who subsequently was the valued general manager of the Messrs. Fairfax's newspapers in Sydney. Of all those connected prominently with the *Argus* when Marcus Clarke was its brightest ornament, Mr. Hugh George alone remained to the end the generous advocate of his exceptional abilities, of which he never lost an opportunity to avail himself in the Sydney journals, over which he exercised a control. And about the last negotiations Clarke entered into, only a few weeks before his unexpected death, were with that gentleman, in connection with a proposal that he should start on a tour through the colonies and South Sea Islands as the accredited "Special" of the Messrs. Fairfax's newspapers, and of the London *Daily Telegraph*, for which brilliantly written journal he had been acting for some years as "Australian Correspondent;" and that he was held in high estimation by the authorities of that remarkable paper the following letter, written by its proprietor and editor, speaks for itself. Wrote Mr. Lawson Levy :—

"Without having the pleasure of your personal acquaintance, I am sure you will pardon me if I venture to address you on a subject which may not be without interest. I have read your books with very great pleasure, and it has occurred to me that you possess most of the qualifications for journalism of the highest order. Has the idea ever occurred to you of adopting this branch of literature, and would it suit your views to come to England? I am, of course, ignorant of what your position may be, and ignorant of any feeling that you may have upon the subject. It is quite possible that ties may bind you to Australia—ties that you cannot break. If, however, the idea should have entered into your mind, tell me in a letter what your position is, what income you would require to entice you to come to London, whether you feel yourself competent for journalistic work, whether you have ever done any, and if you have, you would perhaps think it advisable to send me by the next mail, samples of such work. If, moreover, for the moment, the notion should seem acceptable to you, sit down and write me three or four leading articles on any subjects that may seem best to you—articles that will make about a column of our newspaper matter; and put into them as much of your force and vigor as you can command. Under any circumstances, whether my ideas waken any sympathy in your mind or not, I am sure you will permit me to congratulate you on the success your works have met with here."

Why Marcus Clarke did not avail himself of the chance of going to London under such auspices it is difficult to imagine, the more particularly that he was well aware that such talent as his had no possible scope in this, a new country, whereas in London literary circles it would have been appreciated at its proper value.

Surely, in the face of such encouragement, a genius, well nigh suffocated by the denseness of the *quasi*-intellectual atmosphere surrounding it, should have seized the opportunity to move from scenes clouded over with trouble, and from a community which gave but a feeble response to its bright efforts? But, somehow, it did not, or could not.

Returning to the year 1876, an event happened which deeply affected Marcus Clarke. In August of that year his father-in-law, genial, witty John Dunn, for whom he had a sincere affection, fell down dead in the street. The bitterness of this loss was greatly aggravated by his inability to publish the autobiography of the deceased actor, which he had together with Dr. Neild revised at the author's request, with a view to its publication after his death. But the wish of the deceased was not carried out, owing, it is said, to an objection taken by a daughter of the actor, who had married into so-called Society circles, to have the ups and downs of a poor player's family career submitted to public view.

Accordingly, the autobiography of Australia's clever comedian was not brought out, and the early history of the Australian stage has been lost to the public. For the next three years, besides the journalistic work alluded to, Clarke was busy at dramatic composition, producing, in conjunction with Mr. Keely, *Alfred the Great*, a burlesque, which achieved a success at the Bijou Theatre, during the Christmas season of 1877. This was followed by the adaptation for the Theatre Royal of Wilkie Collins' sensational novel *Moonstone*. This play was not the success anticipated, but it must be said in justice to the author that it was considerably spoiled by the pruning-knife of the management, which did its slashing with little judgment. Another piece, a comedietta, styled, *Baby's Luck*, was subsequently written for Mr. J. L. Hall, in which that popular actor appeared to great advantage. *Fernande*, a clever adaptation of Sardou's emotional drama of that name, was also written about this time, but never produced owing to a disagreement over the matter. Of this adaptation Miss Genevieve Ward expressed to the writer a high opinion of its merits, which, coming from so great an artist and one who had read the play in the original, is no small compliment to the author. It may also be surmised that it was during this period that the fanciful extravaganza of *The King of the Genii* was composed. This piece is written in a Gilbertean manner, and is not unlike that author's *Palace of Truth*. Yet Clarke's ability as a playright was thrown away, as theatrical managers in the colonies had not, unfortunately, either the capacity to know a good thing, or the enterprise to encourage local talent. But not only was Clarke's pen busy at dramas—it was tempted into an entirely new field—that of history. At the suggestion of the then Minister of Education, the late Mr. Justice Wilberforce Stephen, he was engaged to write a history of Australia for the State-schools, which had just come under the new secular, compulsory, and free Education Act. This work entailed upon the writer more routine labour than was to his taste, and consequently, instead of devoting himself to the somewhat tedious task, he, after commencing the book, handed it over, in his usual good-hearted way to some impecunious friends, who did not possess any literary qualification for such work, the consequence being that the book turned out to be a miserable *fiasco*, and was never used in the schools for which it was intended. Some notion of its value may be gleaned from the following critical notice of it in a leading journal:—"In short, the book before us is calculated to impress the reader with the idea that it has been compiled by some literary charlatan rather than by an author of Mr. Marcus Clarke's ability and reputation." But because little or no attention was given by the supposed author of the history to the work, it must not be imagined that the fertile mind was inactive. That clever, though eccentric, *brochure, The Future Australian Race*, was written at this period. Of it an English paper wrote:— "It deals with a subject of considerable ethnological and social interest in language more forcible than philosophical. Mr. Clarke considers that vegetarians are Conservatives, and 'Red Radicals,' for the most part meat-eaters, while 'fish-eaters are invariably moderate Whigs.' He thinks that 'the Australasians will be content with nothing short of a *turbulent democracy*,' and that in five hundred years the Australasian race will have 'changed the face of nature, and swallowed up all our contemporary civilisation,' but it is fortunately 'impossible that we should live to see this stupendous climax. *Après nous, le déluge.*'" Besides this his restless mind was weekly giving out articles, reviews, and sketches, bearing his own mint mark, in the *Age*, the *Leader*, the *Sydney Mail* and *Morning Herald*, and *London Daily Telegraph*. It was also at work on the *Melbourne* and *Victorian Reviews*, in a somewhat significant, albeit imprudent manner, for it was in the *Victorian* that his "disturbing" article on "Civilisation Without Delusion" appeared, and in the *Melbourne* his clever rejoinder, to Dr. Moorhouse's reply to the original article, saw light.

The last efforts of Clarke in the direction of dramatic work, were the two comedies written for his wife on her re-appearance, after an absence of some years, at the Bijou in the winter of 1880. Of the two, the one, *A Daughter of Eve*, was original; the other, *Forbidden Fruit*, being an adaptation from the French. The former is undoubtedly clever, being on the lines of Sheridan's comedies; and in the leading character of "Dorothy Dove," Mrs. Clarke did every justice to her histrionic abilities.

Besides these comedies, the author left unfinished the libretto of *Queen Venus* an *Opera Bouffe* on which he was engaged with M. Kowalski, the eminent pianist, at the time of his death; also the plots and a portion of the matter of the following;—*Reverses*, an Australian Comedy; *Paul and Virginia*, a burlesque; *Fridoline*, an opera comique, and *Salome*, a comedy.

And now reference has to be made to that which more than any other single cause led to the unfortunate pecuniary and other complications in which the subject of this memoir became involved during the last year or two of his short life —namely his appointment as agent with power-of-attorney to act as he deemed desirable for his cousin, Sir Andrew Clarke, in connection with some landed property owned by that gentleman in this colony. Paradoxical as this statement may appear it is nevertheless too true that the confidence placed by Sir Andrew Clarke in his cousin's ability to act as his sole and unchecked agent in business matters was one of the most fatal errors ever committed both for the principal and the agent. For the former it meant pecuniary loss, for the latter neglect of all literary work. That Marcus Clarke was altogether to blame for the "mixed" condition into which the business affairs of his cousin got is simply absurd. All that can be urged against him in the matter is that he was negligent and thoughtless in connection with them as he had always been with his own. However, the less said the better in connection with this episode of the brilliant *littérateur's* life for after all it was not his fault but misfortune, as he has said himself, that he was not a Business Man. Indeed, no reference would have been made to this matter were it not that it was the greatest misfortune that ever happened to Clarke that he had anything to do with this business, as it not only led him to abandon his proper duties, but led him, also, deeper into the clutches of usurers, who eventually wrought him to death before his time. And it is probably owing to this "bungle" that Sir Andrew Clarke has not seen his way to help (although receiving a handsome pension from this colony) the widow and children of him of whose abilities he could think so highly as to induce the Prince of Wales, when on his visit to India where Sir Andrew was Minister of Public Works, to read *His Natural Life*. The Prince did read the book, and was so struck by its powers that he expressed a desire to meet the author, who, he suggested, ought to go to that intellectual centre of the world—London.

It may be assumed that it was owing to this unfortunate business craze which had seized hold of our author, that there had been left behind in an unfinished state a novel which began so brilliantly as *Felix and Felicitas*. Commenced years before, it was allowed to lie by during his "landlord" days, and until a few months previous to his demise, when it was re-commenced ; but too late, for the hand of Death was already upon him, as he himself too well knew and frequently remarked during the last few weeks of his life—notably on the Queen's Birthday, preceding his decease—when, walking with a friend in the vicinity of the Yarra Bend Asylum he mournfully remarked, "Which shall it be—the Mad Asylum or the Pauper Grave? Let a toss of the coin decide—head, grave ; tail, asylum." And forthwith a florin was tossed, and fell tail uppermost. "Not if I know it, my festive coin. No gibbering idiot shall I e'er be ; rather the gleeful, gallows-tree."

That English literature has lost through the incompletion of *Felix and Felicitas*, no judge who has perused the opening chapters can deny ; and that the promise of artistic merit held out by these chapters was fully realised by authorities on the subject is proved by the anxiety of Messrs. Bentley and Sons to urge on the writer to complete the work for publication in London ; and so capable a critic as Mrs. Cashel Hoey, writing from London to the *Australasian* of the story, remarked :—

> The literary world here has received with great regret the intelligence of Mr. Marcus Clarke's death. His tales of the early days of the colonies, and his very striking novel, *His Natural Life*, made a deep impression here. We were always expecting another powerful fiction from his pen. I fear he has not left any finished work, and I regret the fact all the more deeply that I have been allowed the privilege of reading a few chapters of a novel begun by Mr. Marcus Clarke, under the title of *Felix and Felicitas*. The promise of those chapters is quite exceptional ; they equal in brilliancy and vivacity the best writing of Edward Whitty, and they surpass that vivid writer in construction. It is difficult to believe, while reading the opening chapters of this, I fear, unfinished work, that the author lived at the other side of the world from the scenes and the society which he depicts with such accuracy, lightness, grace, and humour.

In order to enable the reader to have some idea of the interesting nature of the plot of the story ideally drawn, it is said, from the author's own experiences, the following sketch of it written by him for the publishers will doubtless be welcome :—

> The following is a synopsis of my novel now in MS. The title is FELIX AND FELICITAS. Those who were in the Academy Exhibition of 18— remember the picture " Martha and Mary."

The artist was a Mr. Felix Germaine, the Son of a country parson having a rectory near Deal. I know the place well. The brother of this clergyman is travelling tutor and friend to Lord Godwin (one like Lord Pembroke), who has just returned from a cruise in the South Seas in his yacht. Ampersand, the idler (everybody knows him), meets Godwin on his return, and tells him of the success of his old schoolfellow—Felix. He brings both to a concert at Raphael Delevyra's, the famous pianoforte maker; and there they hear some good musical and witty talk. Stivelyn, Carbeth, Storton,—not unlike Swinburne, Buchanan, and Albert Grant—are there amongst others. Felix, who is married to a charmingly domesticated wife, falls in love with Mrs. Delevyra, who, as all the world knows, was Felicitas Carmel—the niece of Carmel, the violinist, who retired from public life, having paralysis of the left hand. (N.B.—The great Beethoven was deaf; but his torments were nothing to Carmel's.) Mr. Delevyra is a rich, thriving man—some say that his name is really Levi—but Felicitas doesn't care for him. She and Felix you see—want to live that Higher Life of which we have heard so much lately; and consequently they resolve to break the Seventh Commandment. They get away in Godwin's yacht; and now begins my effort at mental analysis. In a little time they grow weary; then blame each other; then they are poor; and finally they hate each other—each blaming each for causing the terrible fall from the high standard of Ideality settled by them in their early interviews. In the midst of this Delevyra arrives. The Jew has made up his mind. He loves his wife; but she has betrayed him. He will not forgive her; or rather he cannot forgive himself. He explains the common-sense view of the matter. He shows her that she has spent two-thirds of his income—that her desertion was not only treacherous, but foolish, inasmuch as she loses respect, position, and money. In fine, with some sarcasm and power, he strips adultery of its poetic veil, and shows it to be worse than a crime—a blunder. Felix expects a duel—not at all. Delevyra discourses him sweetly upon the "Higher Life," and says to his wife—"If this is the congenial soul you pine for I will allow him £300 a year to live with you and make you happy." Felicitas travels—divorced and allowanced (Teresa Perugino did the same). She writes books, poems, and travels—very recondite stuff they say. Felix, utterly shamed, goes home in Godwin's yacht. He is wrecked at Deal, near his own house, and his body is brought to his wife. He, however, recovers and lives happily. Ampersand says in the last chapter—"You ask what the Modern Devil is." It is an Anti-Climax. We haven't the strength to carry anything to the end. These people ought to have taken poison or murdered somebody. I saw Felix the other day. He is quite fat and rubicund. His wife henpecks him. He makes lots of money by pictures—but they are not as good as "Martha and Mary."

The romance is musical, æsthetic, and sensational. It is not written *virginibus puerisque*, but the effect is a moral one. Some of the characters may be recognised, but I have avoided direct personality.

And now comes the last scene of all, and it is with a sorrowful heart I pen these lines, for Memory flies back to the bright days of our early friendship, when, boys together, we never found "the longest day too long," and whispers, in mournful tones, "Ah! what might have been." But it was not to be, and I bow in silent submission to the Omnipotent Will.

Some months before the end came the never strong constitution of my friend began to give forth ominous signs of an early break-up. The once-active brain became by degrees more lethargic, and the work which at one time could be executed with rapidity and force became a task not to be undertaken without effort. The vivid, humorous imagination of the Peripatetic Philosopher assumed a more sombre hue, yielding itself up to the unravelling of psychological puzzles. The keen vein of playful satire which was so marked a feature of his mental calibre turned into a bitterness that but reflected the disappointed mind of this son of genius; and hence, for upwards of six months, from the opening of the year 1881 to the day of his death in the August of that year no literary work of consequence was done with the exception of the *Mystery of Major Molineux*, which opened in his usual finished style, but which through force of untoward pecuniary circumstances was wound up suddenly, leaving the mystery as mysterious as ever. But above all other matters that occupied his thoughts during the few weeks preceding his death and the one which may be set down as the chief cause of that death, was the compulsory sequestration of his estate by Aaron Waxman, usurer (since gone to render his account before the Almighty Tribunal), which meant the loss of his position in the Public Library. All these mental troubles came upon the broken-down body in a cluster, and the burden was too heavy to bear. Struggling against his bitter fate—the more bitter that he knew he was himself greatly to blame—he fell by the way, crushed in mind and body, and the bright spirit passed away from the weakly tenement of clay which held it, to, let us hope, more congenial realms, leaving behind it a blank in the social and literary circles it was wont to frequent, which cannot be filled up, for that spirit was *sui generis*.

The illness which immediately caused his decease commenced with an attack of pleurisy, and this developing into congestion of the liver, and finally into erysipelas, carried him off in the space of one short week. Indeed he had, during the last year of his life, suffered so frequently from attacks brought on by a disordered liver, that little heed was given to the final attack till a day or two previous to his death, when the wife, who had so unwearyingly attended him night and day, found that matters were more serious than anticipated and sent for an old companion and friend of her husband's, Dr. Patrick Moloney. From the beginning he held out little hopes, as the constitution was sadly worn out, and the mental worry of the latter weeks had completed the task of dissolution. But the dying man himself did not evidently realise his position even up to the time of the insensibility which preceded death setting in, for only a few hours before his decease he remarked jocularly to his watchful wife, "When I get up I will be a different man with a new liver," and then asked for and put on his coat. But the end came upon him rapidly. Losing his speech he beckoned for pencil and paper, and seizing hold of the sheets moved his hand over them as if writing. Shortly afterwards the mind began to wander, but still the hand continued moving with increasing velocity, and every now and then a futile attempt to speak was made. But the tongue could not utter what the fevered brain wished apparently to explain; and then, by degrees, the arms grew weary, the body fell back on the pillows, the large, beautiful eyes, with a far off gaze in them, opened widely for a second—then closed—and all was over on this earth with—Marcus Clarke.

At 4 o'clock on the afternoon of Tuesday, 2nd August, 1881, he died, aged 35.

Reader, let us draw the veil over this sad scene. The sorrow caused by the passing away of so bright a spirit is too mournful to dwell upon.

# A MONOGRAPH:

THE foregoing biographical sketch of my friend having been written immediately subsequent to his death, and when the sorrow occasioned by it overshadowed all feeling in respect to him that dealt with the brighter and lighter sides of his nature, I have deemed it would not come amiss to his many admirers to learn more of the man and author than could be gleaned from a brief outline of his birth, life and death. But in attempting this, I feel I have set myself to do no easy task, for of a verity a more contradictory and many-sided brain could scarcely be found. Only to those few who knew him intimately was it vouchsafed to fully recognise the vividness of his imagination, the lightness of his fancy, the bitterness of his satire, the depth of his pathos. To the outside world, or even to his many acquaintances, he was an enigma they vainly tried to solve, for one of the predominating features of his character was a marked reticence, allied with a desire to mystify by inuendoes and exaggerations, those whom he casually met, or who sought his company out of curiosity. Despite however all these apparent contradictions of character the underlying trait of his nature was a dreamy melancholy. To the close observer this marked feature of his temperament was to be seen in his soulful eyes, even when they were sparkling with humour or flashing with anger, while in his thinking mood this trait was almost painful to contemplate, lending as it did a mournfulness to the expression of the eyes that was unspeakably sad. It was when in this mood that the real pathos of his nature spoke out with a power as pure as true. In proof of this, take the following heart-breaking passage from his great work *His Natural Life*, descriptive of the suicide of two poor little child-convicts, to whom even at so early a stage of their young lives death was preferable to existence.

Just outside this room Sylvia met with a little adventure. Meekin had stopped behind, and Burgess, being suddenly summoned for some official duty, Frere had gone with him, leaving his wife to rest on a bench that (placed at the summit of the cliff) overlooked the sea. While resting thus, she became aware of another presence, and, turning her head, beheld a small boy, with his cap in one hand and a hammer in the other. The appearance of the little creature, clad in a uniform of grey cloth that was too large for him, and holding in his withered little hand a hammer that was too heavy for him, had something pathetic about it.

"What is it, you mite?" asked Sylvia.

"We thought you might have seen him, mum,' said the little figure, opening its blue eyes with wonder at the kindness of the tone.

"Him! Whom?"

"Cranky Brown, mum," returned the child; "him as did it this morning. Me and Billy knowed him, mum; he was a mate of ours, and we wanted to know if he looked happy."

"What do you mean, child?" said she, with a strange terror at her heart; and then, filled with pity at the aspect of the little being, she drew him to her, with sudden womanly instinct, and kissed him.

He looked up at her with joyful surprise.

"Oh!" he said.

Sylvia kissed him again.

"Does nobody ever kiss you, poor little man?" said she.

"Mother used to," was the reply, "but she's at home. Oh, mum," with a sudden crimsoning of the little face, "may I fetch Billy?"

"This is Billy, mum," he said. "Billy never had no mother. Kiss Billy."

The young wife felt the tears rush to her eyes. "You two poor babies!" she cried. And then, forgetting that she was a lady, dressed in silk and lace, she fell on her knees in the dust, and, folding the friendless pair in her arms, wept over them.

"What is the matter, Sylvia?" said Frere, when he came up. "You've been crying."

"Nothing Maurice; at least, I will tell you by-and-by."

* * * * *

Unfortunately, when Sylvia went away, Tommy and Billy put into execution a plan which they had carried in their poor little heads for some weeks.

"I can do it now," said Tommy. "I feel strong."

"Will it hurt much, Tommy?" said Billy, who was not so courageous.

"Not so much as a whipping."

"I'm afraid! Oh, Tom, it's so deep! Don't leave me, Tom!"

The bigger boy took his little handkerchief from his neck, and with it bound his own left hand to his companion's right.

"Now I can't leave you."

"What was it the lady that kissed us said, Tommy?"

"Lord, have pity of them two fatherless children!" repeated Tommy.

"Let's say it, Tom."

And so the two babies knelt on the brink of the cliff, and raising the bound hands together, looked up at the sky, and ungrammatically said, "Lord, have pity on we two fatherless children!" And then they kissed each other, and did it.

Again we have real pathos in those sorrowful idylls, *Pretty Dick* and *Poor Joe*; and the remorse and agony depicted in *A Sad Christmas Eve* compel pity for the sufferer, albeit his grief is the outcome of his own selfishness. Turning to the brighter side of his nature, who can deny him the possession of a rare humour, light as laughter, and bright as sunshine. In his *Humbug* papers it bubbles up unconsciously, as when he writes *apropos* of thieving: "Borrowing may be reduced to a science or elevated to an art. Borrowing an umbrella is a science; borrowing half-a-crown is an art. The man who begins with an umbrella may get to half-a-crown or—even a 'crown;'" or, "Friends as a rule are a mistake. They are too expensive. No poor man can afford to have many friends. They would ruin him. Indeed, friendship is a luxury which should be indulged in with caution even by the rich;" or, of a man in New South Wales who borrowed his friend's horse and then sold it, on being remonstrated with, saying —" What did you lend it for? Do you expect a man in *this* colony to be an icicle?" or, "Mothers-in-law are ladies with daughters. A mother-in-law may be considered as the beard on the matrimonial oyster;" or, "Cordials, as a general rule, are worse than liquor. There is more *spirit* in them. A teetotaler who has been drinking Balm of Gilead is a terrible sight. I have calculated that a teetotaler could not possibly live through more than ten years of *cordiality*;" or, in reference to "loafing!" "Some people take time to acquire this art, but it is inherent in other people, like Original Sin, or buck-jumping in horses that you buy as bargains." But, apart from his humorous writings, Clarke was one of the most entertainingly amusing conversationalists one could meet if the spirit of fun possessed him. He could verily keep a company of clever men (amongst women he was a mute) listening enchanted to his quaint and original descriptions of character or incidents, so uttered that time was forgotten. It was this habit of his which greatly induced him to neglect more important duties, in the to him pleasant excitement of amusing others without giving heed to the fleeting hours. It is at this length of time difficult to recall the many gems of humour—mostly satirical—that fell from his lips, but one or two come to memory—to wit: When expostulated with for placing himself in the clutches of usurers, he would gravely remark that his banking experience had taught him that men who kept "double sets" of books were the safest to deal with financially as their consciences were more elastic. On another occasion, when an artist friend who had lent him money demanded payment, peremptorily threatening legal proceedings, he wrote across the angry letter, "Dear T———, 'Don't.' Yrs., M. C," and returned it. This laconic treatment meted out to the trusting friend served its purpose, as instead of further demands for payment, that friend, who enjoyed a point even to his own loss, showed the reply to his acquaintances, adding, "Who could after this sue him?" But as this conduct on Clarke's part may appear to some as ungrateful and selfish, let me assure such that he did to others in respect to similar transactions what he expected to be done, and was done, by others to himself. Whatever his financial position he could not refuse a call of charity, and although this might not be considered being just before being generous, still it showed that the heart was in the right place, albeit his notions of the value of money were, to say the least, peculiar, taken by the common standard accepted by the world at large. Many are the kind acts that my friend did unknown to anyone save those benefited or relieved. In confirmation of this, and in justice to his memory, let me relate one or two of these acts. Meeting one evening a literary friend of his—a prodigal Bohemian somewhat akin to himself—and learning from him that his family had eaten no food that day, Clarke, having no coin of the realm to give, unhesitatingly took off valuable solitaires, and gave them to his foodless brother in Bohemia to pawn, and so obtain sustenance. This act and others like it came to the writer's knowledge after the author's death, and when he went round taking a variety of articles out of "Uncle's" grasp. And to show how even those astute dealers felt towards their victim, it may be told that they as a rule gave up the articles pawned without charging the interest due thereon. So it will be seen there are "some bowels of compassion" in Israel yet! Another kindly act of my much misconstrued friend I must relate. Hearing one night late that a poor friend's wife was about being confined in a house devoid of blankets, &c., he took the clothes off his own bed, and hoisting them on his back, walked (it being then too late for cabs) over a mile to the unfortunate one's cottage, and there deposited the bundle, merely knocking at the door to let the fact be known, and leaving without further intruding on the delicate and sad scene. Surely much will be forgiven him who hath so acted, be his failings as the sands of the sea?

After learning such reminiscences as these of the author's life, my readers will not be surprised that by those to whom his innermost nature was known he was *beloved*—this word exactly expresses the feeling, for the object of it was in some respects more of woman's delicate than of man's rougher fibre. In proof of this feeling, let me quote a few love-offerings of friends in verse and prose—in addition to the dirge of Kendall's, printed elsewhere in this volume. Such utterances give a stranger to Clarke's nature a better insight into it than columns of description. Wrote of him Mr. Frank Hutchinson, a brilliant *littérateur* of Sydney:—

" After life's fitful fever he sleeps well !"
What needs there more his brief, bright tale to tell?
The merry heart that mocked at Fortune's spite,
The "lips of laughter" and the eyes of light,
Once known and seen, must keep the memory green
Of all he was and all he might have been.
For those who knew him not, enough to know
He shared the poet's joy, the poet's woe.
Life's cup of gladness not content to skim,
He tossed it off in bumpers to the brim ;
Careless as child that knows no after day,
He laughed and sang his happy life away ;
Sketched men and manners ; drew with deftest hand
Bright, living pictures of this latest land,
Or grave or gay, in colour all akin,
Lit by the selfsame "sacred fire" within ;
His wit with wisdom mixed his years belied ;
Cheered ; charmed ; himself immortalised and died.

Mr. Garnet Walch, a friend and brother journalist, adds his meed of praise in these lines:—

The brightest genius that our land could boast,
Whose gifts outweigh'd the gathered golden ore
Of thrice ten years—is dead at half Life's span.
Dead ! when coy August-buds are whisp'ring "Spring,
And nature wakes to trill her matin song.
Asleep ; asleep too soon ! For thee, dear friend,
No golden harvest and no aftermath.
No ripened vintage of the full globed grape ;
No luscious Wine of Life—no fruited Fame,
No flowers, save those pale blooms that deck thy grave.
Oh ! cruel blast—oh ! keen-edged, callous frost ;
Killing the tree that blossomed earliest, best—
The one brave tree, whose growth we watched with pride.

Another member of the same fraternity of Bohemians wrote on the first anniversary of his death.

He was an idler and a dreamer, they
Who little knew that noble heart may deem.
He was a soulless cynic, so may say
Those who judge only things by what they seem.
The love we bore him tells a different tale,
We, his companions in life's bitter fight ;
We, who have fought so oft and hard, to fail,
And still to struggle onward to the light.
We, who his generous heart and kindly soul have read,
Can only give our all—a moment with the dead.

But while intimate friends, and they alone can speak to the lovableness of Clarke's nature, which lay hidden to the outside world, men of acknowledged intellectual position have spoken with no uncertain voice as to his literary power—his undoubted genius. In reference to this subject the Earl of Rosebery sent the author's widow the following letter in accepting the dedication to him of the Memorial Volume of her husband's works.

"There can, indeed, I think, be no two opinions as to the horrible fascination of the work (*His Natural Life.*) The reader, though he cannot but be harrowed by the long agony of the story and the human anguish of every page, is unable to lay it down ; almost in spite of himself he has to read and to suffer to the bitter end. To me, I confess, it is the most terrible of all novels, more terrible than *Oliver Twist*, or Victor Hugo's most startling effects, for the simple reason that it is more real. It has all the solemn ghastliness of truth.

"Since I have been in Australia I have employed some of the little time at my disposal in carefully examining the blue-books on which *His Natural Life* is founded, and during my recent visit to Tasmania I made some personal inquiries on the same subject. The result has been to bring conviction to my mind that the case is not one whit over-stated—nay that the fact in some particulars is more frightful than the fiction. The materials for great works of imagination lie all round us; but it is genius that selects and transposes them.

"It is rare, I think, that so young a country has produced so great a literary force. I cannot believe but that the time must soon come when Australians will feel a melancholy pride in this true son of genius, and Australian genius. While as they read his greatest work (written when he was but twenty-five) they cannot but be thrilled at the thought that the bright present they enjoy is separated by so narrow an interval of time from the infernal tragedy portrayed therein. And in England you may find that he may have made up to him in posthumous honour what was lacking in his lifetime."

And here it is my pleasant duty to record that not only did Lord Rosebery show his appreciation of Marcus Clarke's genius, but he testified to the genuineness of that feeling by sympathy with his widow and children in seeking them out when passing through Melbourne, and giving them a practical illustration of what that sympathy meant.

The once King of English Journalists—Mr. George Augustus Sala—in expressing his opinion of the author—wrote to a friend thus:—

"It is a thousand pities that a man who could produce a book of such extraordinary genius as is displayed in *His Natural Life* did not avail himself of the splendid opportunities awaiting him in London. Of local fame he had no lack; but fortune—and splendid fortune—would have been at his beck and call in London, whether he had laboured in the field of journalism, or of fiction, or of the drama. Assuredly Charles Reade never wrote so powerful a romance as *His Natural Life*. As assuredly Reade, Sims, and Tom Tayler would have had to look to their laurels had your friend seriously grappled with the craft of the playwright, and most assuredly he would have taken a very high place as a descriptive journalist."

While on this subject I cannot do better than quote from an article written upon Clarke by the late brilliant William Bede Dalley, of Sydney. Referring to his literary ability he says, "He was almost universally regarded as by far the brightest, readiest, and most gifted writer of Victoria." Of *His Natural Life* he writes—

"He made as intense and exhaustive a study of the old well-nigh forgotten records of prison experiences, of gaol sufferings, and horrors, as could have been undertaken by the most laborious philanthropist animated with a generous desire to reform institutions of anguish and terrors. No great humanitarian could have been more industrious and conscientious, more exact and sympathetic. He patiently accumulated the materials of history, and employed them in the construction of a romance."

In a characteristically pathetic manner the great lawyer, brilliant orator, and charming *littérateur* concludes his review of the memorial volume of Clarke's works:—

"We lay down this brief memorial of powers and faculties, which formed through circumstances so incomplete an expression, with a feeling of sadness that one so richly gifted, so capable of the noblest service in the cause of social refinement, was afforded so few opportunities, and was swept away so soon, before, to borrow the words of Matthew Arnold, the stars have come out, and 'the night wind brought up the stream murmurs and scent of the infinite sea.'"

And reader, it is of one thus written of by such men that two would-be political leaders of the Colony of Victoria, Thomas Bent and J. B. Patterson, spoke from their places in Parliament in brutal and coarse language (unfit for publication) when the subject of a grant of £1000 to the widow and orphans of the deceased author was under discussion at the instigation of one who is justly the pride of his country—Alfred Deakin. But assuredly Posterity will adjust the balance, and sift the grain from the chaff as regards what constitutes a National Representative.

I do not think I can conclude this monograph more appropriately than by quoting the character given of the author, as revealed by his hand-writing, by a gentleman formerly resident here who had acquired a mastery of the foolishly despised art of graphiology—namely, Mr. Noel Conway:—

"A man of a highly cultivated intellect and possessing much refined poetical feeling and eloquence of mind with considerable penetration and clearness of ideas; also having a certain simplicity and severity of taste, with a judgment formed rather by intuitive observation than from sequence of ideas. A cheerful, ardent disposition with strong passions, straightforward and truthful, so far as a most vivid imagination would allow. Possessing a strong, obstinate, despotic will, and a quick, hot temper; in fact, where indifference was felt, a most provoking man to deal with. Should think he would pay the greatest attention to detail in any cause or work that interested him. Finally, a man with much force of character, very marked originality of thought, and eccentricity of manner. Still, without the affectation and pretension often seen with such a lively imagination."

*Christmas*, 1889.                                       H. M.

# AUSTRALIA OF THE PAST.

───◆───

## WILLIAM DAMPIER: NAVIGATOR.

THE notion of giving to the great reading public a series of sketches of the lives and exploits of the early voyagers to Australia, is so excellent a one that I wish the execution of it had been entrusted to an abler pen than mine. Difficulties arise at the outset. The information to be obtained concerning these old Australian Worthies—if I may call them so—is scanty and often unreliable. The major portion of their journals is occupied by descriptions of dangers and perils, which tempt one to turn aside from the bare narration of facts ; while the space at command compels to brevity and condensation. Having read the wonderful adventures of some of these sea-kings, one feels more inclined to expand one's knowledge into a romance of three volumes than to compress it into an article of three pages, and I must beg that these brief, bald notes may be considered but as hints to those who desire to gain for themselves full information concerning some of the gallant and heroic souls who have gone before us.

In the seventeenth century existed a condition of mundane affairs which was altogether unique in the history of the world. The genius of navigation had seized upon men. Americus Vespucius and the great Columbus had discovered a new earth where the skies were balmier, the waters bluer, the soil more fruitful than in Europe. To this favoured land—teeming with plenty and rich in mineral treasure— came the desperate, the reckless, the daring of all nations. The young nobles, the impoverished gentry, the broken soldiers, who in former times would have lived and fought [the hired comrades of some lawless prince or usurping monarch], eagerly betook themselves to the El Dorado of the West, to the islands of the Pacific, to the country where blood bought both gold and glory. They found it occupied by the Spaniard.

The history of the government of New Spain is the history of a torture-chamber. Putting aside the question of religious intolerance, there is no doubt whatever but that the conquerors were merciless to the conquered. Nor would they suffer other nations to share with them the spoil so rudely seized. Along the shores of the forest-coasts had encamped some daring spirits, tired of civilization and eager for the free life of the savannah and the jungle. These men

A

lived upon jerked flesh, *boucan*, and were called buccaneers—a name to be hereafter spoken with dread by many a Spaniard. To dislodge these men of the woods was the incessant task of the governors of the settlements round the coast, and a wood-warfare began, which was carried on with such bloodthirsty fury on both sides that the report of it soon spread to Europe. The resistance of the logwood-cutters of Campeachy Bay was interpreted to mean the protest of all free nations against the increasing power of Old Castile, and from all sides flocked to their aid those daring adventurers whose hopes of treasure and renown had been dashed at sight of the guns of Carthagena, or checked at the report of the grandeur of Panama. The buccaneers became the rovers of the South Seas, the pirates of the Pacific, the Norsemen of the New World.

The history of these heroes demands for itself a whole encyclopædia. They were the ancestors of the men who fought at Navarino and Trafalgar. They beat the Armada. They laid the foundation of Britain's naval glory, and the memory of their prowess is perpetuated by every breeze that waves the shot-tattered Union Jack of England. The exploits they performed savour of the miraculous. Sir Henry Morgan crossed the Isthmus of Darien, sacked Panama, and marched back with his plunder. Van Horn took Vera Cruz in five hours, and sailed through the Spanish fleet with a booty of £437,500 without the loss of one of his six small ships. In 1670, thirty-seven vessels rendezvoused at Cape Tribaron and disembogued an army of 2000 men, each sworn to kill a Spaniard for the glory of the English arms. Stories of the greatness, the desperation, the piety, and the iniquity of these sea-rovers were in the mouths of every boy in every English fishing village. The glories of Captain Montbars and Raveneau de Lussan were compared with the tigerish ferocity of Morgan, and the piety of honest Captain Watling, who swore his men to give no quarter and to keep the Sabbath-day.

In the year 1669, such legends as these fired the mind of a boy of seventeen years of age at the Latin School of East Coker in Somersetshire. This youngster, one William Dampier, was an orphan, a friendless youth with a large heritage of hopes and of but little beside. He longed for the sea, for the Spanish Main, for wild adventure and spirit-stirring change. Placed with the master of a ship at Weymouth, he made voyage to Newfoundland, but the bleak regions of the cod-banks chilled his spirit. The marvellous land of the West tempted him. Returned a sturdy and self-confident youth to his native town, he engaged as a common sailor in a voyage to the "Indies." His voyage brought him adventures. He was in the Dutch war under Sir Edward Sprague. He was an overseer on a logwood factory at Campeachy Bay. He was a speculator at Bantam. In 1678 he returned, brown, careless, worldly-wise, a past-master in the freemasonry of the ocean. Colonel Hellier, of Jamaica, had lost a good servant, and England gained a great navigator.

From this date began William Dampier's career of fortune. In 1679 he sailed with one of the numerous semi-mercantile, semi-piratical expeditions of the time, to the West Indies, and falling in with the bold hearts and ready blades of the coast, snapped fingers at merchandise, choosing rather to seek for El Dorado. It was a weary search. In company with Captain Ringrove and Surgeon Wafer he crossed the isthmus of Darien, plundered the rich townships on the Pacific Coast, recrossed the isthmus, and joining (in 1683) with Cook and Eaton, sailed conquering and to conquer for the Undiscovered Islands. Cook died, raving of buried treasure, and Davis took command. Davis was a man of courage, but lacked brains; Swan, who, commanding the "Cygnet" (duly furnished by staid London merchants), met the pirate fleet at Guayaquil, was a man of stratagem. "Let us," cried he, "force the whole Pacific Coast to pay tribute to our arms! We, with our lively craft, our agile vessels, can steal upon their towns, swoop into their harbours, harry them 'twixt midnight and morning!"

A nobler ambition was Dampier's. His plan was to attack, capture, and hold Santa Maria, thus locking the coast to Quito. "We must organize," said he, at a meeting of the Captains. "The Spanish flag droops before the united banners of our comrades. Give me the silver mines of Darien with a thousand slaves to work them and I will defy the yellow ensign of old Spain till death shall clutch me." Swan embraced the scheme with eagerness, but was overruled. So with the memories of the great Darien expedition of Basil, Ringrove, Barty Sharp, and Wafer, our hero turned his vessel's beak and made for open sea.

His fortune deserted him. He lost fifty men in forays upon the coast. On the last day of March, 1686, he took his departure from Cape Corrientes, and starved in deadly calms to the Ladrones. It was proposed to kill and eat Swan and other malcontents, but as the fatal lot was drawn, rose into view the purple shore of Guam, and the victims breathed again. At Mindanao awoke a mutiny, and Dampier, with others, left his incapable co-adventurer to his fate. The next year saw them at Manilla, and having careened their vessels at Pulo Condore, they made for the Chinese coast, were driven through the Spice Islands, and in February, 1688, sighted New Holland. Nothing in the account of this continent was then of interest. The natives were dirty and stupid, the vegetation and soil uninviting after the glorious prodigality of the tropic seas. Dampier says of them:— "The inhabitants are the most miserable wretches in the universe, having no houses but the heavens, and no garments but the bark of a tree tied round the waist. . . . . Their eyelids are half-closed to keep out flies, which are here very numerous and troublesome, and we saw no fruit trees, nor so much as the track of any animal, except one footstep of a beast which seemed the size of a large mastiff." This *beast* was, without doubt, the kangaroo. From this unhospitable shore they crossed to Sumatra, and having vainly attempted to establish a trade in ambergris, Dampier, broken in credit and health, started with Hall and Ambrose for Acheen, in an open boat. After a terrible voyage they reached the harbour. Dampier remained there, baffled and defeated, an unsuccessful man, until 1690, when (acting as gunner to the English fort of Bencoolen) he was offered a passage to England by Captain Heath of the "Defence." He sailed on the 25th January, 1691, and cast anchor in the Downs on 16th September, 1691, having been absent more than twelve years from his native country.

The *eidolon* of Dampier appears now in fashionable society. The sailor had brought with him a curiosity—a tattoed chieftain ! This savage—one Jeoly—called in the slang of the day "The Painted Prince," was bought a slave at Mindano by a planter named Moody, and when Dampier left Bencoolen, the owner presented him with his serf. "Jeoly was curiously painted," says Dampier, "down the breast, behind, between the shoulders, and most of all on the fore part of the thigh, in the nature of flower-work. This was done by pricking the skin and rubbing in the gum of a tree called *damuser*." Poor Jeoly was carried about and "shown for money," and finally died of the small-pox at Oxford. Those interested in the memoirs of the time can find frequent mention of this unhappy barbarian in the *Gazettes*, papers, and contemporary correspondence of the day.

A lapse of eight years—amply accounted for, doubtless in tavern bills—now occurs in the history of Adventurer—Sailor—Showman—Navigator Dampier. In 1699, we find him engaged in command of the "Roebuck" sloop of eight guns, which, with fifty men aboard, and provisions for twenty months, sailed in the King's service for New Guinea. The records of this voyage have perished. Dampier touched at Brazil, ran across to New Holland (arriving there 1st August, in lat. 26°), and in 1701 sprung a leak at Ascension on his homeward voyage, and was conveyed by a returning East Indiaman ingloriously to England.

One more voyage only was he destined to command. It had been reported that his rashness or vanity precluded others from working with him, and the respectable merchants of London were loth to trust so furious a commander. At the beginning of the Succession War, however, the hopes of performing great feats against the Spaniards urged the merchants, who, in the bitter words of Funnell, "believed that a profitable expedition might be made into those parts, if the buccaneers with ill-provided vessels had performed such extraordinary things." So the good men fitted out two ships of twenty-six guns and one hundred and twenty men each, one the "Fame," commanded by John Pulling, the other, the "St. George," commanded by Dampier. Both ships were amply supplied with warlike stores and well victualled for nine months, having commissions from Prince George, the Queen's husband, against the French and Spaniards. The expedition was a failure for Dampier, who was "broken" over it. Funnell (a self-seeking and lying fellow) relates the story of the cruise, which can be read by the antiquarian in the "Voyages" of Harris. He says, "Dampier returned naked to his owners with a melancholy relation of his unfortunate expedition. . . . Even in his distress he was received as an eminent man, and was introduced to Queen Anne,

. . . The merchants were so sensible of his want of conduct that they resolved never to trust him again with a command."

So disappears Dampier, drunken and desperate as "pilot" to Captain Rogers, in a final expedition to "those seas where his name had long been a terror to Spaniards." Despite his faults he was a greatly daring man, one suited to the times, bold, fearless, and English. Humbolt calls him "the Prince of Navigators." He not only extended the power of British arms, but enriched science and history by his discoveries. An author of much picturesque and graphic power, his works are accurate and interesting. His portrait hangs in Trinity House for all good mariners to admire.

\* \* \* \* \* \*

I would not have the boys who read this copy William Dampier in his drunkenness or in his desperation. I would, however, be glad to hope that the rapid narration of his stirring history may win from the bar-counter, or the cheap cigar shop, some young English-blooded boy, who reminded of the ancient glory of his race, will fling his tobacco out of the window, stop his silly lass's mouth with a kiss, and manfully hoist sail for the Southern Archipelago, the future El Dorado of Federated Australasia.

# ABEL JANSEN TASMAN: EXPLORER.

THE seventeenth century may be called the century of Companies. The English, the French, the Spaniards, and the Dutch seem almost simultaneously to have recognised the great principle of Co-operation in the furtherance of commercial enterprise. In the year 1600, Queen Elizabeth granted to certain merchants of the city of London a charter to trade to the Eastern Indies, reserving to them all rights and privileges and constituting them a body corporate. This charter was the foundation of that great power, afterwards known as "John Company." Eleven years afterwards, Gerard le Roy, an adventurer of daring and genius, obtained a similar privilege for the French. Still later the Emperor Charles VI. created at Ostend a commission known as the "Imperial Company" which died strangled in its birth by political intrigue, while the Danes, under Christian IV., established a trading company in 1612.

The Co-operative Society that at present concerns us, however, is that of the Dutch. The greed of Phillip of Spain strove to secure to himself all the commerce of those magnificent islands of the Pacific to which the daring spirits of the old world were hastening. Phillip knew that a monopoly of trade was the first step to universal Empire. He seized upon the passage into the Baltic hoping to become master of the commerce of the North. He intended to build a city at the straits of Magellan, and there establish such a colony as might, to use the words of old Harris, "put it out of the Power of other Nations to trouble the Commerce of the South Seas or find a passage that way to the Indies." Now Phillip's revolted subjects in the Netherlands had already begun to make a figure in trade, and the instant Spain mastered Portugal she forbade the Dutch to purchase those commodities of the East, which, by their commerce with Lisbon they had hitherto procured and advantageously spread over Europe. This prohibition created men like Abel Tasman, and made the Dutch lords of the Indies.

The merchants of Amsterdam, considering the profits already made by the English who had run successfully the Spanish blockade, took up a resolution to open for themselves a passage to those countries from which they were so contemptuously excluded, and in 1595, they organized a co-operative, offensive, and defensive society called "The Company for Remote Countries." The proceedings of the captains employed by this first company savour of the piratical. Stephen Van der Hagan, the gallant Heemskirk and dashing Oliver van Noort did not stick at trifles. They were on the decks of their own ships, and woe betide any adventurous Spaniard or Portuguese who crossed the range of their fat cannon. The ships of the Hague merchants were little better than subsidised privateers, and it was not until by repeated battles they established a claim to settlement and trade, that the great East Indian Company of the Netherlands can be regarded as respectably existent. The first charter was dated 20th March, 1602, and was to continue for twenty-one years. The second charter was granted on the year that the former expired and terminated in 1644. The third terminated on the 7th February, 1665. The company obtained five charters in all, and in lieu of the fifth, which expired in 1717, procured from the States-General a monopoly of trade within the limits of the original charter, thus making themselves, not only masters of the rich commerce of Japan, but absolute monarchs of Batavia and the smaller islands of the East.

To understand precisely the position which the subject of this monograph held when he first became notable in history, we must take a rapid survey of the condition and economy of the settlements of the company. The government was carried on by a Governor-General and Council, who had their head-quarters at Batavia, or at Amboyna. Banda, Malacca, Ceylon, and Cochin were ruled by lieutenant-governors, who reported directly to head-quarters at Batavia. The Governor and his Council were specially instructed from Holland to use the ships at their disposal in the exploration of the adjoining seas, and when the captains of the Dutch-Indian fleet were not chasing Spaniards or subjugating refractory savage monarchs, they were cruising about the unknown waters of the South seas in obedience to the orders of the Governor. Now, in 1642, that astute and ambitious man, General Antony Van Diemen, was Governor at Batavia, and one of his most trusted captains was a Hollander of obscure birth known as Abel Jansen Tasman.

It is remarkable that the Dutch biographers have neglected to record particulars of the life of their countryman. Notwithstanding the magnitude and importance of his discoveries his name is but briefly mentioned in the histories of the settlements of Dutch-India. Nothing is said of his birth or death; the narrative of his first voyage only survives, and that but by the accident that Valentyn the historian and author of the notable *Omstanding Verbaal van de Geschiedenissen en Zaaken, etc.*, had married into the family of the Secretary of Batavia and obtained access to the neglected private journal of the navigator. Even this narration is open to suspicion, for though the Dutch had treated Tasman with a silence which was either contempt or policy, other nations had recognised the value of his explorations, and several accounts, each purporting to be the only correct one, had appeared in England and France. The editor of *De Hondt's Collection of Voyages* asserts that he himself possessed the manuscript journal, though his transcript differs in many important particulars from that of Valentyn. An English translation from *Dirk Rembrandt*, published in London in 1711, again differs from the French of Thevenot, and the earlier translation (1682), in *Dr. Hook's Philosophical Collection*. In the standard work upon the lives of the great men of the Dutch Indies—*Dubois, Vies des Gouverneurs*

*Hollandois aux Indes Orientales*—Tasman is dismissed with a paragraph in the *Life of Anthony Van Diemen*; and no known book contains any records of his second voyage. I have taken the following account of the first voyage from Dalrymple [*Voyages to the South Pacific Ocean*, Lond. MDCCLXX.] collating with Harris. [*Navigatiarum Bibliotheca*, 1744.] Thevenot, and the *Terra Australis Cognita* published in Edinburgh, 1766. Dalrymple asserts that his narrative is a transcript of Valentyn's reprinted M.S. corrected by De Hondt's quarto, published at the Hague, 1749; Thevenot's folio of 1663; *Nasborough's Voyage*, 1711; and Campbell's *Navig. et Itiner Bibliotheca* (the London folio of 1744.)

On the 14th August, 1642, Tasman sailed from Batavia with two vessels of the Company, the "Heemskirk" and the "Zeehan" (named as are the two peaks which overlook Macquarie Harbour after the two great adventurers who laid the foundation of the Dutch Empire in the South), his instructions being to discover the extent of that Australian continent which previous navigators had already discovered. Touching at the Isle of France, he shaped his course south, then south-east, meeting with stormy weather. On the 22nd November, in lat. 42° 58′ S., the compasses traversed eight points, so that they imagined themselves near some magnetic mines, and on the 24th, land was discovered ten miles distant, which Tasman named "Van Diemen's Land" after the Governor-General.

Stress of weather drove them out to sea, and they did not attempt a landing until the 2nd of December, when, having anchored in Frederick Henry Bay, they sent Francis Jacobez, the master of the "Heemskirk," with a guard of four musqueteers, and attended by the prauw of the "Zeehan," to look for water. In three hours Jacobez returned without accident, and reported abundance of wood and water, but had seen no human being, hearing only a noise as of a gong at a little distance. Prudent Tasman waited all that day, observing from the ship smoke towards the W. by N. and "seeing plainly men of extraordinary size" moving along the shore. On the 3rd, he attempted a landing on the east side of the bay, taking with him a boat's crew and six men, but the surf being dangerous the carpenter, Peter Jacobez, swam ashore, towing with him a pole and the Dutch flag. Making shift to set up his pole near four high trees, the new-found territory was formally taken possession of by our saturated carpenter, and two days after Tasman sailed to the east, thinking it not worth while to prosecute enquiries into the customs of the inhabitants. Calculating his latitude and longitude by the new notation [longitude east and west from the meridian of Greenwich], it would appear that the land first seen was Point Hibbs, and that had Tasman run up Storm Bay he would have reached the present site of Hobart Town. In any case, if, instead of sailing out eastward he had continued his course northerly about four degrees, he would have struck the continent some three degrees east of the present site of Melbourne, midway between Wilson's Promontory and Cape Howe, while less than a single degree north from this point of divergence would have brought him into the straits which divide Van

Diemen's Land from Terra Australis, and anticipated the discovery of Bass. It is probable, however, that his instructions were so framed as to induce him to rather sail for the south, where it was believed existed islands as rich in spices as those of the Javan Archipelago.

On the 13th of December, in latitude 42° 10′ S., and longitude 178° 28′ E., he discovered a mountainous country, which he named Staaten Land, and anchored in what he calls a "fine bay," but which was really the straits between the north and middle islands of New Zealand. When thus at anchor, a disturbance took place with the natives who approached in their canoes and surrounded the two vessels. Seven canoes full of Maories in war costume lay off the "Zeehan," and five canoes, each containing seventeen men, put off to the "Heemskirk." Tasman describes the natives as of a colour between brown and yellow, their hair twisted on their heads like that of the Japanese, and their bodies covered round the loins with a sort of mat. The plates in Dalrymple's work portray the natives as Maories. An affray took place in which the Maories upset the prauw of the "Zeehan," killing three men, and forcing the others to swim for their lives. The weather being rough, Tasman thought it prudent to depart without risking further combat, so, naming the ill-omened spot "Murderers' Bay," he sailed to the eastward.

Here again the Dutchman was just on the point of anticipating the discovery of Cook's Straits. He sailed to the north to Three King's Island, in latitude 34° 25′ S., and longtitude 172° 40′, naming a cape to the eastward (the north-west coast of Auckland) Maria Van Diemen, in honour of the daughter of the Governor-General. Being in stress for provisions, he did not land, and sailed north for the islands of Cocos and Hoorn (discovered by Schonten in 1616) for a supply of food. After passing a rock which he named High Pylstaarts Island, from the abundance of its fowl, he sighted, on the 21st January, 1643, two islands called Amsterdam and Middleberg (part of the Friendly Islands), the inhabitants of which brought fruit, pigs, and poultry. The navigators went ashore here and held a festival. Tasman gives a most picturesque description of his reception by the King, which I regret I have not space to quote, regretting even more also that I cannot reproduce the fantastic and charming illustration of the "Harbour of Amsterdam Island," and the bird's eye view of the anchored fleet lying outside the palisaded and populous town.

On the 1st of February, he discovered the islands of Prince William, and on the the 22nd an easterly trade wind in latitude 5° 2′ S., and longitude 178° 32′ E., brought him in sight of the group of islands called Ontong-Java, by Le Maire, and set down by him as ninety miles from New Guinea. From thence he sailed to New Britain, which he erroneously called New Guinea, and passing by Seram-Bourg and Boston, arrived at Batavia on the 15th of June, having accomplished his voyage in ten months. A map of his discoveries was sent to Amsterdam.

As I have before said, no complete memoir exists of the second voyage of Tasman, though there is little doubt but that it was more important in its results than the first one. Mr. Major supposes that these records were wantonly destroyed. There is some reason for this supposition, for the Company was unreasonably jealous of the progress made by its West India rival, and carefully locked up all charts which might give aid to foreign mariners adventuring into those seas which it regarded as its own. The works from which historians compiled their narratives were few in number. Almost all that was publicly known concerning the discoveries of the Batavian governors was to be found in Thevenot's folio of 1663-72; the *Nord en Oost Tartarye* of Witsen, 1692-1705; Valentyn's *Oud en Nieuw Oost Indien* 1724-26; in the *Inleidning tot de algemeen Geographie*; Nicolas Struyk, 1740, and the celebrated *Book of Despatches* quoted by Flinders in the introduction to his *Voyages*.

In this last-named work, the instructions to Tasman for his second voyage in 1644, are set down with a phlegmatic and money-making caution which is curious to contemplate. No ardour for science or for discovery for discovery's sake stirred the mercantile souls of the "Company." Tasman was to "put up signs of possession" on such countries as he might discover, by "planting European trees, and carving the arms of the Netherlands and the Company on posts, stones, and rocks." He was to institute trade with the natives, but "to keep them ignorant of the value of precious metals," showing samples of lead, tin, or pewter as of more value than gold. He was to bring home samples of everything likely to be of mercantile value and to make treaties with the natives to exclude in trading transactions all other nations but the Dutch. He was to make drawings and descriptions of the bays, capes, rivers, etc., for which purpose a draughtsman accompanied him, and he was desired to note most carefully the latitude and longitude, and prevailing currents of wind. His sailing directions were as follow :—He was to proceed to Amboyna and Banda, thence by Tenimber, Key, and Aroun to Point Ture on the south coast of New Guinea. From that place he was to continue eastward to 9° south latitude, and endeavour to ascertain if within the great inlet of Spratt's River there is not an entrance into the South Sea. Thence to coast along the west coast of New Guinea to the farthest known spots in 17° south latitude, and follow the coast, despite all opposing winds, in order "that we may be sure whether this land is divided from the great known south continent or not." If he found that the great south land *was* so divided his instructions were to circumnavigate it, but if—as the Council believed—no opening existed between New Guinea and New Holland, Tasman was to run down the north coast to south latitude 22°, proceed to Houtman's Abrolhos, fish up a chest of dollars lost in Pelsart's wreck, pick up two Dutchmen who had been there put ashore for mutiny, and obtain from them all particulars of the country. If the weather did not permit him to go to Houtman's Abrolhos, he was to complete the discovery of Arnhem and Van Diemen's Lands and return by Java and the Straits of Sunda. So he departed some time in January,

1644, with three ships, the "Limmen," the "Zeemeuw" and the "Brak," and disappears for ever out of human history.

There is no doubt but that the cool-headed navigator fulfilled his mission with honour and credit and brought back numerous drawings and plans. These together with his charts and journal were carefully concealed or destroyed by the Company. The only fragment of anything which looks like an authentic record is some four paragraphs of a journal published in 1705, by Witsen, and purporting to be written by Tasman. These paragraphs are understood to refer to Papua, though the latitude is given 17° 12' south, and longitude 121° east. They describe the natives as very populous and possessing bows and arrows. It is more than probable that the assumption of Burgomaster Witsen is unwarranted. Better evidence of Tasman's fortune are the maps of 1648-60. In the same year in which the map of Australia was inscribed in the floor of the Stadthouse in Amsterdam (1648), Louis Mayerne Turquet published at Paris a *mappemonde*, which is evidently based upon observations similar to those which Tasman was directed to make. So also in the *Mar di India* in the 1650 edition of Janssen's *Atlas*, in the *Atlas* of Klencke of Amsterdam, in the sixteenth chart of *Thevenot's Relation de divers voyages curieux* (1663), distinct reference is made to discoveries which it is most reasonable to suppose were made by Tasman. In one of the early maps of Van Keulen a portion of Tasman's track with his soundings is given, and in the British Museum is a chart which Mr. Major regards as a *copy* of Tasman's own [See *Major's Early Voyages to Terra Australis: Introduction*, p. xcvi], and which appears to give evidence that, missing the discovery that New Guinea and New Holland were separated by sea, he took the alternative afforded him and continued sounding down the Gulf of Carpentaria, sounded ingloriously all the way to De Witt's Land and then returned in a direct line north-west for Java.

So ends all that is at present known of a man who was without doubt a prudent commander and a competent, well-skilled navigator. That he did not leave a larger memory is perhaps due to the system which created him—a system which cultivated human sponges to be filled, squeezed and thrown away.

# THE SETTLEMENT OF PORT JACKSON (N.S.W.).

AT daylight on the 13th May, 1787, His Majesty's ship "Sirius" made signal to sail to a little fleet that had been lying off the Mother Bank since the 16th of March. This little fleet was destined to carry Governor Phillip to take formal possession of Botany Bay, a place recommended to the Government as suitable for a convict station.

The fleet was not a large one. It consisted of His Majesty's ships "Sirius," "Supply," and "Hyena" (the latter only acting as convoy for a certain distance), three victualling ships with two years' stores and provisions for the settlement, and six transports with troops and convicts. The Major-Commandant and his staff were on board the "Sirius," and the transports carried about 200 officers and soldiers, together with 775 convicts, consisting of 565 men, 192 women, and 18 children. The list of the military force, as given by Captain Watkin French, of the marines (from whose account of the expedition the minuter details of this paper are derived), is worth noting—four captains, twelve subalterns, twenty-four sergeants and corporals, eight drummers, and 160 private marines, and he adds that the majority of the prisoners were mechanics and husbandmen specially selected by order of the Government. Having got through the Needles with a "fresh leading breeze, the convicts began to repine at their lot, but on the morning of the 20th, getting their irons knocked off by order of the Commandant, and sending a few messages to England by the "Hyena," which parted company that afternoon, matters began to assume a more cheerful aspect.

Let us glance for a moment at the state of affairs in Europe. It was seven years after the Gordon riots and the burning of Newgate. American independence had been already declared, and the bloodshed at Bunker's Hill had caused the tree of liberty to blossom and bud. Admiral Kempenfelt and the "Royal George" had gone down at Spithead. William Pitt was twenty-nine years old, and had been Premier of England for four years. The steam-engine had supplanted the hand-loom in the cotton mills for nearly three years. Poor Peg Nicholson had just stabbed at George III., and Edmund Burke had thrown the first stone at Warren Hastings. Washington was on the eve of his presidency, and the Convocation of Notables was waiting to be convoked. It was the age of mail coaches, knee-breeches, frogs, Frenchmen, taxation, and wooden shoes. England was yet bleeding from her struggle with her colonies, and the thundercloud of revolution hung over France. Napoleon had just got his commission as sub-lieutenant, and the Bastille had not yet fallen.

After touching at Teneriffe on the 3rd June—where a convict made a desperate attempt to escape by seizing a boat in the night and rowing off to a small cove, from which he intended to "cross to the Great Canaries"—and Rio de Janeiro on the 7th August, the fleet cast anchor in Table Bay on the 13th of October, and found the harbour crowded with shipping. At the Cape they remained until the 12th of November, and took on board two bulls, seven cows, three horses, forty-four sheep, thirty-two hogs, besides goats and poultry, for the purpose of stocking the settlement. A few officers also purchased live stock, but found it an inconvenient proceeding, as hay cost 16s. the hundredweight. It was also gratifying to the expedition to be informed by the master of an American ship—140 days from Boston, on a trading voyage to the East Indies, and rescuer of the officers and crew of the "Harcourt," wrecked on the Cape de Verde Islands—that "if a reception could be secured, emigration would take place to New South Wales, not only from the old continent but the new one, where the spirit of adventure and thirst for novelty were excessive."

Meeting with contrary winds, Governor Phillip resolved to change his pennant from the "Sirius" to the "Supply," and proceed on his way without waiting for the rest of the fleet. On the 25th, therefore, the separation took place, several sawyers, carpenters, blacksmiths, and other mechanics being drafted from various ships into the "Supply," in order that His Excellency might get a few buildings run up by the time the fleet should arrive. The fleet itself was put into two divisions, the first, consisting of three transports, under the command of Lieutenant Bird; and the second, comprising the victuallers and remaining transports, was left in charge of Captain Hunter of the "Sirius." Sailing in this order, on the 7th of January, 1788, the expedition sighted the shore of New South Wales, but the westerly wind dying away, the little squadron was compelled to hold off the shore, and did not get sight of it again until the 19th, and on the morning of the 20th—a dull, heavy, and cloudy day—the last division cast anchor in the harbour, and was welcomed by the already-arrived "Supply" and her illustrious passenger. The voyage had taken exactly thirty-five weeks, and out of 112 marines His Majesty had lost but one, making up for it, however, by the death of twenty-four out of the 700 convicts.

The stay in the bay was not of long duration. The Governor and Lieutenant-Governor (Mr. Robert Ross) started to explore the country the next morning, and getting into an opening called by Captain Cook "Port Jackson," were so struck with the advantages of the place that it was determined instantly to remove thither. On setting sail the next morning, however, a great alarm spread through the fleet,—two large ships were seen standing in for the mouth of the bay! All sorts of rumours were afloat. It was the vanguard of a Dutch fleet coming to dispossess them. It was an armed vessel of war, and her consort. It was a store-ship from England. Governor Phillip, however, stayed the panic by making public announcement that the strange sail were French ships under the command of

M. de La Perrouse. The next morning the two nations saluted each other as they passed with flags flying in the solitary bay. After a few hours run to Port Jackson, during which time the party admired the luxuriant prospect of its shores, among which many of the "Indians" were frequently seen, they anchored in a snug cove, and on the next day commenced to disembark.

Setting vigorously to work to cut down the trees, set up the tents, and mark out the dimensions of their future home, the expedition passed away some weeks pleasantly enough. The Governor fixed his residence on the eastern side of a small rivulet at the head of the cove, with a large body of convicts encamped near him, and on the western side were stationed the remaining body of prisoners, with guards posted over them night and day. The pressure of business—that is to say, the making of huts and daubing of wattles—prevented the immediate reading of the commissions, but on the 7th of February the colony was taken possession of in due form. On that day the officers of the guard took post in the Marine battalion, which was drawn up and marched off the parade, with colours flying and music playing, to an adjoining ground which had been cleared for the occasion, and upon which the convicts were assembled. The Judge-Advocate, David Collins, Esq., then read His Majesty's commission, which appointed His Excellency, Arthur Phillip, Esq., Governor and Captain-General in and over the territory of New South Wales and its dependencies; together with an Act of Parliament for the establishment of laws, and patents for holding civil and criminal courts. Upon this His Excellency made a judicious speech to the convicts, assuring them of his desire to treat them fairly and kindly. Three volleys were fired by the troops, who then marched back to their parade, and were reviewed by His Excellency, and the day's proceedings wound up by a "cold collation" in His Excellency's newly-erected tent, and the "drinking of many loyal and public toasts." We can imagine the happy little picnic party in the cool of the evening drinking prosperity to Port Jackson, with the "Indians" handy in the adjoining bush, and about 1,200 square feet of cleared land round about them, all unwitting of goldfields, Bathurst rushes, separation of Victoria, land acts, universal suffrage, and the like.

The extent of the Governor's authority by this commission is defined to reach from 43° 39' south to latitude 10° 37' south, and commencing again at the 135° of longitude, east of Greenwich, it proceeds in an easterly direction, and includes all islands within the limits of the specified latitudes in the Pacific Ocean. As far as regarded his authority over his governed subjects he was absolute; he had no council, he could imprison at will and pardon at will.

He was soon called upon to exercise his power. Four days after the conciliatory speech, three convicts were brought to trial. One was convicted of striking a marine with a cooper's adze, and received 150 lashes for his pains. Another, for theft, was marooned on an adjoining island, and kept there on bread and water for a week; while a third, sentenced to receive fifty lashes, was pardoned by the grace of the Governor. On the 28th of February a "mutinous" plot was discovered among the convicts, who had planned to steal the provisions and take to the bush. Four were arraigned, three sentenced to death, and the fourth to be flogged. Only one, however, was executed—the ringleader, Thomas Barrett, "an old and desperate offender, who died with a hardy spirit." He was swung off the limb of a big tree, near which were assembled the whole body of convicts, guarded by the battalion of Marines.

The constitution of the Court by which these fellows were tried was rather peculiar. The number of members, including the Judge-Advocate, was limited to seven, who are expressly ordered to be officers of either army or navy. The Court being met in military fashion—armed, the Judge-Advocate swears in the members in the manner adopted towards jurymen, and is afterwards sworn in himself in the same manner. The crime is then put to the prisoner, and the prosecution is left entirely to the person at whose suit he is tried. The witnesses are all examined on oath, and the decision is directed to be given according to the laws of England, "or as nearly as may be, allowing for the circumstances and situation of the settlement," by a majority of votes. In capital cases, however, five out of the seven members must concur to make a verdict. During the sitting of the Court, the court-house was surrounded by a guard under arms, and admission granted to any one who might choose to enter it.

On the 15th February, Lieutenant Ball sailed for Norfolk Island, a place concerning which the "Ministry" had heard great reports, and took with him Lieutenant King as commandant, a surgeon, a midshipman, a weaver, two marines, and sixteen convicts, of whom six were women. Events went on quietly enough. The natives, or "Indians" as they seem to have been called, were friendly, and viewed with astonishment the white skins and shaven chins of the new comers. Governor Phillip seems to have protected them from insult, and they in return behaved with some civility, though occasionally breaking out and knocking in the skull of some aggressive convict. They were a poor set of creatures, going entirely naked, sleeping in a sort of coffin of bark, eating roots, and refusing rum, but when roused they could be dangerous. Their weapons were stone hatchets, wooden swords, spears, and clubs. The dingo, that pest of the early squatters, was quite domesticated in those days. Governor Phillip had one given to him as a present by a friendly native, and thought it something like a fox. With the aspect and appearance of the colony the settlers seemed more than satisfied, but they complained bitterly at first of the bad grain of the wood. Snakes were plentiful, and the emu and kangaroo alarmed the female convicts greatly. The soil seemed well adapted for agriculture, and the vegetables planted by the garrison grew very successfully. The notion of "mines," which it would appear had possessed the brain of some wild dreamer in England, was speedily laughed to scorn, although Governor Phillips observed a "prodigious chain of mountains," running north and south, at a distance of some sixty miles inland, which he thought might be worth exploring.

In the middle of March the French departed on the prosecution of their voyage. Their ships—under the command of M. De La Perrouse—had sailed from France on the 1st August, 1785, and as all the world knows, were not destined to get back again. While at Botany Bay, Abbé Receveur—the naturalist attached to the expedition—died, and was buried on the north shore, with a plate of copper attached to a tree above his grave.

On the 20th March the "Supply" returned from Norfolk Island, having safely landed Lieutenant King. Lieutenant Bull reported that the Norfolk pines were very large, but regretted much that he could not find any New Zealand Flax, arguing badly for the future commercial prosperity of the Colony from that circumstance.

Winter now coming on, the erection of barracks was set about with great vigour, and the privates of each company undertook to build for themselves two wooden houses, 68ft. in length and 23ft. in breadth, but were compelled to abandon the undertaking and proceed on a more limited scale. The plan of the town, moreover, was drawn out, and it being agreed that "to proceed on a narrow confined scale in a country of the extensive limits we possess would be unpardonable, extent of empire commanding grandeur of design," the principal street was laid down 200 ft. in breadth, and the rest in corresponding proportion. Possessed with the same admirable notions, His Excellency undertook an expedition into the interior. His party consisted of eleven persons, but at the end of four days, provisions growing scarce, it was deemed prudent to return.

Now the troubles began. Fresh meat began to fail. The "Supply" went to Howe's Island (discovered on her former trip) to look for turtle, but found none. Fish became scarce. It was not thought prudent to kill the live stock bought at so great an expense at the Cape, and the settlement was compelled to live almost entirely on salt provisions. As a natural consequence, scurvy broke out; vegetables were scarce, and the garrison fell sick. It drew near the time for the departure of the ships for Europe, and earnest representations were made concerning the supply of fresh meat. But there was a hopeful spirit abroad.

On the anniversary of the King's birthday all the officers dined with the Governor, and among other toasts drunk was that of "Prosperity of Sydney Cove in Cumberland County." At daylight the ships fired twenty-one guns each, which was repeated at noon, and answered by three volleys from the battalion of Marines. Each prisoner received an allowance of grog, and—glorious day—"every non-commissioned officer and private soldier had the honour of drinking His Majesty's health in a pint of porter, served out at the flag-staff." Three days' holiday were given to every convict on the Island, and four felons who had been marooned in irons were allowed to rejoin their comrades. This indulgence, however, was followed by ill effects. A prisoner named Samuel Peyton, twenty years of age, broke open an officer's marquee with intent to commit robbery, for which offence he was tried and hung, together with another man named Corbett, who had attempted to escape

On the 14th of July, 1788, the ships, with the exception of the "Sirius" and the "Supply," which had gone to Norfolk Island, sailed for England, to report to the British Government that the Colony of Port Jackson had been successfully established.

Looking back—while a boy yells latest Sydney telegrams under my window—from the new story of 1870 to this old story of 1788, it seems worth the re-telling.

# THE SCOTCH MARTYR CONVICTS.

IN the various histories of Australia reference is made to the story of "The Scotch Martyrs," Messrs. Muir, Palmer, Margarot, and Skirving. These gentlemen were sent as felons to Sydney in the year 1794, and their crime was inciting certain citizens of Edinburgh to present a petition to the Crown for Universal Suffrage. The accounts given of their sufferings and adventures differ materially; the fullest is written by Mr. Samuel Bennett, in his *Australian Discovery and Exploration;*—and even the report of the trial by Howell is not corroborated in all particulars by other authorities. Unfortunately books which ought to throw further light on the matter are not accessible. Mr. Palmer wrote an account of his voyage to Sydney in the "Surprise" transport, which was published by Mr. Joyce, and a letter of his, detailing the circumstances of his arrival in New South Wales, appeared in the *Monthly Repository*, but neither work is obtainable in Melbourne. I have done my best to reconcile incongruities and relate the extraordinary history with some degree of coherence.

The year 1793 was an eventful one in Europe. The French Revolution was at its height, and the minds of all men were disturbed with fear of social revolution or with hope of political reform. The National Convention sitting at Paris had, on the 21st of January, ordered the execution of Louis XVI., and the feeling of terror and insecurity became intensified. London had just seen the Gordon riots, and had pronounced Thomas Paine guilty of libel in publishing the *Rights of Man*. All over the Kingdom were societies calling themselves "The Society for Constitutional Information," "The London Corresponding Society," "The Revolutionary Society," "The Society of Friends of the People;" and the Government were unusually active in prosecuting the vendors of pamphlets printed by these bodies. On the 23rd of February, Thomas Holland, a printseller in Oxford Street, was sentenced to a year's imprisonment and a fine of £100, for publishing *An Address to the Addresses on the late Proclamation*—an expression of opinion concerning war with France— and the following day Daniel Eaton was arrested for circulating a pamphlet entitled *Political Hog's-wash*. On the 1st of March, Butler and Bond were fined £500 and sentenced to six months in Newgate, for printing a publication animadverting on the Secret Committee of the House of Lords; and on the 11th the Lord-Lieutenant of Ireland issued a proclamation commanding magistrates to disperse by firearms all private political assemblies. On the 26th March, Dr. James Reynolds, a physician in good practice at Belfast, was committed to

Kilmainham Gaol for refusing to give evidence "concerning the condition of the district where he resided"—that is, I suppose, to betray his disaffected neighbours; and on the 8th May two booksellers, named Ridgway and Symonds, were imprisoned for three years and fined £300 for publishing the works of the abhorred Paine. On the 19th of June, Frost, the attorney, was struck off the rolls and sentenced to the pillory for "using seditious words;" and on the 30th August one Thomas Muir, Esq., the younger, of Hunter's Hill, was put on his trial for sedition before the High Court of Justiciary at Edinburgh.

Mr. Muir was a young man of true ambition and parts. Born in Glasgow in 1765, he was admitted a member of the Faculty of Advocates, and, being of a liberal disposition, and taking a keen interest in social developments, soon found his sympathies enlisted on the side of political reform. About 1792 one of the numerous societies which I have mentioned established a branch in Glasgow, and Muir became an ardent worker in the cause. Allied with him was a Mr. Palmer—the Rev. Thomas Fyshe Palmer, a native of Bedfordshire, and a Master of Arts of Queen's College, Cambridge. He was ordained a curate in the Church of England, but in 1783 became a convert to Unitarianism, and under the auspices of the celebrated Dr. Priestley, laboured for some eight years as a clergyman of that denomination. He, too, was strongly impressed with liberal views, and was made a member of the "Friends of Liberty," together with Messrs. Skirving, Gerald, and Margarot. The "Friends of Liberty" held meetings in various places, one being in "Berean Meeting House" at Dundee, another, "Laurie's Rooms" in Edinburgh, and another, an inn in Archintilloch. The meetings in themselves were harmless enough, but it happened that the dreaded Thomas Paine was quoted, and that in the speeches made by Palmer and Margarot language less guarded than the times demanded was too often used. "We are oppressed with taxes." "We are spending the blood and treasure of the nation in an unholy war against a people who seek but the right of every man—liberty." "Universal suffrage and annual parliaments are the only means to enable the people to govern." "No man has a right to acquire land in fee simple from the State." "The overgrown estates of nobles and rich commons originated in rapine, murder, desolation, and proscription." "Those who have no votes in the election of representatives are not free," &c.;—all of which seems tame enough in these days, but all of which in July, 1793—when Charlotte Corday had just stabbed Marat—was very terrible treason indeed.

Mr. Muir was tried first. He was accused of having by his speeches, publications and acts, excited the citizens to sedition, and of having absconded from the Kingdom when called upon to stand his trial. His seditious practices consisted in holding meetings of the "Society of Friends of the People," in corresponding with the "United Irishmen," "and in printing the rude remarks of Thomas Paine." His absconding consisted in his having taken a passage for New York, and landing again in Ireland when the vessel in which he shipped put into Belfast for cargo. The evidence against him, so far as these circumstances were concerned, was undeniable. He lent Thomas Paine's book to many people, and spoke of it highly. He read an address from the "United Irishmen" to the "Scotch Society," and openly pronounced himself a friend of Hamilton Rowan, and an ally to the Irish cause. He had in his pocket when arrested, a passport from General Mausry in favour of "Citizen Muir," given "in the first year of the French Republic." He had given orders that letters were to be sent to him under cover "*Au citoyen de Coudille, Hotel de Toulon, No. 1 rue des Fosses du Temple.*" All sorts of witnesses gave evidence as to his unguarded language, and the gravest attention was paid to their trumpery. A servant lass named Annie Fisher was complimented by the Court upon her honesty when she said that she heard her young master tell his hairdresser to buy Paine's *Rights of Man*, and keep it in the shop to enlighten the people. Another witness said that the prisoner stated that members of Parliament should have forty shillings a day, and none but honest men sit in the Legislature. A third was permitted to allege, as a proof of the young man's hatred of the Government, that he had termed the Irish Catholics "men taxed without being represented, bound by laws to which they had given no consent, and politically dead in their native land." The High Court—Lord Justice Clerk (M'Queen), Lord Henderland, Lord Swinton, Lord Dunsinnan, and Lord Abercrombie—found the "panel" guilty with one voice, and sentenced him to transportation beyond seas for fourteen years, under penalty of death should he return before the expiration of that term.

Palmer fared equally ill. An attempt by his counsel to overthrow the indictment on account of the misspelling of his name— Fische—was promptly rebutted. There was no evidence that he *wrote* the MS. of the "libel" complained of, but it was proved that he paid for the printing of it, and he too received his sentence—seven years merely—for an offence which Lord Eskgrove characterized as "dangerous to society and dangerous to himself—an attack upon the King, Parliament, and the Constitution."

Skirving, Gerald, and Margarot were arrested together in their room at the "Black Bull," and their papers and effects seized. Margarot was one of the most active members of the society which met in a room in Black Friar's Wynd, in Edinburgh, and both he and Skirving frequently took the chair. The business of the meeting— the minutes of which were read at the trial—was to urge upon the people the necessity for petitioning for Universal Suffrage and Annual Parliaments. In fact, the "Friends of Liberty" were the forerunners of the Chartists. Constables twice attended to disperse these meetings, and on one occasion the Provost himself appeared on the scene. The assemblage, however, protested against interference, and went away peaceably enough, to continue the debate elsewhere. The tenor of the arguments and of the documents was the same as those circulated and used by Muir, and the three prisoners were sentenced to fourteen years' transportation. Margarot made a most eloquent, and—for one in his situation—a most imprudent speech.

He defended his own conduct, and that of his friends, with warmth and roundly attacked the system of boroughmongering and aristocratic patronage which a few years more saw happily abolished. The Lord Justice Clerk in summing up the case, said, "The panel has been accused of sedition, and he has defended himself in a speech which is nothing but sedition from beginning to end." Lord Abercrombie said, "the right to enjoy universal suffrage and annual parliaments would bring ruin and destruction on England," and gave it as his opinion, that the " punishment was, on the whole, perhaps the mildest that ought to be pronounced."

The only place of transportation beyond seas, which was at the disposal of Great Britain in 1794 was the six-year-old settlement of Botany Bay, and thither the unfortunate victims of bigotry and fear were conveyed by the transport "Surprise," Patrick Campbell, master, in April, 1794. But, there were not wanting humane men to plead the cause of the enthusiasts. On the 10th March the Right Hon. W. Adam brought the case before the House of Commons, and, seconded by Mr. Fox, strove to procure a remission of the sentence. But in vain. Hansard records briefly, "The motion was negatived without a division." After a long voyage, during which they would appear to have been treated with unusual severity, the five victims of advanced ideas arrived in Sydney. Palmer's inaccessible pamphlet, doubtless, gives full particulars of the journey and the reception. On the authority of Howell, I may say that the Governor (Hunter) extended his protection to the exiles, and gave them permission to cultivate land, and employ their capital in hiring labour. Gerald, however, whose health had been broken by continued confinement in a close cell in Newgate, died soon after his arrival, and Skirving, a delicate man, did not long survive. Gerald was buried in Farm Cove, now part of the Botanic Gardens, but I do not know if any record marks his tomb. Margarot lived to return to England in 1815. Howell says that "he seemed to have behaved throughout with the most shameless profligacy," but I can find no reason for such an assertion, save that the staunch old Scotchman persistently denounced the infamous traffic in rum, by which many of the officers and early settlers laid the foundation of their fortunes. Margarot gave evidence before the First Committee of the House of Commons on Transportation, in 1812, and is described by Lord Strangford as "Old Maurice Margarot, one of the Aboriginal reformers." "I saw him," says his lordship, " with his wife and an old cat, the faithful companions of his exile." According to Howell he died in November, 1816, while a subscription was being raised for his relief.

Palmer lived quietly enough in Sydney until the year 1799, when he began to make preparations for his homeward voyage. In conjunction with Captain Reid, Mr. Boston, and Mr. Ellis, he purchased a small vessel, and set sail from Port Jackson on the 20th January, 1800, with the intention of taking in timber at New Zealand for sale at the Cape. They spent, however, twenty-six weeks in New Zealand, and exhausted their stores. Pressed for provisions, they ran for the Tonga Islands, but were not allowed to land. At Fiji they obtained some fruit and yams, and after narrowly escaping shipwreck on a reef at Goraa, they sailed for Macao, but were compelled to put into Guam, although aware that it was a hostile port. The Spanish Governor seized them as prisoners of war, but treated them kindly. The exposure he had suffered caused Palmer to be seized with dysentery, and though keeping life flickering for nearly eight months, he died early in June, 1802, two years after his sentence expired.

The end of Thomas Muir's life was as romantic as the beginning. He had been in "correspondence" with France from early boyhood, and it was destined that after many adventures his bones should rest in the land he loved so well. On his settlement in Sydney he built a house on some land which he had purchased, and named the little estate "Hunter's Hill," after his paternal acres in the Scotland he had left for ever. It is remarkable that Tuckey, who knew nothing about the story of Muir, copies in a note to his voyage to Port Phillip, an inscription in an English book presented to the library of Antonian monks, in St. Sebastian, by the unhappy exile during the stay of the "Surprise." The opening lines show how thoughts of his home still wrung the poor fellow's heart :

"O Scotia ! O longum felix, longumque superba
Ante alias patria, Heroum sanctissima tellus !"

The book is inscribed as presented to the monastery by Thomas Muir, Gente Scotus, animâ orbis terrarum civis. He employed his leisure by instructing the convicts in certain portions of the Bible, and even set up a little printing press, and circulated copies of texts struck off by his own hand. In America, says Mr. Bennett, the story of the trial had excited much interest. Muir had many friends in New York, and General Washington, then in the seventh year of his Presidentship, permitted a sloop named the "Otter" to be fitted out and put under the command of Captain Dawes, for the express purpose of rescuing Muir. The "Otter" anchored in Port Jackson in January, 1796, and after about a fortnight the captain succeeded in getting speech with his man. There was no time to lose if escape was meant. The "Otter" had put in, presumedly, for water, and folks wondered why she stayed so long. Muir went home, wrote a letter of thanks to Hunter, and carrying with him only his pocket-Bible, embarked under cover of night in the friendly vessel. But his adventures had only just began.

After a voyage of four months, the "Otter" made Nootka Sound, struck on a rock, and went to pieces. None survived of all the ship's company save Muir and two sailors. The three were captured, when in a starving state, by a tribe of Indians. Muir won the affection of the savages by his bold bearing and by his compliance with their customs. His companions were killed, but Muir managed to escape, and after a walk of nearly four thousand miles he reached Panama, naked, and covered with wounds. The Governor treated him civilly, and after a little rest, the undaunted man started for Vera Cruz, across the Isthmus. Here the Governor offered to send him to the Havannas in a vessel that was about to sail for that port, but the unfortunate man was attacked by yellow fever, and, as Mr. Bennett pathetically says, "laid on a bed of sickness, a stranger, and penniless." On his recovery he was sent to Cuba, but was there imprisoned, and finally put on bard a Spanish frigate, the "Nymph," as a common sailor. The "Nymph" and her consort were sighted off Cadiz by the "Emerald" and the "Irresistible," part of Sir John Jarvis's squadron, on the look-out for treasure ships. A fight of two hours took place in Camille Bay, and, after a bloody battle the Spaniards surrendered. The last shot from the "Irresistible" struck Muir on the head, and he fell as one dead upon the deck. When the English officers boarded their prize, they were struck with the curious fact, that one of the bodies which lay on its face held, clasped in both hands, a pocket-Bible. The sailors raised the apparent corpse, and, seeing that one eye was knocked out, and part of the cheek carried away, made as though to fling it overboard, when the man uttered a sigh, and the book fell from his hands. An English officer picked it up, and read in the title-page the name of his old schoolfellow, Thomas Muir. Keeping his own counsel, he got his friend conveyed ashore as a wounded Spaniard; and after some months of suffering, the iron constitution of the hardy Scotchman triumphed. He found means to communicate with his friends in Paris, and was invited by the Directory to "make his home, as one of the friends of liberty, in the land which liberty had chosen for her own."

His entrance into France was a sort of triumph. At Bordeaux he was entertained at a banquet of five hundred citizens, the Mayor of the town presiding. His health was drunk with enthusiasm, and, supported in the arms of the American Consul, he attempted to return thanks, but fainted. On the 4th of February, 1789, he reached Paris, but, despite the most devoted care and attention, gradually sank from the effects of his frightful wound in the head. He died at Chantilly on the 27th of September, and was buried by the French nation with every mark of respect.

Thomas Muir was a brave and pious man. If he erred from zeal in his youth, he surely atoned for his indiscretions by his bitter punishment. In the stories of himself and his companions, I can find little to rebuke and much to pity. Victims to the popular fury of the hour, they yet watered the tree of political liberty with their blood. The residents of "Hunter's Hill" may surely think, with a blameless sigh, of the sad fate of its quondam owner. As was said of a greater martyr than Thomas Muir, "His crime was that he lived too soon."

# BARRINGTON: PRINCE OF PICKPOCKETS.

MOST people have heard of George Barrington, the pickpocket. His name has become notorious—I had almost written famous—for gentlemanly larceny. Bulwer has dished up an imitation of him in *Paul Clifford*, and Lever introduced him bodily into *The O'Donoghue*. I read once a highly-spiced romance called by his name, and purporting to be an account of his doings, in that oracle of nurserymaids the *London Journal*, and I came very near to seeing a sensation drama in five acts, of which he was the intelligent hero. I have heard his name mentioned with almost as much admiration as that of Jack Sheppard by pipe-smoking "old hands," yarning while the sheep were camped; and I have seen a picture of him—Claude Duval dashed with Almaviva—presiding at a banquet as the Prince of Prigs. That he *was* the prince of prigs in the age of the First Gentleman in Europe there can be no doubt. He robbed with grace, and broke the eighth commandment with an air. He was not such a grand speculator as Price, otherwise Old Patch; he did not ride so dashingly as Claude Duval; he had not the more solid qualities of M. Vidocq, nor the enterprising financial ability of Sir John Dean Paul; but he was, in his way, as smart a fellow as any of them. He lived merrily all his life, and having been transported, made the best of his altered circumstances, took the goods the gods provided him, became superintendent of convicts at Parramatta, wrote a history of his adopted country, and died in the odour of respectability.

It is on account of his latter exploit in the way of authorship that I have elected to tell the true story of his life in these pages. Strangely enough, however, though Messrs. Sherwood, Neily, and Jones, of 5, Newgate Street, London, published, in the year 1810, in two volumes quarto, a *History of New South Wales*, by George Barrington, superintendent of convicts, the literary fame of its author was not much enhanced. His speeches at his trials, were excellent, but his writing is execrable. The *History* is a very slip-slop piece of work; and is, moreover, according to Dr. Lang, untrustworthy. As a thief, Mr. Barrington was not above suspicion. As an author, he is beneath contempt. One would have thought that so ingenious a stealer of other men's property could not but have succeeded in literature: but, strange to say, he neglected the advantages afforded by his early training, and consequently has not achieved literary distinction.

George Barrington was born in the year 1755, at Maynooth, in Kildare. His real name was Waldron, and his parents seem to have occupied the position of respectable cottagers. They were themselves in straitened circumstances, and their son would have grown up without education had not his precocious talents attracted the attention of a benevolent clergyman, who placed the lad at school in Dublin. He was liberally supplied with money by his patron, who announced his intention of starting him in life. At sixteen years of age, however, he quarrelled with another lad, and stabbed him with a penknife. For this, Waldron was severely flogged, and smarting as much from wounded vanity as from loss of cuticle, he determined to run away. The same night he packed up his clothes, stole twelve guineas from his master, and a gold repeater from his master's sister, and scaling the school wall, set out in the middle of the night to seek his fortune. Such as it was, he soon found it. Putting up the next evening at a small inn in the town of Drogheda, he heard that a company of strolling players were to perform that night, and, boy-like, went to see them.

The manager of this company was a man named Price. He was of gentlemanly exterior, of reputed good family, and agreeable figure, but having been detected in the commission of some fraud, was outlawed to Ireland. Price fell in with the boy, took a fancy to him, heard his story, and enrolled him as a member of his company. Burning with theatrical ambition, Barrington—as he now called himself—essayed the part of Jaffier in *Venice Preserved*, and made a hit. He had a speaking eye, a good figure, a handsome face, some talent, and a prodigious memory. The last two qualities gave him success in his new rôle; the first three gained him the heart of the Belvidera of the night. This was a young girl of respectable connections and some education, who had been seduced and deserted by a lieutenant of marines and thrown upon her own resources for a livelihood. She appears, however, to have been more sinned against than sinning, and to have in some degree merited the affection which the ardent, impulsive youth showed for her. Into this *liaison* Barrington fell, like the young gentleman in *Disowned*— or jumped—headlong, and the troop secured his services.

For some time life seemed cheery enough. With love in the person of the lively actress, and fame in the shape of the thumpings of the thick sticks of an Irish audience, Barrington was satisfied. But soon there came a change. At Londonderry, Manager Price announced that he was in difficulties, Barrington's stolen watch had long ago disappeared, and the twelve guineas had quickly melted in the sun of Belvidera's smiles. The "company" —poor devils—had not a sou amongst them. In this dilemma Mr. Price suggested pocket-picking, and Barrington—with Belvidera in tears—consented. What with pocket-picking and play-acting the winter of 1771 passed pleasantly enough, but falling sick of a fever, Barrington was left behind by the ungrateful Price and came near dying. Belvidera, however, refused to desert her lover, and nursed him to a recovery. A few weeks after, the poor faithful wicked little soul—she was only eighteen—was drowned crossing the Boyne

Barrington, upon this, set out to look for Price, and found him at Cork, picking pockets. He told him of his loss.

"Join your fortunes with mine, lad!" says Price over a bowl of punch. "Fools were made for men like us to live upon."

The compact was soon made. Barrington took the part of a young gentleman of fashion, and Price that of his tutor. They frequented assemblies, balls, and races, and by the end of the year made £1,000. Emboldened by success, Price became less cautious in his operations, and was detected, convicted, and sent to the plantations. His hopeful pupil, turning his head from the card table, saw the arrest of his friend, and with a plausible excuse, rose, slipped out, and took horse for Dublin.

At Dublin, *he* was caught on the racecourse, but, restoring the snatched purse to its owner, was permitted to escape. Judging that the story would soon get wind, he wisely started for London.

Now begins a new phase in his career. He had been the Bohemian, the strolling player, the *bon camarado* of bullyrooks and swindlers. He would take a new line of action. He would be the gentleman, the gamester, the man of fashion. He sailed in the "Dorset" yacht (which had on board the Duke of Leinster), and there he made the acquaintance of a Mr. H. Mr. H. was a pigeon of admirable feather. Rich, and of good family, he was well worth the plucking. Young, vain, and innocent, he was easy to be plucked. To this young man Barrington introduced himself as a man of fortune "travelling for his health," and they soon became firm friends. With the remnant of his Irish booty, Barrington rivalled his friend in extravagance, and the two seem to have seen the usual round of London dissipation. When Mr. H. wanted money, he drew a cheque on his bankers; when Mr. Barrington's funds were low, he picked a pocket. Meanwhile, the dice-box rattled, and the cards were dealt frequently. *Ecarté* was a favourite game of the fashionable Mr. Barrington, and he had a knack of "turning the king" that was both curious and profitable. It was not fated, however, that he should keep his dish all to himself. One night at Ranelagh, while indulging in his usual depredations, he was accosted by a stranger. "I know you," said this man, "I came over in the yacht with you from Ireland. I saw you pick that gentleman's pocket. You are a scoundrel, sir; and unless you *divide* I hand you over to the police!"

The booty was nearly £100 in gold, and some five watches, but the virtuous stranger was firm. They adjourned to a tavern and Barrington divided the spoil.

The stranger turned out to be a swindler named James, who had been the possessor of £300 a year, but having ruined himself at the gaming table, had turned highwayman. A bullet wound received on Finchley Common incapacitated him for his profession, and he then turned parson, and pickpocket. With this worthy, Barrington joined his fortunes, and introducing him to poor H. as "Captain" James, the two rooked him without mercy.

The "Thatched House" and the "Devil's Tavern" at Temple Bar were the favourite resorts of the two friends, and they soon became famous for their easy bearing and gentlemanly address. Cautious and cool, Barrington mixed in the best society, and picked its aristocratic pockets without detection. The noblemen of his acquaintance bewailed their losses to him, and he cheered them with his sympathy, or roused them with his wit. The memory which enabled him to play Jaffier at twelve hours' notice stood him in stead in his new part of gentleman of quality. He read largely, and remembered what he read. His natural talents were great, his impudence unbounded, his nerve admirable; he was Barry Lyndon varnished; he wanted but a touch of genius to become Vautrin.

In the summer of 1775, he visited the "waters" in company with other dandies, and at Brighton—then called Brightelmstone, and only in the bud of its Georgian blossom—he fell in with Lord Ancaster and Sir Alexander Leith, and was entertained by them with much gravity. During this time he still continued his partnership with James, who acted as jackall to the more noble beast of prey and found out his game for him. Moreover, in his late profession of high toby man, Mr. James had become acquainted with that useful creature, a "fence" or receiver of stolen goods, who purchased the commodities which the firm had for sale and asked no questions. It is just probable that Barrington imagined that his partner, jackall as he was, retained the lion's share of the booty, for in the beginning of the next spring I find him employing a Mr. Lowe as his chancellor of the exchequer.

Lowe had been a livery-stable keeper, landlord of a sporting public-house, and usurer. His last speculation, while it enriched him considerably, enlarged his circle of acquaintance. He took a respectable house in Bloomsbury, lived like a man of easy fortune, and "put away" large quantities of stolen goods. To him Barrington linked his fortunes. James, at first disgusted, and then indignant, appears to have accepted the inevitable, and retired into private life. Like the wicked *marquise* of the old, or the Becky Sharpe of the modern Balzac, he "sought the consolations of religion." He retired to a monastery, and left all his earnings to the Church. Lowe, by the way, was not so fortunate. He was tried for firing a hospital at Kentish Town, of which he was treasurer, and poisoned himself in prison in 1779.

In conjunction with this worthy man Barrington rapidly rose to eminence. He went to Court on the Queen's birthday, and in addition to the innumerable snuff-boxes and purses, cut off the collar of an Order of the Garter, and sold the diamonds to a Dutch Jew who came over from Holland each year to purchase stolen jewels. Encouraged by his success, he next attempted to steal Prince Orloff's diamond snuff-box, at Covent Garden Theatre. This box was of gold, thickly studded with brilliants, and was presented to the illustrious Russian by the Empress Catherine. It was supposed to be worth £30,000. Barrington seated himself next the Prince and secured the box, but the Russian caught him by the collar and handed him over to the police. Being brought before Sir John Fielding, the wily prisoner set forth a sad case with such semblance of truth that the good-natured Prince declined to press the charge, and he escaped with a caution. This *exposé*, however, ruined his social reputation, and, being turned out of his old haunts, he was compelled to hunt smaller game. In 1777 he was detected picking the pocket of a trull at Drury Lane Theatre, and was sentenced to three years' hard labour in the hulks. Here his behaviour was so good that he was released after twelve months, and six months after his liberation was again detected picking pockets at St. Sepulchre's Church, and sentenced for five years. The "hulks" of those days was a terrible place. Men and women were crowded together. Oaths, dirt, drink, and the cat embroidered the prison garments. Prisoners were treated like beasts, and behaved like beasts. The lash cut their manhood out of them. Here Barrington seems to have suffered severely in mind and body. He tried to escape twice and to stab himself once, but was unsuccessful in all three efforts. His misery, however, attracted the attention of a wealthy associate of former days, who, exerting his influence with the Government, succeeded in getting Barrington's release, on condition that he should exile himself, as his old patron manager Price had done, to Ireland. Here he resumed his old occupation, until Dublin was too hot to hold him; and then, taking Scotland by the way, returned to England.

His star shone brighter now than ever. He stole £600 at Chester, £1,000 at York, and 500 guineas at Bath. He was the chat of the coffee-houses, the scandal of the wells. His person was well known. He was the hero of a hundred stories. He achieved a reputation for gallantry. Fine ladies were in love with him, or professed to be. He was reported to have robbed the King's coach, and to have intrigued with a Royal duchess. He was captured once or twice, but always escaped. He had plenty of money, and turnkeys—in those days, at all events—were not angels. He jumped from one disguise to another with the nimbleness of a harlequin. Now he was here, now there. One day he would be a quack doctor at Bath, the next a respectable bagman at Gloucester. He kept an E.O. table at the races on Monday, and on Tuesday borrowed £20 as a Methodist missionary desirous of turning heathen souls to God. Even when arrested, his wit and manners saved him from the ready rope. Being seized at Newcastle, he was sent in irons to Newgate, but pleaded so successfully with his friends, that they raised 100 guineas for him, and spending it in feeing an astute counsel, he escaped again through some legal quibble.

At last he was caught and held tight.

A Mr. Henry Hare Townsend, having entered a nag for the Enfield races, had gone down to see how fortune would turn. He had his watch and seals with him, in his waistcoat pocket. As he was leading his horse down the course, he was jostled by a person in light-coloured clothes, from whom he demanded, with an oath, what he wanted, but got no reply. A few moments after a Mr. Blades— a sporting friend of his—came up and asked him if he had not been robbed. Clapping his hand to his pocket, he discovered the loss of his watch, and instantly suspected the awkward gentleman in buff. This was Barrington. Seeing him the other side of the course, Townsend and Blades went round and seized him, Townsend saying, "You d——d rascal, you've got my watch!" They took him into a booth, and there several witnesses of credibility swore that they saw him drop the stolen property. On Wednesday morning, 15th September, 1790, he was tried and convicted.

Barrington made an able defence, commenting on the unfavourable opinion which the jury entertained of him, and the facts that no one saw him *take* the watch, nor could absolutely swear that he dropped it. Referring to his expectation of a death sentence, he said that he should bear it with fortitude, as he was innocent and maligned, but that if time were given him to repent he would do so without delay. The jury, impressed by his eloquence, sentenced him to seven years' transportation. They *could* have hung him if they chose. On Wednesday, the 22nd of September, the Recorder pronounced sentence on him, and the accomplished scoundrel took leave of him in the following neat and appropriate speech, to which Mr. Owen Suffolk, late of this colony, could perhaps alone supply a parallel:—

" My Lord,—I have a great deal to say in extenuation of the crime for which I now stand convicted at this bar; but, upon consideration, I will not arrest the attention of the honourable Court too long. Among the extraordinary vicissitudes incident to human nature, it is the peculiar and unfortunate lot of some devoted persons to have their best wishes and their most earnest endeavours to deserve the good opinion of the most respectable part of society frustrated. Whatever they say, or whatever they do, every word and its meaning, every action and its motive, is represented in an unfavourable light, and is distorted from the real intention of the speaker or the actor. That this has been my unhappy fate does not seem to need much confirmation. Every effort to deserve well of mankind that my heart bore witness to, its rectitude has been frustrated by such measures as these, and consequently rendered abortive. Many of the circumstances of my life I can, without any violation of the truth, declare to have therefore happened absolutely in spite of myself. The world, my lord, has given me credit for abilities, indeed much greater than I possess, and therefore much more than I deserved: but I had never found any kind hand to foster those abilities. I might ask where was the generous and powerful hand that was ever stretched forth to rescue George Barrington from infamy? In an age like this, which in several respects is so justly famed for liberal sentiments, it was my severe lot that no noble-minded gentleman stepped forward and said 'Barrington, you are possessed of talents which may be useful to society. I feel for your situation, and as long as you act the part of a good citizen, I will be your protector; you will have time and opportunity to rescue yourself from the obloquy of your former conduct.' Alas, my lord, George Barrington had never the supreme felicity of having such comfort administered to his wounded spirit. As matters have unfortunately turned out, the die is cast; and as it is, I am resigned to my fate without one murmur of complaint."

Being shipped off to his new home, Mr. Barrington not only conducted himself with propriety but did the State some service. A mutiny broke out on board the convict-ship. The convicts attempted to seize the vessel and take her to America, "where," says Barrington in his account of the voyage, "they expected to not only attain their liberty, but receive a tract of land from Congress." The plot was laid with some ingenuity, and on an occasion when the captain and officers were below examining the stowage of the wine, the mutineers attempted to get possession of the ship; but Barrington, snatching up a handspike, kept the hatchway until the officers came to his assistance. The two ringleaders were hung at the yard-arm that very afternoon, and the others severely flogged. This service caused the gentlemanly convict to receive some attention. He had the run of the store-room on board, and was recommended to Governor Phillip as soon as the ship anchored at Sydney.

The Governor received him with kindness, and appointed him superintendent of convicts, and in November, 1792, he entered upon that office by virtue of one of the first warrants of emancipation granted in the colony.

From this time Mr. Barrington seems to have conducted himself with propriety, and to have given up the follies of his youth. It is possible, indeed, that police were more plentiful than purses in the land of his adoption. However, he made an admirable superintendent of convicts, and would address his petty officers in tones which yet faintly smacked of the Phœnix and Ranelagh. At the expiration of his sentence he was but forty-four years of age, but he settled in Parramatta and lived to a good old age, though I cannot find the precise date of his death. The author of a little book called *Australian Discovery and Colonization*, published 1850, says that at that time the interesting thief was still remembered by some of the early residents as a very gentlemanly old man, scrupulously neat in dress and courteous in deportment. In addition to his "history," which he dedicated with characteristic impudence to "His Gracious Majesty," Barrington was the reputed author of the celebrated prologue to the "Revenge," spoken on the 16th January, 1796, at the first dramatic performance given in the colony, and which, from the neatness of the couplet—

"True patriots we, for be it understood,
We left our country for our country's good"—

has been often quoted. There is more reason, however, to suppose that some officer of literary ability and cultivated tastes was the author. No convict would have written such a cutting satire upon colonial society and his own pretensions to respectability. Moreover, the neatness of the prologue is in striking contrast to the slovenliness of the history. It is impossible to imagine that the same hand wrote both.

# GOVERNOR BLIGH AND THE "RUM" REVOLT.

THE social condition of Sydney in 1807 was somewhat curious. The place being under military discipline, and controlled by military officers, the army was at a premium. The Governor was a sort of pro-consul with absolute power, and his officers monopolised all the good things of the colony. Among the principal of these good things was the rum-trade. From the first settlement of New South Wales the unrestrained importation of ardent spirits had prevailed to an alarming extent. Rum poured into the colony in barrels, in hogsheads, in puncheons. Rum flowed like water, and was drunk like wine. Rum was taken morning, noon, and night, was paid as "boot" in exchanges, and received as payment for purchases. Rum at last became a colonial currency. The Governor, clergy, and officers, civil and military, all bartered rum. The New South Wales Veteran Corps (a regiment of pensioners tempted by promise of privilege to emigrate) was called the "Rum-Puncheon Corps." Mr. Macarthur (the chief actor in the drama about to open) says in his evidence on the trial of Major Johnstone, that such barter "was universal. Officers, civil, and military, clergy, every description of inhabitants, were under the necessity of paying for the necessaries of life, for every article of consumption in that sort of commodity which the people who had to sell were inclined to take: in many cases you could not get labour performed without it."

This being the case, one may judge of the disgust that prevailed among the rum-storers when it was reported that a new Governor was to replace Governor King—a bluff sailor, who loved rum—with strict injunctions from the Home Government to put down the monopolists. The name of this new Governor was Captain Bligh, a bold and daring, though somewhat nigheaded post-captain, who had gained some notoriety by reason of the famous mutiny of the "Bounty." This story is so well known that I will do no more than glance at it. The "Bounty" was sent to collect seeds of the breadfruit tree of the South Sea Islands, for the purpose of planting them in the West Indies. Tired of this botanical exploration, and seduced by the black eyes of the Tahitian damsels, the crew of the "Bounty," led by a lazy old reprobate named John Adams, mutinied, and putting Bligh and his officers adrift in a longboat, gave themselves up to unrestrained licentiousness on one of the lovely islands of the South Pacific. Here they lived for some years, until Adams, worn out by debauchery, achieved patriarchal dignity, and preached the Gospel to his numerous family of half-caste children. Although it is more than probable that he never heard of Byron, the old gentleman verified the poet's statement anent "rum and true religion," for he tried the charms of both, and died in the odour of sanctity. His companions, ultimately found, were given the convict settlement of Norfolk Island as a residence. They—with Adams at their head—have since been canonized by the low Church missionary story-books and the "Mutiny of the 'Bounty,'" was for some time the strong point of the *Sunday at Home*. Bligh displayed much ability in navigating his boat to safety, and, as a sort of recompense for the sufferings he had endured, was made Governor of New South Wales. His previous history was a good one. He had been for nineteen years a post-captain; had fought under Parker, Howe, and Nelson. At Copenhagen he commanded the Glatton, and was thanked by Nelson publicly on the quarter-deck for his services. He was said to be a tyrant, and to have ill-treated the crew of the "Bounty." It is possible he did so, but it is also possible that they deserved it.

The expectations of the colonists were realised. Bligh landed in 1806, and forthwith announced his intention of travelling through the colony in order to ascertain the condition of its inhabitants. Now, but four months before his arrival, occurred the great March flood of 1806, and the colony was suffering from scarcity of grain. According to Dr. Lang (*History of New South Wales*) maize meal and coarse flour were sold in Sydney at 2s. 6d. the pound, the two-pound loaf being 4s. 6d., and sometimes 5s., while "whole families on the Hawkesbury had often no bread in their houses for months together." Bligh riding round, like the King of Yvetôt, made personal inquiries into the condition of each settler, and volunteered to take from each a certain quantity of wheat or produce, giving in payment orders in *advance* on the King's Stores at Sydney. This arrangement, however beneficial to the settlers, did not accord with the interests of the military and civil importers of rum and tobacco. No settler who could obtain tea, sugar, and woollen stuffs at nearly cost price from the King's stores would sell his crop for the fiery Jamaica compound of the monopolists, or accept as part payment the usual puncheon of strong waters at the usual high rate of valuation. The merchants of Sydney were most indignant, and their indignation was not decreased by the publication on February 14th, 1807, of a general order prohibiting the rum-puncheon trade altogether. By this alarming order the monopoly was at once crushed. Bligh prohibited "the exchange of spirits or other liquors as payment for grain, animal food, labour, wearing apparel, or any other commodity whatever." A prisoner convicted of such sale or purchase rendered himself liable to 100 lashes and twelve months' hard labour. A settler, free by servitude, pardon, or emancipation, was deprived of all indulgences from the Crown, fined £20, and imprisoned for three months. Free settlers and masters of ships were fined £50, and deprived of indulgences from the Crown. This sledge-hammer proclamation at once knocked to shivers the brittle pot of profitable monopoly which had hitherto boiled so briskly, and the merchants and trading members of the New South Wales Corps began to mutter curses against the popular despot of Government House.

At last a spark from an unexpected quarter fired the train. In March, 1807, the ship "Dart" arrived in Sydney. Among her cargo were two large stills, one addressed to Captain Abbott, of the New South Wales Corps, and the other to Mr. Macarthur. It seems that Mr. Macarthur was part owner of the "Dart," and that the agent to whom Captain Abbott had written for the still, thinking that the speculation would be a profitable one, took upon himself to send another to the owner of the vessel. In these stills a wondrous potion was about to be brewed.

According to custom the manifest of the "Dart" was exhibited to the Governor, who, observing the unlucky stills, ordered them to be both placed in the King's stores, in order that they might be shipped back to England on the first opportunity. It so happened that the coppers of the stills had been filled with drugs, and the naval officer to whom the execution of the Governor's mandate was entrusted, retained only the heads and worms, allowing the coppers to be placed in Mr. Macarthur's stores.

Mr. Macarthur, formerly captain and paymaster of the New South Wales Corps, and then a merchant of respectability, was not on good terms with the Governor. As might naturally be expected, he sided with the monopolists. Indeed, he was bound to the "opposition" by a threefold band. As an old member of the military corps he possessed all the *camaraderie* by which a regiment hangs together, and resented the proclamation of the Governor as injurious to the interests of his old companions. As a merchant, with whom the rum puncheon trade was necessarily a source of income, he saw himself deprived of large and sure profits. As a private gentleman of wealth and station, holding a position universally admitted to be only inferior to that of the Governor, he had imagined himself injured by the action of Bligh with reference to an appeal from the law courts, and refused to visit at Government House. At this distance of time, and in the absence of anything like satisfactory evidence, it is impossible to decide how far the conduct of Macarthur was dictated by petulance or vanity. Mr. Flanagan, in his *History of New South Wales*, warmly supports the course he took, and declares that Bligh's pretended affection for the people but veiled his quarter-deck detestation of all interference, and that he tyrannized grossly over Macarthur and his friends; while Dr. Lang contends that Bligh was an honest, rough, and well-meaning man, who opposed himself sturdily to a monstrous system of mercantile robbery. Having due regard to Bligh's former career, I feel inclined to agree with Dr. Lang.

Macarthur, annoyed at the order of the Governor, was yet to be subjected to another act of oppression. The "Duke of Portland" being about to sail for London, it was discovered that the stills were not on board her, and the Governor ordered them to be shipped forthwith. Macarthur replied that he had nothing to do with Captain Abbott's still, and that he intended to dispose of his own to some ship going to India or China, but that if that should be objected to, the head and worm could be disposed of as His Excellency thought fit, and that he would apply the copper to some domestic use. His Excellency but reiterated his former order, and after some complication and correspondence, a Mr. Campbell was sent to "take the stills." The merchant showed him where they were placed, and told him that he might take them at his own risk if he chose. Campbell did choose, and Macarthur prosecuted him instantly for illegal seizure of property, asking in Court, "if an Englishman in New South Wales was to have his property wrested from him on the mere sign manual of the Governor." The rebellion against despotism had begun.

Now another complication arose. In the month of June, a convict named Hoare had escaped in the "Parramatta" to Tahiti. Macarthur was part owner of this vessel, and the English inhabitants of Tahiti (that is to say, a few missionaries who had usurped the lands of the natives under the pretence of converting them) complained to the Governor. Proceedings were taken against Macarthur by the Governor, and a bond of £900 given by the owners of the "Parramatta" to the Government declared forfeited. Macarthur appealed to the Governor against this sentence, but without effect, and thereupon refused to pay the fine. In default of payment, the vessel was seized, and Macarthur hearing of the seizure, informed the captain and the crew that as they had "abandoned" the vessel, they might expect nothing more from him. By the colonial regulations, no seamen were allowed ashore in Sydney unless under certain conditions, and the men were therefore compelled to make affidavit of their owner's procedure. In consequence of this affidavit, the Judge-Advocate sent a summons commanding the appearance of Macarthur at court on the following day.

Unfortunately Richard Atkins, the Advocate-General, was himself involved in Macarthur's personal quarrels, and an action at law was then pending between them. Moreover, Atkins was a man of intemperate habits, and profligate character. He is characterized by Dr. Lang as "the broken-down relative of a person in power," and was notoriously incapable of fulfilling his legal duties. Governor Bligh, indeed, having been desired by the Secretary of State to inform him privately of the characters of individuals holding office, wrote thus of Mr. Atkins :—"He is accustomed to inebriety. He has been the ridicule of the community. Sentence of death has been pronounced in moments of intoxication. His determination is weak, and his opinion floating and infirm. His knowledge of the law is insignificant, and subject to private inclination ; and confidential causes of the Crown, where due secrecy is required, he is not to be trusted with." The result of this mingled ignorance and intemperance on the part of Atkins was, that he was obliged to have recourse to a convict named Crossley in order to prepare his indictments and aid his wavering judgment. Crossley had originally been an attorney, but was transported for perjury, and having been pardoned by Governor King, was living on his acquired property on the Hawkesbury River.

As may be easily imagined, the scandal anent Atkins and his friend was considerable, and Macarthur in his quarrel was supported by the majority of the officers under Government. Desirous of pushing matters to a crisis, and, I am afraid, not without a certain malice prepense against his enemy the Governor, Macarthur replied to the Judge-Advocate's summons by a cold and stinging letter, briefly refusing to attend. Upon this Atkins committed an error. Galled by the contumacy of the wealthy merchant, he determined to put a slight upon him which he would not easily forget. He issued a warrant for his arrest. The execution of this warrant was entrusted to a man named Francis Oakes, who had been a "missionary" to Tahiti, but was now head-constable at Parramatta. Oakes, having thus from a fisher of souls become a fisher of bodies, repaired to Macarthur's residence on the 15th December, 1807, and, "after many humble apologies," presented the warrant. Macarthur read it, and—remarking to Oakes that "if he came a second time to enforce it, to come well armed, for he would never submit until his blood was shed"—refused to comply. "I have been already robbed of ten thousand pounds," said he, "but let them alone and they will soon make a rope to hang themselves." Poor Oakes then requested that the great man would give him some document to show that the warrant had been duly executed, and Macarthur wrote the following:—

"Parramatta,
"December 15th, 1807.
"Mr. Oakes,—You will inform the person who sent you here with the warrant you have now shown me, and given me a copy of, that I never will submit to the horrid tyranny that is attempted until I am forced; that I consider it with scorn and contempt, as I do the persons who have directed it to be executed.
"(Signed) J. MACARTHUR."

Oakes having obtained this document, posted off to Atkins, and (doubtless chuckling at the speedy humiliation of his superior) recapitulated all that had passed. Atkins, furious with rage, sought the Governor; and Mr. Oakes' deposition having been taken, a warrant was issued for Macarthur's arrest. The next day three constables, armed with cutlasses, apprehended the "monopolist" in the house of Mr. Grimes, the surveyor-general, and he being brought on the 17th before a bench of magistrates, was duly committed for trial for "high misdemeanours" before a special criminal court to be summoned for the purpose. To the inhabitants this intelligence was as startling as the news of the arrest of the Five Members had been to their ancestors. The despot had accomplished a *coup d'état*.

Macarthur, however, was liberated on bail, and in the interim between the 17th of December and the 25th of January the greatest excitement prevailed. The ill-feeling between the prisoner and the Judge-Advocate was well known and freely commented upon. Macarthur himself was not idle. He enlisted the sympathies of the New South Wales corps, and seems to have informed its officers (who were to try him) that he relied upon their favourable verdict. This reliance was not unfounded. The officers rallied round their old comrade, and it is on record that the night before the trial Macarthur's son and nephew and two of the bailsmen dined at a public mess dinner of the corps. The colours of the regiment were displayed and the regimental band playing, Mr. Macarthur himself walking up and down the parade and listening to the music. History again suggests a distant parallel in the "white cockade" Opera House dinner of bodyguards at the Œil de Bœuf.

It is, I am afraid, beyond question that Macarthur, not content with the knowledge that the six jurors would acquit him, to the confusion of the Government party, determined to strike a final blow at his old enemy the Judge-Advocate; nay, it is possible that, strong in his own position, he meditated nothing less than the downfall of Governor Bligh himself. On the 25th January, 1807, the Court was crowded, not only with civilians, but with many soldiers of the Veteran Corps, muttering discontent, and fingering their side-arms. It was generally understood that the prisoner had, in a letter addressed to the Governor, protested against the presence of the Judge-Advocate; and as it was evident that the Judge-Advocate was about to preside, the action of Macarthur was anxiously looked for. The indictment, prepared by Crossley, charging Macarthur with contempt and sedition, was then read, and the six officers having been sworn, Atkins was preparing to take the oath himself, when the prisoner challenged him. The point was argued, and Atkins declaring that by the terms of the patent the Court could not be formed without him (which was perfectly true), Captain Kemp replied that the Judge-Advocate was nothing more than a juror, and Lieutenant Lawson desired the prisoner to state his objections, calling out, "We *will* hear him!"

Amid the greatest confusion, Atkins vacated his seat as President, and Macarthur harangued the Court. He stated that he had been brought to trial in ignorance of the charge against him, that he had in vain attempted to obtain from Atkins a copy of the indictment, and that he objected to him on six grounds:—First, that a suit was pending between them. Second, that Atkins cherished a "rancorous inveteracy against him." Third, that having given evidence to support an accusation against Atkins, he was therefore exposed to his enmity. Fourth, because Atkins had "associated and combined with that well-known dismembered limb of the law, George Crossley," to accomplish his destruction. Fifth, because Atkins knew that should he fail to procure a conviction, he would be prosecuted for false imprisonment. Sixth, because Atkins had already pronounced sentence against him at the bench of magistrates, and, consequently came into Court with the intention to convict. This speech contained a quotation of eight "authorities" on the question of challenge, and ended with an *ad captandum* appeal to the New South Wales Corps.

At the conclusion of the harangue Atkins swore he would commit the speaker for contempt, but Captain Kemp cried, "You, you commit! No, Sir; but I will commit you to jail." The soldiers began to cheer, and Atkins, apprehensive of violence, called out that he had adjourned the Court, but the six refused to listen, and told the people not to disperse, saying, "*We* are a Court. Tell them not to go out."

The Judge-Advocate having left, Macarthur demanded protection, stating that he had been informed that a force of armed ruffians had been prepared against him, and begging for a military guard. As perhaps had been previously agreed upon, this request was instantly granted. The Provost-Marshal, however, considering this proceeding a rescue, left the Court in search of Atkins and three magistrates, in order to get a warrant for the apprehension of Macarthur.

The six, thus left masters of the situation, desired to proceed *pro formâ*, and solemnly then and there concocted a letter to the Governor, requesting that another Judge-Advocate might be appointed in the place of Atkins. At half-past twelve the reply came. The Governor refused. "Willing to wound, but yet afraid to strike," the six sent another letter, reiterating their opinion, and begging further consideration.

Atkins, however, had not been idle. He, too, sent a memorial to the Governor, giving his version of the story, and complaining that the six had impounded his papers. Upon the receipt of this letter the Governor, at a quarter-past two, sent his secretary, Mr. Edmund Griffin, to the court house with a peremptory order to bring away all papers. The six, however, respectfully refused to comply with this command, unless "His Excellency would be pleased to appoint another Judge-Advocate." At a quarter to four the Governor played his last card. He sent a letter "finally demanding an answer in writing" as to the intentions of the six, and with italics "*repeating* that they were *no* Court without the Judge-Advocate." The six at 5 p.m. closed the campaign by formally informing His Excellency that they intended to retain the original correspondence, and had adjourned to the following day.

That evening was one of intense excitement in Sydney. The recalcitrant six were in some tremor as to the result of their proceedings, and one may not unreasonably think that the mess-table talk was not of the brightest. Mr. Macarthur snatched out of the hands of the fowler, and exultant in his temporary triumph, could not but be alarmed as to the ultimate issue of the struggle; Richard Atkins, Esq., and Crossley, his companion, were indignant and revengeful, breathing threats and warrants; while His Excellency, Governor Bligh—whose fits of rage were notorious—paced the dining-room of the verandah cottage called "Government House," waiting with furious impatience for the arrival of his allies. The Prussians of this Waterloo were represented by Major Johnstone, commanding the New South Wales corps; and immediately upon the receipt of the last manifesto of the six, Bligh had sent a despatch commanding his appearance. If the presence of their commander-in-chief did not quell the rebellious officers, Bligh's quarter-deck knowledge was good for nothing. Unluckily, Major Johnstone had been thrown out of his chaise some time before, and was unable to come. He lived four miles from town, and returned merely a verbal message, regretting his inability to comply with His Excellency's order. "He was too ill to come, and too weak to write." This was the *coup de grace*. It was evident that the major sided with his comrades. Nothing now remained but to try conclusions with Macarthur.

Early the next morning (January 26) Macarthur was arrested and lodged in gaol. The Court re-assembling, demanded that he should be restored to his former bail, and at 10 o'clock addressed another letter to the Governor, asserting that the deposition of the Provost-Marshal was false, and that the prisoner ought in law to be released. No answer was vouchsafed to this document, and at 3 p.m. the Court adjourned, wondering what His Excellency would do next. They were soon informed. In the course of the afternoon Bligh had decided upon war, and before dinner each of the six received a letter summoning him to Government House on the morrow to answer for "treasonable practices." It was also rumoured that Major Johnstone had received another letter, containing a tacit threat that, unless he appeared to support constituted authority, he would be virtually superseded in his command by Captain Abbott.

The utmost dismay now prevailed. It was urged that Bligh intended to set aside all forms of law, and ignoring the powers and jurisdiction of the Criminal Court, would seize upon his enemies in virtue of his untempered despotism. The barracks were in a ferment. Officers and men were alike ready for resistance. In the midst of the turmoil, at 5 p.m., a chaise containing the injured Johnstone drove up to the barracks. Lafayette's white horse could not have produced a greater sensation. The crowd on the barrack steps received him with open arms, and, amid a storm of mingled cheers and hisses, demanded whether he was come to ruin or to save the State. Johnstone, whose action would seem to point to a foregone conclusion, vowed that he had no intention of injuring his old companions in arms, and his utterance was received with intense enthusiasm. Presently the waiting mob outside the gates, eager to know the result of the noisy council within, were gladdened by a visible sign of power. Two merchants, Messrs. Bloxcell and Bayley, appeared flourishing a folded paper and took the way to the gaol. Major Johnstone, the "Lieutenant Governor," had signed an order for Macarthur's release, and was ready to back it with the muskets of the regiment under his command. Presently Macarthur appeared amid more cheering, and was conducted by his rescuers to the Council Chamber. For more than an hour the Council deliberated, and at last a strange noise was heard in the barrack-yard. The soldiers were getting under arms. It was more than a revolt; it was a revolution.

At half-past six the drums beat hard and loud, and the regiment, having been formed in the barrack-square, marched down to Government House with colours flying and fixed bayonets. Government House was a verandahed-cottage in O'Connell Street (in 1852 it was still standing), and was guarded by the usual guard of honour, under Lieutenant Bell. As the regiment approached Bell was heard to order his men to prime and load, and the instant after joined his comrades. In another moment the house was surrounded. The Bligh dynasty had fallen. Major Johnstone was Governor of New South Wales.

The entrance of the revolutionary army was opposed by but one person—and that a woman. Mrs. Putland, the widowed daughter of the Governor, ran down to the gate and endeavoured to dissuade Johnstone from entering, but she was put aside, and a search was made for the Governor. It has been stated that Bligh took refuge under a bed, and was dragged thence in a condition of craven terror; but this statement is stoutly denied by many persons. It seems, indeed, almost impossible to suppose that a man of Bligh's well-known courage would be guilty of such an act of gross cowardice. All that we know of his past life militates against such a supposition. In times of danger he had always been found brave to rashness. His very vices were those which spring from an overweening self-confidence, combined with strong personal courage. It is not likely that a captain who had fought his ship so as to merit the thanks of Nelson, and had lived through such a voyage as that which followed upon the mutiny of the Bounty, would hide beneath a bed to escape from the violence of officers who had dined at his own table. Moreover, there was nothing in the aspect of affairs to warrant such a display of timidity. The "revolution" was after all but a civil matter. There was no infuriated mob waiting to tear him in pieces. No threats of personal violence had been used, and Bligh must have known that his life was never in danger. Apart from the evidence of "character," which is directly opposed to the supposition of rank cowardice, there is not the shadow of motive for such a dastardly act as that with which he is charged, while the story is in itself precisely one of those coarse lies which are so easily invented and so readily believed by the vulgarer sort. Bligh and his bed is only another version of James II. and his warming pan.

What really took place is—as nearly as I can discover—as follows:—

On entering the house Major Johnstone despatched Lieutenant Minchin to summon the Governor to his presence, and calling for pens and paper composed in Bligh's dining room a formal letter of dismissal. This letter stated that Bligh "having been charged by the respectable inhabitants of (*sic*) crimes that render him unfit to exercise supreme authority," it was the painful duty of the writer to require him "in His Majesty's sacred name" to resign his authority and submit to arrest. This letter was addressed to "William Bligh, Esq., F.R.S.," and signed "George Johnstone, acting Lieutenant-Governor, and Major commanding the New South Wales Corps."

Bligh, in the meantime, had resolved on his course of action. Seeing that resistance was hopeless, he called to his orderly to saddle his horses, and ran upstairs to put on his uniform. His idea was to escape from the house and get to the region of the Hawkesbury, where he believed that the people, remembering the benefits he had formerly bestowed upon them, would rise in his behalf. While standing on the stairs, waiting for a servant who had gone for his sword, he was surprised by a number of soldiers with fixed bayonets, who made their way up stairs. Conceiving at once that Johnstone wished to take him prisoner, he stepped back into a bedroom adjoining, and attempted to get from a cupboard some papers which he wished to destroy. In this position he was found by Lieutenant Minchin, who arrested him in the name of the king.

Minchin brought his prisoner into the drawing-room, "crowded," says Bligh, "with soldiers under arms, many of whom appeared to be intoxicated." The letter written by Johnstone was then brought by Lieutenant Moore, and while Bligh was in the act of reading it, the new Governor appeared in the doorway, surrounded by officers, and verbally confirmed the contents of the letter.

Martial law was then proclaimed; all official papers and letters, together with Bligh's commission as Governor, and the "great seal" of the colony were seized, and Bligh left with his daughter and another lady, sentries being placed round the house to prevent his escape. Strangely enough, this eventful evening was the 26th January, 1805, the twentieth anniversary of the founding of the colony.

On the 27th a general order was published, headed with the following Napoleonic fustian :—

"Soldiers! your conduct has endeared you to every well-disposed inhabitant in this settlement. Persevere in the same honourable path, and you will establish the credit of the New South Wales Corps on a basis not to be shaken. God save the King!"

By the general order all the officers of the late Government were deposed, Atkins heading the list. The ringleaders of the revolution were appointed magistrates, and Mr. Campbell, the Treasurer, was dismissed, with directions to balance his accounts without delay.

Nor was this all. Three days afterwards Mr. Fulton, the Chaplain, was suspended, and all civil and military officers, and every well-disposed inhabitant were ordered to join in giving thanks to Almighty God for his merciful interposition in their favour by relieving them without bloodshed from the awful situation in which they stood before the memorable 26th inst.

On the 2nd of February Mr. Macarthur was tried over again before the same court which had already sat upon his case, Mr. Grimes acting as Advocate-General in the place of Atkins, and was unanimously acquitted. Ten days afterwards he was made Colonial Secretary and Territorial Magistrate.

Not satisfied, however, with advancing their friends, the successful revolutionists determined to take vengeance on their enemies. Mr. Lowe, the Provost-Marshal, who had arrested Macarthur, was imprisoned for nearly three months on a charge of perjury, and finally sent for four months to the coal mines at Newcastle. Atkins was too high to be assailed, but Crossley, the attorney, was sentenced to transportation for seven years.

These arbitrary acts caused some sensation among the free settlers, and the Government went the length of prohibiting all public meetings, fearing lest a demonstration might be got up in favour of Bligh. Notwithstanding this, however, a memorial was drawn up, and signed by a large number of persons, and forwarded secretly to England. This proceeding was discovered, and the most active mover in the business, Mr. George Suttor, was imprisoned for six months.

Notwithstanding the enthusiasm with which the rum-puncheoners had hailed the accession of Major Johnstone (bonfires had been blazing in all directions), the disaffected mustered largely, and it was rumoured that a conspiracy was on foot to reinstate Bligh. The illustrious prisoner was the white elephant of the Johnstone Government. He was kept at Government House, and followed by a sentry wherever he went; but upon these rumours gaining ground, was with his daughter placed as a close prisoner in the military barracks. At last it was decided to send him to England, and in March, 1809, he was permitted to go on board the "Porpoise," on the condition that he sailed straight for Great Britain, and did not attempt to land on any part of the Australian coast. Bligh gave his word to this effect; but I am sorry to say that he broke it immediately, and landed at Hobart Town, Van Diemen's Land being then a dependency of New South Wales. His coming created considerable excitement, and for some time he received the honour due to his rank; but before long an attempt was made to seize him, and he was compelled to lie on and off the coast in the "Porpoise" hoping for despatches from England.

For nearly nine months the "Porpoise" beat about the Van Diemen's Land coast, and at last the wished-for succour arrived. On the 25th of December Colonel Macquarie arrived in Sydney with orders to reinstate Captain Bligh for twenty-four hours, and to then assume the command. Johnstone was to be sent home in strict arrest, and the New South Wales Corps was to be replaced by the 73rd Regiment. In January, 1810, Bligh arrived from Adventure Bay, where he had been lying when the news of the arrival came to him, and was received with due honour by Colonel Macquarie. The former officers were reinstated, and a special act passed to legalise proceedings taken under the usurped Government.

On the 12th May Bligh sailed for England, and was followed by Johnstone and Macarthur, together with a cloud of witnesses of all kinds. The Government—caring but little for its convict colonies—was willing to deal gently with the culprits. Bligh was certainly made rear-admiral, and sent on active service, but Major Johnstone was not prevented from becoming lieutenant-colonel. At length, on the 7th May, 1811, the trial took place. The Court sat at Chelsea, the Right Hon. Charles Manners Sutton (father of the present Lord Canterbury, Governor of Victoria), being Judge Advocate General. Colonel Johnstone was found guilty, and cashiered. In publishing this sentence in the general orders the following rider was added:—

"The court in passing a sentence so inadequate to the enormity of the crime of which the prisoner has been found guilty, have apparently been actuated by a consideration of the novel and extraordinary circumstances which by the evidence on the face of the proceedings may have appeared to them to have existed during the administration of Governor Bligh."

Colonel Johnstone returned to the colony, and died there universally respected, during the Government of Macquarie. Mr. Macarthur, after a compulsory absence of eight years, also returned, and died better than poor Johnstone—he founded a family.

So ended the Rum-Puncheon Revolution. To us it may seem something like a storm in a teapot, but to the worthy residents of New South Wales in 1807, it was a very terrible hurricane indeed!

# GOVERNOR RALPH DARLING'S "IRON COLLAR."

AT the Sydney Quarter Sessions, held on the 8th November, 1826, two soldiers of the 57th Regiment were indicted for stealing calico from the shop of a Jew named Michael Napthali, and sentenced to seven years' transportation.

The circumstances of the offence were peculiar. In December, 1826, Lieutenant-General Sir Ralph Darling succeeded to the governorship of New South Wales, and was clever enough to become in twelve months the most unpopular personage in the Colony. A detailed disquisition upon his character would be out of place here, but a very excellent and brief summary of it is given by Mr. Sidney in his *Three Colonies of Australia:*—"He was a man of forms and precedents of the true red-tape school—neat, exact, punctual, industrious, arbitrary, spiteful, and common-place." Impressed with a marvellous sense of his own importance, and obstinate to desperation, Sir Ralph Darling brought the severest military discipline to bear upon the social relations of governor and governed. He was Sir Oracle, and if any unhappy dog dared bark when *his* august lips were open, instant annihilation was the punishment of his temerity. He ruled the convicts with a rod of iron, and surrounded by a tribe of parasites, flatterers and knaves, stretched the authority he possessed to the verge of abuse. A violent opposition to Government House and its belongings had been growing ever since the days of Bligh, and the bureaucratic despotism of the military Governor gave to this opposition a weapon which it was not slow to use. The more he was abused, the more arbitrary did the Governor become ; and at last he perpetrated an act of tyranny, which went near to bracket him in history with Governor Wall.

The condition of the military forces in the colony was not an enviable one. The privates of the 57th Regiment saw around them many wealthy men whom they remembered as convicts, and startled by the strangely lenient sentences passed by many magistrates, began to murmur at the severe punishment and strict discipline meted out to themselves by the Governor's orders. The convict population of Sydney was, in 1827, in one of two positions. A prisoner of the Crown was either better or worse treated than his deserts. The cat was used unsparingly. A county magistrate was "permitted to award any number of lashes for insolence, idleness, and other indefinite offences." Men were flogged until they died, or abused until they committed suicide to escape the weariness of living. The newly established settlement of Moreton Bay rivalled the infamies of Macquarie Harbour, and was only exceeded in terror by that lowest of deeps, Norfolk Island. But the corrupt condition of officialdom rendered immunity from punishment sufficiently easy to a patient and designing convict. Money could do everything, and instances are not wanting of murderers and thieves who succeeded in establishing themselves in snug shops and snugger farms. Convict jurors sat upon convict prisoners, and the *bon camaraderie* of the chain-gang and the hulks was not invariably forgotten. The military, not always composed of the best materials—viewed with disgust the social success of the men whom they had in former times helped to guard, and a pernicious and dangerous feeling ran current in the garrison that to be a soldier was not always to be better off than a convict. During the residence of the 57th Regiment in the colony more suicides took place in it than in any other corps quartered there before or since—five men had already committed robberies in order to obtain their discharge, while two had incurably mutilated themselves for the same purpose.

Darling was aware of this notion, and unreasonably irritated at what he considered an insult to his own judgment, instead of lightening the military yoke, caused it to press the heavier, vowing that he would take dire vengeance on any exponent of the rebellious doctrine.

Sudds and Thompson were fated to be the martyrs of a military reformation. Discontented with their position, and eager for their discharge from a service which the peddling tyranny of the Governor had made worse than penal, the two silly fellows determined to commit an offence which should, by rendering them amenable to transportation for five or seven years, secure them their discharge at the end of that time. Thompson who bore a good character in the regiment, appears to have been drawn into the scheme by the arguments of Sudds, who had a wife in England, and was doubly anxious to escape from the bondage of the Barrack-square. Sudds had been for a long time discontented and was regarded as a "loose fellow" by his officers; that is to say his discontent took the usual shape of rebellion against constituted authority. The military stock had become too tight for Sudds and Thompson.

On the evening of the 20th September, 1826, the two men determined to put their project into execution. They went into the shop of a Jew named Napthali, and asked to see some shirting. Several pieces were shown them, and Sudds selecting twelve yards of calico placed the bundle under his arm and walked out of the shop, remarking that his companion would pay. Thompson chatted with the shopman for a while, and being at last certain that Sudds was beyond pursuit, declined to pay anything, and walked out. The pair having met, bestowed the calico about their persons, and awaited the arrival of the constables. They did not wait long. As they had anticipated, they were soon apprehended, and giving up the calico, laughingly, told the officer that they were weary of military service, and had taken this means of quitting it. On the 8th of November they were tried, and sentenced to seven years' transportation. All had turned out as they had hoped, and Thompson on leaving the dock said, with a smile, "I hope your Honour will let me take my firelock, it may be useful to me in the bush!"

Thus far nothing in the case called for public comment, and beyond the ordinary newspaper paragraphs concerning "daring conduct," and "robbery in open day," the case of the two men passed unnoticed. But on the 21st of November it began to be rumoured that General Darling intended to make "an example of the two prisoners," and that some extraordinary punishment was in store for them. On the 22nd of November a general order was issued, which stated that—" The Lieutenant-General, in virtue of the power with which he is invested as Governor-in-chief, has thought fit to commute (!) the sentence, and to direct that privates Joseph Sudds and Patrick Thompson shall be worked in chains on the public roads for the period of their sentence, after which they will rejoin their corps. The garrison has been assembled to witness the degradation of these men from the honourable station of soldiers to that of felons doomed to labour in chains. It is ordered that the prisoners be immediately stripped of their uniform in the presence of the troops, and be dressed in felon clothing! That they be put in chains, and delivered in charge to the overseers of the 'chain gangs,' in order to their being removed to the interior, and worked on the mountain roads, being drummed as rogues out of the garrison.

Now the usual way to "drum a man out of the garrison" is to put a rope round his neck, cut off the facings of his uniform, and place on his back a piece of paper on which is written the name of the offence which the culprit has committed, and it was supposed that such had been the course pursued in regard to Sudds and Thompson. On the evening of the 22nd of November (Thursday), however, the officers and soldiers of the garrison began to let fall hints respecting some more imposing ceremony, and it was rumoured that the prisoners had undergone some extraordinary punishment which had seriously injured one of them. These rumours gained ground until Monday the 27th, when it became known that Sudds had died on the previous night. The Opposition papers published an exaggerated account of ironing, chaining, and flogging, and after some bickering between the democratic *Australian* and the Government paper, an inquiry was held, at which General Darling most indecently presided—and it was given forth that Sudds had died from combined dropsy and bronchitis. Mr. Wentworth—a native-born Australian barrister of some eloquence and intense capacity for hating—would not rest satisfied with this explanation, and little by little the facts of the case leaked out.

Sudds and Thompson had been loaded with heavier irons than those placed upon the most desperate convicts, and the ingenious Darling had placed round their necks spiked iron collars attached by another set of chains to the ankle fetters. The projecting spikes prevented the unhappy men from lying down at ease, and the connecting chains were short enough to prevent them from standing upright. Under the effects of this treatment Sudds had died.

Public fury now knew no bounds. Tradesmen put up their shutters as though in mourning for some national calamity. The fiercest denunciations met the Governor on all sides, and he was accused of wilful murder. A full investigation of the case was demanded, and granted, but in the meantime Darling's parasites had *made away with the irons.* At the sitting of the Executive Council lighter ones were substituted. A Captain Robison, however, had, unluckily for himself, found the original irons at the Government station at Emu Plains, and gave a full description of them. Shortly after this he was sent to Norfolk Island, and, after many harassing changes, finally cashiered by a court-martial convened by Darling, on a frivolous pretence. Wentworth published in England a series of pamphlets, containing an account of the whole transaction, and it is from these pamphlets (taken in connection with the Parliamentary papers of the day) that I have attempted to compile an impartial history of the case.

While awaiting trial Sudds had complained of illness. On the 8th of November the two prisoners were removed to the gaol. On the 11th, Sudds, being in irons, complained of pains in the bowels, and was admitted as an out-patient of the gaol hospital. A few days after he was brought into the sick ward, suffering from pains in his head and bowels. The irons were removed, and the following morning his legs, belly, and thighs were greatly swollen. John Thompson, the gaol attendant, ordered fomentations of hot water, which removed the pain in the bowels, and the surgeon arriving that afternoon ordered him to be discharged. The next day he was brought back worse than before. "My belly is like a drum," he said. Medicines were given to him, and he remained in the hospital with gaol irons on until the morning of the 22nd. On the 22nd the order arrived for the two prisoners to be sent to the barracks. Wilson, the under-gaoler, and two constables thereupon came for Sudds, and dressed him in his regimentals. Outside the ward he met Thompson, and the two were sent down to the parade-ground. The day was one of extreme heat, and most oppressive. Sudds was unable to stand, and was supported by a man under each arm while the order was read. Captain Robison, who was present at the ceremony, says of Sudds: "His whole body was much puffed and swollen, particularly his legs and feet." The order having been read, the regimentals were stripped off their backs, and replaced by the yellow convict clothing, while a set of irons was placed upon each of them. During this operation Sudds was obliged to sit upon the grass. "These irons," says the editor of the *Australian,* "were of a peculiar kind. The rings from the ankles are made after a peculiar fashion, and are of an uncommon size. In place of having chains attached to them in the common way, they are connected by means of long and slender chains with another ring, which is put round the neck, and serves as a collar. Two thin pieces of iron, each about eight inches long, protrude from the ring collar, in front under the chin, behind under the nape of the neck. This is the position of the pieces of iron (they are not spikes, not being sharp at the end) when the chains are put on and adjusted as intended. From this it is evident that the degree of ease or torture experienced by the wearer must depend entirely upon the length of the several chains. He can't lie down on his back or on his belly without twisting round the collar, in order to remove the projecting irons to the side. If the chains be not longer than that part of the body between the ankles and the neck, he never can extend himself at full length, but must remain partly doubled up, and become cramped in the course of a short time; for, in turning the collar in order to lie down, the chains wind, and form a curvature round the body, thus diminishing in effect their length." The weight of these irons was, according to Captain Robison, between thirty and forty pounds.

Having been thus bound, the pair were conducted to the barrack gate, and given over to the constables. Sudds was obliged to lean against the wall, and complained that the basils of the fetters cut his legs. Being placed in the cell the torture commenced. Sudd's neck began to swell, and he found that he could barely breathe. Thompson offered to "turn" the collar for him, but his offer was refused. Sudds said it hurt him if it was stirred. "It would admit nothing between it and the neck but a cotton handkerchief." As for Thompson, he says, at his examination on board the "Phœnix" hulk, "The projecting irons would not allow me to stretch myself at full length on my back. I could sleep on my back by contracting my legs; I could not lie on either side without contracting my legs. I could not stand upright with the irons on; the basil of the irons would not slip up my legs, and the chains were too short to allow me to stand upright." This was the "little cage" of the Power, or the stone cage of the Bastille over again. We can imagine without much difficulty the torture that would be produced by such compulsory contraction of the body.

That night Sudds was taken so ill that Thompson borrowed a candle from Wilson the under gaoler, fearing lest his companion should suddenly die. He also gave him some tea which he had purchased. A little after midnight the poor wretch became so bad that Thompson, thinking he was dying, asked a fellow-prisoner to come and look at him. The man looked, and said, "He's not dead, but I do not think he'll live long." Upon this Thompson asked Sudds if he had any friends to whom he would wish to write, Sudds replied that he had a wife and child at Gloucester, and begged Thompson to "get some pious book and read to him," adding that "they had put him in irons until they killed him." Shortly after this, Thompson, worn out with fatigue, fell asleep, and a man named Moreton, who was in gaol for an assault upon his mother, undertook to sit up with the dying man. At eight o'clock the next morning, Thursday, Sudds was taken to the hospital; his irons were removed when the doctor came round at twelve o'clock. That day he ate nothing but a piece of fish brought him by Thompson. Mr. M'Intyre, the surgeon, said to him, "You have brought yourself into pretty disgrace. You will be a fine figure with those irons at work." To which he replied, "I will never work in irons." "You would be better out of the world," says M'Intyre, and the poor creature with a groan said, " I wish to God I was."

His wish was fulfilled on Sunday night. Had he died within the precincts of the gaol, an inquest could have been demanded, and General Darling, hearing of the precarious condition of the prisoner, absolutely ordered him to be removed on Sunday afternoon to the General Hospital, whither he was taken in a small cart about an hour before he expired. The necessity for an inquest was thus obviated, and Mr. M'Intyre, the assistant-surgeon of the gaol, went down to the hospital to make a *post-mortem* examination of the body. He found the organs healthy, but "discovered in the throat mucus of a slimy, frothy description. The wind-pipe was rather inclined to a reddish colour." It is tolerably clear that this appearance was caused by inflammation, induced by the tight and heavy collar; but Mr. M'Intyre, who held his post at the Governor's pleasure, obligingly considered it the effect of bronchitis.

The *Australian* newspaper, however, thought otherwise, and said so. Upon this Mr. M'Leay, Colonial Secretary, at the Governor's request wrote to the editor and put him in possession of what he was pleased to term the "facts of the case," to wit, that the punishment inflicted was, in reality, a *mitigation* of the original sentence; that Sudds died from dropsy, that the chains weighed exactly 13lb. 12oz., and could be seen at his office. Public feeling was still rampant, and on the 5th of December Darling brought the case under the consideration of the Executive Council. At this meeting Mr. M'Intyre reiterated his statements about bronchitis, saying that he had been most particular in his observations as he knew that "this was a case which the rascally newspapers would take up." Captain Dumaresq, acting civil engineer, and son-in-law to the Governor, produced a set of 13lb. irons, and said they were the ones worn by Sudds. A soldier of the 57th, named Jesse Geer, who was in waiting, was then called in, and the Governor remarking that Geer was as nearly as possible of the same size and stature as Sudds, ordered the irons to be put upon him, and called the assembled council to witness how easily they fitted !

Everything now seemed explained, and Darling as a last precaution, wrote to Earl Bathurst on the 12th reporting the case and the decision of the Council, and adding that "being satisfied from what had occurred that the conduct of the hospital requires investigation he would immediately appoint a Board to ' inquire into the management and system generally,' and report upon the same for his lordship's information."

But tenacious Wentworth still held on to the facts of the case, and was presently gratified by a piece of important information. Captain Robison of the Veteran corps had seen the original irons which had been placed on Thompson, and had tried them on out of curiosity. To that gentleman, on the 1st of January, does Wentworth write, requesting a full account of the circumstance. Robison replied on the 3rd, and after giving in his letter the particulars concerning the "drumming out" already quoted, says, "A few months after Sudd's punishment and death (May or June, 1827), I was returning from the command of the Bathurst district in company with Lieutenant Christie, of the Buffs, and we stopped a night at the Government station on Emu Plains. The chains which Private Thompson worked in, as above mentioned, had been left at Emu, and were brought for us to see. They were of a very unusual description, and the iron collar reminding me of those I had seen on condemned slaves, &c., in South America, I was anxious to examine them, and from this motive was induced to put them on my own person, as did also Lieutenant Christie, of the Buffs. *We had but one opinion as to the torture they must have produced.* . . . I found it quite impossible whilst I had the collar and irons on me to lie down, except on my back or face, there being two long iron spikes projecting from the iron collar which was rivetted round the neck, which put it quite out of my power to turn over to the other side; independently of which there were two chains on either side extending from the collar and communicating with those on the legs. . . . I guessed the weight at about 30lbs. or 40lbs., or even upwards."

Mr. Mackaness, the Sheriff, stated also that calling at Government House with Colonel Mills a few days prior to the punishment of Sudds and Thompson, he saw on the right hand of the hall after entering the door, "either one or two sets of irons, having collars and iron spikes projecting from them," which now, he has no doubt were the same he afterwards saw upon the men in gaol. Mackaness "took them to be newly-invented man-traps."

Armed with this fresh information Wentworth succeeded in getting a sort of Commission to examine Thompson. This Commission, consisting of M'Leay, the Colonial Secretary; W. H. Moore, the acting Attorney-General, and Wentworth himself sat on board the "Phœnix" hulk on the 23rd April, 1827. Thompson in his examinations spoke boldly, and confident in popular support, did not hesitate to expatiate upon the cruelties to which he had been subjected. The day before the death of Sudds, Thompson could endure the torture of the collar no longer. On Saturday, the 25th November, he broke the chain, "so as to turn the collar, and lie at ease." The chains remained broken until Monday morning, when Wilson, the under-gaoler, took him to the yard, and had Sudds' irons put on him. It so happened that the chains of these were a little longer than the others, and Thompson being a smaller man than his companion, could straighten his body. He remained in the gaol until Tuesday, when he was placed in a boat and taken to the prisoners' barracks at Parramatta. On Wednesday, he was taken in a bullock-cart to Penrith Gaol, and on Thursday morning conveyed to "No. 1 Iron-chain-gang party" on Lapstone Hill, being the first range of the Blue Mountains. At three o'clock the same day he was taken out and set to work with the gang, having the spiked collar that had killed Sudds on his neck the whole time. After eight days of this work he gave in. It was very hot weather, and the heat of the iron collar became intolerable, "compelling me," he says, "to sit down frequently in order to hold it with my hands off my neck." The overseer ordered him to continue work; but he refused, and asked to be taken to gaol, where he could get "rest from the heat of the sun." To gaol he went accordingly, and on the following morning the collar was removed by Mr. M'Henry, "by order of the Governor." Having had his irons removed, he was sent back to the overseer, carrying the collar, &c., with him, and on the arrival of the gang at Emu Plains, was invested with "the usual irons of the gang." A week after this he refused to work, and being lodged in gaol, fell sick of dysentery, and was finally sent on board the hulks. What became of him at last I do not know, and cannot discover. Having played his little part in the drama, he retires. His exit is doubtless noted in the prison records of New South Wales.

Thus informed, Wentworth wrote to Sir George Murray, the Secretary of State, and forwarded to him a long bill of indictment against the detested Governor. On the 8th July, 1828, Mr. Stewart, a member of the British House of Commons, rose to move for "papers connected with the case of Joseph Sudds and Patrick Thompson." Sir G. Cole bore testimony to "the excellent and humane character of the Governor of New South Wales," but the motion was agreed to.

In the meantime, "the rascally newspapers" had not been idle. "Miles," a correspondent of the *Morning Chronicle*, at that time edited by Black, took up the cudgels for Mr. Wentworth, and commented severely on the conduct of the Tory Governor of New South Wales. The Tory papers retaliated, and after some fierce fighting, Darling seems to have received a hint to resign. The facts of the case came out but too clearly, and the motion of Mr. Stewart was fatal. But the struggle lasted four years—long enough to ruin Robison, who was bandied from post to pillar, and finally cashiered. On Darling's resignation in 1831, Robison attempted to obtain redress from the Home Government but failed. The Whig party still clamoured for vengeance, and "Miles," persistently chronicling all Darling's misdeeds, vowed that unless he was tried for his life Picton would have been an ill-used hero and Wall a murdered man. The crowning stroke was delivered in a letter published in 1832. On Wednesday the 14th December, 1831, a savage letter from "Miles" in the *Chronicle*, called forth a silly and abusive reply in the *John Bull* from Lieutenant-Colonel Darling, the brother of Sir Ralph. The writer averred that "Miles" would not dare to attack the Governor of New South Wales when that much-injured man arrived in London in May. "Miles" waited quietly until June, and then came out with a clear exposition of the whole case, couched in the most bitter language, and gives a little bit of information which sets the question of Governor Darling's veracity at rest for ever. John Head, who was hut-keeper at Emu Plains, deposed upon oath in Sydney, on the 29th July, 1829, that, "being at the hut when Thompson arrived he was desired by Plumley, the overseer of the gang (he not being able to read), to read to him a letter which he said Plumley had received purporting to be signed by Alexander M'Leay, Colonial

Secretary, by command of the Governor, and that it directed the said Plumley to take the chains and collar off the said Patrick Thompson, and to convey the same *privately* to Government House, and that the said Plumley did accordingly take the chains and put them in a bag, which the deponent, Head, carried on his back above half-a-mile to the Government House at Emu, and delivered them to Mr. James Kinghorn, and it is his opinion that they could not have weighed less than from 30lbs. to 40lbs." However, there was no "trial for murder." The Government expressed itself fully satisfied with the conduct of Sir Ralph, who was Tory to the back-bone. Robison was cashiered, and Mr. Wentworth having got for Governor Major-General Sir Richard Bourke (unquestionably the ablest man that had yet occupied that office), turned his attention to other pursuits.

Meanwhile, if some official in Sydney Gaol will turn up the records for 1826, he may solve the mystery of poor Thompson's fate.

# A LEAF FROM AN OLD NEWSPAPER.

ON Saturday, the 23rd September, 1820, the free residents of Hobart Town, on opening the moist folio of the *Hobart Town Gazette* and *Southern Reporter* found a startling proclamation. The *Hobart Town Gazette*, let us note, was the paper authorised by the Government, and assisted by those agreeable evidences of patronage, Government advertisements. It was published "by authority," and printed by Mr. Andrew Bent—the father of the Tasmanian press, who was at that time the leading printer in Hobart Town. Mr. Bent, however, fell out with Governor Arthur, and venturing to attack the Government, was summarily deprived of his office, and eventually ruined.

In the year 1820, however, Mr. Bent was in good favour, and headed his *Gazette* with the following notice:—

"His Honour the Lieutenant-Governor has thought proper to direct that all Public Communications which may appear in the *Hobart Town Gazette* and *Southern Reporter*, signed with any Official Signature, are to be considered as Official Communications made to those persons to whom they may relate.

"By command of His Honour,
"E. ROBINSON, Secretary.

The proclamation which greeted the readers of this issue of the 23rd of September, fifty years ago, was nothing less than an announcement of the death of the late "Sovereign Lord, King George III.," and accession to the crown of that "High and Mighty Prince, George of Wales," and ran to the effect that William Sorrell, Esq., Lieutenant-Governor of the settlements of Van Diemen's Land, together with several other distinguished persons, being assisted by the officers, civil and military, the magistrates, clergy, and principal inhabitants of the colony generally, did publish and proclaim, "with one Voice and consent of Tongue and Heart," the aforesaid High and Mighty Prince, to be *George IV.*, defender and rightful liege lord of all sorts of things and Supreme Liege Lord of Van Diemen's Land among the rest.

The paper in which this piece of news appears is lying before me as I write. It is a broadsheet of the coarsest character, and, with its flourish of Royal Arms at the head of it, looks not unlike a corpulent playbill. The paper is rough in texture and brown in colour, and the imprint is not as clear as it might be. The whole matter is of course surrounded with a deep black border as mourning for poor old George Tertius.

A glance at its columns will give us a glimpse into a curious condition of society. In the first sheet is the Police Fund of Van Diemen's Land "in account current with John Beamont, Esq., Treasurer," in which are some quaint items. Mr. John Petchey receives £10 for firewood supplied to Government House. Mr. R. W. Fyett charges £1 for the use of his cart and bullocks. The superintendent of police receives £6 as "a reward for capturing three absentees," also £5 for "apprehending Blackmore, reward advertised" (Blackmore, I presume, being a convict illegally at large). Mrs. Cullen is paid £2 15s. for accommodating persons in attendance on the Lieutenant-Governor at general muster. Nicholas de Ccurcy claims £1 for tailor's work for the Governor's orderly, and Mr. Lord charges £50 "for a horse supplied to Government." The Government was all in all in those days.

Immediately after this financial statement comes a paragraph that may perhaps surprise one or two of the inhabitants of Hobart Town who think their church has been named in honour of the patron saint of Wales.

"The Lieutenant-Governor directs that the New Church of Hobart Town shall be called 'St. David's Church' out of respect to the memory of the late Colonel David Collins, of the Royal Marines, under whose direction the settlement was founded in the year 1804, and who died Lieutenant-Governor in the year 1810."

Great generals have been canonized before now, and strong men lived before Agamemnon and Colonel David Collins. Though to name a church after a colonel of marines *does* seem rather a liberty with the Calendar.

The Lieutenant-Governor orders a "general muster of inhabitants" (civil officers and military alone excepted), on certain days. This proclamation is interesting because of its pleasant tyranny. It commands all "free men" and "free women," together with "male and female prisoners and ticket-of-leave men," to come together at certain places, at certain dates for the purpose of being counted, like sheep; and further orders that at "all these musters the free women—as well those who came free to this colony as those who are free by absolute or conditional pardon, and by expiration of sentence—are to give in the names and ages of their children."

What a strange sight this "muster" must have presented! Any colonial Frith desirous of painting a picture of the sensational school, might choose a worse subject than of "A General Muster in 1820." Let us imagine for a moment the old town, the old-fashioned dresses, the striving of the "tawdry yellow" of the convict garb with the "dirty red" of His Majesty's uniform, the intermingling of faces, the strong contrasts and curious juxtapositions. There seems room for powerful painting in such a picture.

The *Town Talk* is not very important. An account is given of a procession which took place on Sunday, and was composed of the Lieutenant-Governor, the Deputy Judge-Advocate, the officers and magistrates, and the principal inhabitants of the settlement, all in deep mourning, and it is stated that minute guns, in number corresponding with the years of his late Majesty were fired from Mulgrave Battery. The reporter for the *Gazette* remarks also that the ceremony left a deep impression of the veneration and respect which were felt towards the lamented sovereign, "an impression," he says, "which was much strengthened by the discourse of the Rev. R. Knopwood, M.A., whose allusions to His late Majesty's public and private virtues were most appropriate to the melancholy occasion." "The writer further observes that the memory of the diseased monarch cannot fail to live while Royal Virtue continues to be venerated."

*Le roi est mort ; vive le roi !* The next paragraph relates how the reading of the Proclamation of the new king was received. The document—which is printed at the head of the paper—was read "in front of Government House under a Royal salute from Mulgrave Battery, and three volleys from a detachment of the 48th Regiment."

Commerce goes hand in hand with loyalty. The *Southern Reporter* is happy to hear that "the new flour mill lately erected in Liverpool Street grinds remarkably well." The mill-stones of this remarkable structure are specially mentioned as being "the first yet used in this settlement the production of Van Diemen's Land." A vaguely worded but well-meant support of native industries.

That portion of a paper which *Punch* called the *Hatches, Matches*, and *Dispatches*, is not very well filled. One solitary marriage is alone recorded :—

"Married by special license by the Rev. R. Knopwood, M.A., on Monday, the 11th inst., John Beamont, Esq., Provost Marshal, to Harriett, second daughter of G. W. Evans, Esq., Deputy Surveyor-General."

But close upon the heels of the marriage follows an amusing exposition of the intentions of a Mr. Fergusson.

"Mr. Fergusson hereby Begs leave to make known to those who stand Indebted to him his intention of Looking for the same in the next sitting of the Lieutenant-Governor's Court, and no Favour or Affection will be shown."

Mr. F.'s impartiality is quite touching. Debts appear difficult to collect at this date, for Mrs. Lord, acting as agent to Edward Lord, Esq., acquaints the public that though deeply desirous of "affording them every Facility for discharging their Embarrassments," still she cannot remain wholly unpaid, but is prepared to accept good storeable beef and mutton to the extent in quantity of 250,000lbs. weight at 6d. per lb. in liquidation of their debts. While making this liberal offer, however, Mrs. Lord feels it a duty belonging to her agency to state "that if the present opportunity be *not* embraced by Mr. Lord's creditors "she will not allow the expected Circuit of the Supreme Court to pass without resorting to that and the Lieutenant-Governor's Court as the case may require to *Compel* Payment of the several obligations." A courteous but a severe lady, Mrs. Lord, evidently, and one who will stand no "nonsense," but have her lawful bond or pound of flesh as the case may be.

Here is a curious advertisement:—"Mr. Reiby has the pleasure of informing the public that he has received by the last arrivals the following choice articles, which will be sold at very reduced prices for ready money:—Brass-wire sieves, loom-shirting, flannel, writing-paper, quills, wafers, ink-powder, tortoiseshell combs, spices of all sorts, snuff, ball-cotton, threads, white and coloured handkerchiefs, men's common hats, red cotton shirts, Flushing coats, red caps, waistcoats, pea-jackets, drill frocks, trousers and jackets, chip hats, nankeens, knives and forks, crockeryware, cotton socks, best English chintz, best bottled London porter, cedar in plank, tumblers, English playing-cards, gunpowder, white wine in draught and bottle, rum, tea, sugar, Bengal soap, and various other Useful and Valuable articles. Also, a capital One-horse Gig, with harness complete." Rather a miscellaneous collection of Mr. Reiby's!

The newspapers of that day contained items which would rather startle a modern Tasmanian. For instance:—

"One Hundred and Fifty Pounds Reward."
"Police-office, Hobart Town,
"November 28, 1820.
"Whereas, Thomas Kenny (No. 73), a convict, 5ft. 3¼in. high, brown hair, dark-grey eyes, 18 years of age, a blacksmith by trade, was tried in the county of Dublin in 1818, was sentenced to be transported for life, born in the county of Westmeath, has a crucifix above the elbow on the right arm, T.K. on the left arm, arrived in Sydney in the ship "Bencoolen," and here in the ship "Admiral Cockburn," charged with wilful murder; and Thomas Atkinson, &c., and James Letting, &c., and Thomas Lawton, &c., and Joseph Saunders, &c., charged with divers capital felonies, broke out of His Majesty's gaol at Hobart Town on the night of the 27th of November." And so on.

Beneath this Mr. James Blay puts a
"Caution to the Public.
"Whereas several of my One Shilling promissory Notes have been lately altered into Five Shilling Bills: in order to bring the offender or offenders to public justice, I hereby offer a reward of Five Pounds sterling to any person or persons who will be the means of apprehending them.
"JAMES BLAY."

A glance at the police reports and trials shows a healthy condition of severity:—

Daniel Eachan, charged with forging an order for £3, is sentenced to 200 lashes and transportation to Newcastle. James Flinn and John Griffiths, *alias* Frog, charged with stealing a pocket-book, value 15s., and attempting to steal a watch, are sentenced to fifty lashes and transportation to Newcastle; and John Anthony, James Taylor, and George Howel, charged with "committing divers felonies," are treated to 100 lashes each and twelve months in the gaol gang.

Here is a specimen of female "absconders."

"Ann Darter. May. 5 ft. 1½ in.; brown hair, brown eyes; aged 36; servant. Tried at the Old Bailey, April, 1822—life.

Native place, St. Sepulchre's. Absconded from the service of Dr. Bromley, 17th February."

"Janet Ceflude, Brothers. 5 ft. 4 in.; dark hair, dark eyes; aged 26; dressmaker. Tried at Chester, April 5—life. Native place, Whitehaven."

Constables who permitted convicts to escape were not merely reprimanded or reduced. A sterner punishment was meted out to them, as thus :—

"Thomas Trueman, a Constable, was charged with negligently suffering two prisoners, who were confined in the County Gaol on charges of a very serious nature, to escape, which was clearly proved by various witnesses, and he was sentenced, being a prisoner, to be dismissed his office and to receive 100 lashes."

*Quis custodiet ipse custodes ?*

Amongst other duties of constables was that of seeing to the safe housing of all ticket-of-leave men by a certain hour, and the ancient institution of curfew, or something very like, was in force. A notice in the issue of the 23rd November, signed by Mr. Robinson, says:—

"Commencing on Monday next, the Evening Bell will ring at 9 o'clock until further orders."

Matrimonial matters did not always seem to go happily, even in this primitive condition of things. Gentlemen are constantly advertising their domestic troubles in the *Southern Reporter*, and scarcely a day passes without some husband being left lamenting by his frail spouse. Ladies seem to have been at a premium. I extract two plaints which are touching in their simple woe :—

"CAUTION.

"The public are hereby cautioned against harbouring or concealing or giving credit to my wife, Mary Steele, she having absconded from her home with sundry articles amounting to nearly fifty pounds in property, as I am determined not to pay any debts she may contract, and to prosecute any person or persons who may harbour or conceal her after this notice.
"GEO. STEELE."

The second is even more notable :—"Whereas, my wife, Margaret Banks, having eloped from her home without any just provocation, leaving me with her five small children !—This is to give notice that I will not be responsible for any debts she may contract on my account.
"THOMAS BANKS."

The care with which Mr. Banks distributes his personal pronouns is touching.

"Leading articles" are few and far between in the columns of our journal. Government advertisements, "local news," and lists of "prisoners tried" exhausted the balance of reading matter, which is made up of such items as these :—"Indian marriage in high life," "Singular discovery of a murder by dreaming," "New method of seasoning mahogany," "The honest cook," and "A jest by Mr. Curran." The jest is so exquisitely dull that it is worth extracting:—

"Mr. Curran, cross-examining a horse-jockey's servant, asked his master's age. 'I never put my hand into his mouth to try,' answered the witness. The laugh was against the counsel (mark this!) till he retorted, 'You are perfectly right, friend, for your master is said to be *a great bite!*'"

With this witticism let me close the *Hobart Town Gazette* for 1820. If the reader pleases he can compare it with the *Hobart Town Advertiser* of 1870.

# A SETTLER'S LIFE IN CONVICT DAYS.

"NOW, gentlemen," said the captain, "the boat's all ready for you." "We had come to anchor that morning in Sullivan's Cove," says Dr. Ross, writing in 1836 an account of his landing fourteen years before at Hobart Town, "and for the last hour or two had been doing our best, after a long voyage, to make ourselves decent, in order to pay our respects to the Governor."

Dr. Ross was a gentleman of ability and taste, who had emigrated from England with a view of settling as a farmer in Tasmania—as it was then called, Van Diemen's Land. After many vicissitudes, truthfully recorded in the following narrative, he became editor of a Government paper, and starting the *Hobart Town Chronicle* and *Van Diemen's Land Annual*, occupied a prominent position in the colony until his death. To his exertions the historians of Tasmania have been largely indebted for the material of their books. His *Annual* is —apart from the scarce newspapers of the day—the almost only record left of the earlier days of the colony, and his experiences may be read with interest.

On this memorable morning he seated himself in his well-creased "last new London-made dress-coat" in the bows of the boat, eager to be among the first to call at Government House. His fellow passengers were of a motley character, and he describes with some humour the incidents of the landing :—

"The boat was just shoving off when we were desired to stop (in a stentorian voice, which none of us dared to disobey), in order to take on board an emigrant whom we had all forgotten, and who we wished had also forgotten us, but who now appeared, descending the steps. I do not to this hour know how he managed to get down, for both arms were loaded with articles of the heaviest kind. One embraced a steel mill, on the excellent machinery of which he had enlarged almost every day since he had purchased it in Oxford street. The other held, linked together in a bullock-chain, a huge iron maul, a broad axe, and another very long felling, or rather *falling* one, as it is colonially called, and which it, unfortunately for me in this instance, too truly proved to be. For in spite of all our cries, 'No room, no room !' 'Keep back !' 'Wait till next time !' &c., in an instant he had his foot impressed, with all the superincumbent weight of himself and his iron ware, on the gunwale of the boat, which he at once brought down to the edge of the water, and with the help of the passenger who sat beside me, and by the sweep of his arm, trying to preserve his equilibrium, depriving me of mine, I was as suddenly precipitated about ten or a dozen feet below the water. Thanks to the aquatic acquirements of my early days, however, I was soon again at the surface, where I swam until I caught the end of a rope, by which I returned on board, with the mortification of having my fine *levée* coat steeped in salt water, and seeing the rest of the passengers paddling smoothly on shore to get the first blush of the Governor's patronage. The only consolation I had under my catastrophe was the finding that the whole of the heavy articles which had contributed to it were now lying snugly four fathoms under water, at the bottom of the Derwent."

This unlucky accident, however, procured him the pleasure of a private interview with the Governor, Colonel Sorrell, who seemed much pleased at the intention of the new-comer to settle in Van Diemen's Land instead of going on to Sydney. He was assured that the colony was in urgent need of settlers like himself, and was promised all the assistance the Government could give. The largest grant that the Governor was at that time empowered to make to any settler was 2560 acres. Unfortunately, in sailing from London the doctor had been induced, in order to accommodate some other passengers, to take out of the ship a large quantity of goods, and as grants of land were only made in consideration of, and in proportion to, real property, he could not claim the full allowance. Colonel Sorrell, however, ordered that 1000 acres should be "laid off" for him, with the understanding that he could take it up as soon as the second vessel, containing his property, arrived. This took place six weeks afterwards, but Ross was then "busy with his farm and family in the interior," and was unable to come to town or see after the fulfilment of the promise. This state of things continued until a change of Governors took place, and when Colonel Arthur arrived, Ross came down to enforce his claim. New Governors or Governments are not always eager to confirm the minutes left by their predecessors, and Arthur did not appear to think it necessary to carry out the suggestions of Sorrell in every particular. Poor Ross was informed that "the additions would all come in good time, when he had made the proper improvements on the thousand acres he had already obtained;" and this decision, he says, took him so much aback that he never since stirred in the matter, and—" I have, in consequence, for a series of years been struggling with every colonial difficulty to maintain a numerous family. I have seen many other settlers, with far less original means, and—I say it without disparagement—with certainly no higher claims, enjoying the advantage of maximum and additional maximum grants, and rapidly accumulating large and independent fortunes."

Hobart Town in 1822 was not a very cheerful place. The population, including prisoners and military, barely amounted to 3000 souls. The streets were but just marked out, and consisted for the most part of thinly-scattered cottages standing in the midst of unfenced allotments, while the roots and stumps of primeval gum trees tripped up the unwary foot-passenger. Macquarie Street was distinguished by Government House, several stores, and the "Hope and Anchor public-house," St. David's Church (then but just built), and the "Macquarie Hotel," a store where Ross expended the first money he laid out in the colony in "the purchase of a razor-strop for two dollars." The streets were knee-deep in mud, and undermined with large holes, into which the unwary fell headlong. Even in 1825 —three years later—Dr. Ross states that going home one night he witnessed the sudden plunge of the military band into a mud-hole, and the consequent stoppage of the martial music which they were discoursing.

The "old market-place," where "Mr. Fergusson's granary stood by itself," was an "impassable mud-hole periodically overflowed with the tide." The only inns were Mrs. Kearney's, the "Derwent" and "Macquarie Hotels," and the "Ship Inn"—the last named being at this moment the best hotel in Hobart Town—and the remainder of the town was principally composed of two-roomed cottages, having a "skillion" behind. The only bridge was the "Cross" in Elizabeth Street, which spanned the "town rivulet," and was calculated as the centre of the city. This bridge was the "Under the Verandah" of Hobart Town, and many admirable plans for spoiling the Egyptians were there concocted.

"There were assembled, especially towards evening, gentlemen of various classes, and from various parts of the world, those who had recently left the pocket-picking purlieus of the great metropolis, and those who had added to that experience a few years' sojourn in these colonies. Numerous bargains, assignments, and assignations were there planned and transacted, which made their appearance on the ensuing morning in dismantled and dilapidated stores and other symptoms of 'freedom' in a foreign land."

Mount Wellington overhung the city in all his primeval and barbarous beauty. The forest of gum trees reached down to the edge of the town, and "people cut cartloads and barrowloads of wood for their fires not a hundred yards from their own doors."

It so happened that another vessel had arrived in harbour at the same time with that one which had brought Dr. Ross, and this astonishing and unusual circumstance created a profound sensation. Lodging-house keepers, as rapacious then as now, and as ready to turn an honest penny at some one else's expense, had raised their prices, and Ross found it most difficult to obtain a resting-place for himself and his family. "After a weary search," he succeeded in "hiring a hut of two apartments, in one of the principal streets, at a weekly rent of four dollars, or 20s. currency.

Each room had a glazed window, and one of them a fire-place. It had no other floor but the mother earth, nor roof but the gum shingles, nor door but the entrance one. Such a building, at a moderate estimate, I think, could have been put up in any part of Middlesex for 40s., or two months' rent. Indeed, when I hired the premises, the proprietor said he would prefer selling it to me right out, and that I should have it for £20, or not quite a half-year's rent."

This pleasant and cheap domicile was situated about a quarter of a mile from the town, and Ross set out to find it, carrying his portmanteau in one hand and his little baby on the opposite arm, while his wife and two little ones walked by his side—surely as forlorn a picture of immigration as could be well imagined.

Presently, however, a man, decently dressed in blue trousers and jacket, volunteered to carry the portmanteau, and on arriving at the "hut," demanded payment for his trouble. This good Samaritan was an "assigned servant," and eked out his living by this method of charity. Ross gave him "the only English shilling, with its George the Dragon," which had remained in his pocket since he had paid the boatman at Cox's Quay. Unluckily, English money was at a discount, and the convict did not like the look of it.

"He turned it from side to side, between his finger and his thumb—he looked at the dragon and he looked at the shield with the garter, but neither seemed to please him. I saw by his countenance that he considered them in bad taste in Van Diemen's Land, and he flatly told me that a pillar dollar of the then oppressed country of Spain was the only coin he approved of; which, as I did not choose to give him, he would make me a compliment of the shilling and the job together. As my pride at that time was not very high—I blush to avow it—I was mean enough to pocket the affront, and so we parted, never to meet again."

By dint of using one box as a table and another as a bed, the new settler contrived to give the "hut" a homely look; and, getting out his crockeryware and unpacking his tea and sugar, set to work and made tea for his "poor sick and wearied wife and little family." He had brought with him two servants—the seductive "married couple" of the advertisements—but, like many deluded settlers before and since, he found that his importations were worse than useless. The man was a lout and the wife a ninny, and disgusted, Ross was compelled to get rid of them both.

Being awakened by the cold of the morning air, he got up to stroll around his new premises, and inspected more particularly a little inn which was opposite his door. The servant in this place was sweeping out the remains of last night's feast, and stared so hard at the new arrival that Ross went across to look at him. The description he gives is so characteristic of the time that I extract it bodily:—

"A country settler, whose cart stood before the house, and whose four large oxen I saw grazing in the bush on the hill behind, was turning himself in order to renew his nap, on the long wooden sofa-seat, as it is colonially called, serving as a drinking bench by day and bed by night, on which he lay half undressed, and covered only with a kangaroo rug. I then inspected the garden of this hostelry, for though it had been once inclosed with a paling fence, many panels were already gone or lying prostrate on the ground, and, though so young in existence, it was already bearing the appearance of antiquity and decay. A goat was grazing in the farther corner, and no vestiges of horticulture were apparent, except a sweetbriar bush, a few marigolds in full yellow blossom, and the remains of two cabbage stalks, which had been nibbled by the goat."

The next week was passed in arranging his furniture, unpacking his household goods, and storing them in the town. He had brought with him a small box of dollars for current expenses, and the conveyance of this box to his house cost him infinite pain. Some half-dozen fellows—"some in the garb of gentlemen, others in grey and yellow"—followed him to his hut, and peered suspiciously round the corner, looking with sharp eyes to see where the specie was stowed. Ross, however, purchased a bull-mastiff of one of the soldiers of the 48th, and hung his "trusty Manton" loaded, on a couple of pegs in his bedroom.

Having thus provided for home cares, he determined to fix on a locality for his future farm. Getting letters of introduction from the Governor, he clubbed with three of his fellow-passengers in the hire of a ticket-of-leave man, who would guide the party to its destination. This gentleman was civil and attentive. He had been a burglar, and informed Ross that his last offence—for the commission of which he was then suffering—was the robbing of the picture gallery of a nobleman in England, and that he had received £400 as his share in the booty. Winding along the foot of the Wellington range, with the Derwent on the right hand, Ross took the road towards the present township of New Norfolk, and kept his eye open for farmland. He did not see what he desired, but met with something that frightened him instead of pleasing him. Surmounting the hill where is now the cottage of Beauly Lodge, he was met by three men, one of whom carried a blue bag on which the stains of blood were very conspicuous. Curiosity induced the party to pause, and the strangers good-naturedly opening the bag, showed them a—human head.

"Taking it by the hair, he held it up to our view, with the greatest exultation imaginable, and for a moment we thought we had indeed got amongst murderers, pondering between resistance and the chance of succour or escape, when we were agreeably relieved by the information that the bleeding head had belonged two days ago to the body of the notorious bushranger, Michael Howe, for whom, dead or alive, very large rewards had been offered. He had been caught at a remote solitary hut on the banks of the river Shannon, and in his attempt to break away from the soldiers who apprehended him, had been shot through the back, so that the painful disseverment of the head and trunk, the result of which we now witnessed, had been only a *post-mortem* operation."

After a pleasant journey, with numerous pauses at hospitable settlers' houses, Ross arrived at a beautiful spot on the banks of the Shannon, which he determined to make his future home, and returned to Hobart Town for the purpose of making the necessary arrangements to purchase it.

He found his family well but heard that several attempts had been made to carry off the box of dollars. Robberies at that time were absurdly frequent. The police—such as it was—was inefficient, and the thieves numerous. Scarcely a night pased without some robbery being committed. The assigned burglars, thieves and "burkers" would put their wits together to prey upon their neighbours. They would cut away boards, or pull out a brick from the chimney bottom, and so work a hole large enough to admit their bodies. A foot-passenger walking the streets at night was almost certain to be attacked.

"It was a very common practice to run up behind a well dressed person, and whipping off his hat, to run away with it. This was called 'unshingling,' or taking off a man's roof. To say nothing of the jeopardy in which a watch and other little valuables were placed on such occasions, I have known instances of persons having the very coat taken off their back, especially if it happened to be a good one. For my part I could never discover what use the thieves could possibly put these stolen articles to; for in so small a population not only were the face and person of every individual well known, but the shape and colour of his coat, and even of his hat, were equally familiar. Unquestionably, if I had been so unfortunate as to lose my hat in this way (which I was not), I should have recognised it had I seen it on any man's head in Hobart Town next day. A man much more readily identifies an old friend of this kind, however great the similarity of black hats may be, when encountered in the open air, and in the bright light of day, than he can possibly do in an ante-room by candle light after the dazzle of a dancing party. I say this with the more confidence because one of my fellow-passengers, who had lost his hat in this manner, actually recognised it on the head of a dashing fellow, strutting with gloves and cane in Macquarie-street. The rogue was apprehended and convicted of the theft, and enjoyed as a reward of his 'unshingling' propensities the pleasure of what is called in these ingenious countries a 'second lagging.'"

Tired of these city joys, and having obtained his grant, and purchased tools, a plough, and bullocks, our immigrant started up the country to begin his farmer's life.

The account which Dr. Ross gives of his journey "up the country" does not much vary from the accounts which have been given by early settlers in any colony. The same troubles with refractory bullocks, the same camping out in unexpected places, the same astonishment at the beauties of nature as she appears at dusk, and the same raptures concerning the rising sun, which are common to all suddenly transplanted cockneys, characterise his writings. He is disgusted because his men swear at his bullocks, but admits, with grief, that swearing is, after all, a necessary evil. He finds the same difficulty in using an axe that all town-bred gentlemen have found from time immemorial, and his classical allusions to Tityrus, Melibœus, and Horace's Sabine farm have been made with more or less success by every "settler" of any pretensions to scholarship. But an element enters into Dr. Ross's narrative which is wanting in that of the Canadian backwoodsman or the Victorian "pioneer of civilisation." In addition to straying bullocks and cursing bullock-drivers, Ross had another experience. His servants were convicts, and their manners and customs were not of the most elegant nature.

The spot he selected for his farm was about fifty-six miles from Hobart Town, and was situated in the midst of a "howling wilderness." To reach it a pilgrimage had to be made with "assigned servants," as assistant pilgrims. He purchased two carts, made to order, at a cost of thirty-one guineas each, and with two bullock teams and servants to match, set out from the city. The first cart was filled with baggage, and in the second sat Mrs. Ross and her family. The patriarch himself, sometimes walking, sometimes riding, hovered like the parent bird around this ambulatory nest. The day was oppressively hot, and before the cavalcade had proceeded two miles, Mrs. Ross, tired of the jolting and the flies, determined to walk a little. With the terrible exception of the nursemaid and the baby, the party dismounted, and Ross told the drivers to "proceed slowly." Instantly they cracked their whips, cursed the bullocks, and disappeared over the brow of the hill. "I feel the exertion I made on that occasion," says Ross, "at the moment I am writing. . The hill was steep enough and long enough to my conception. No attempt had then been made to cut down the bank in order to lessen the acclivity. It was to my mind as steep a ridge as any Dame Nature ever left upon her fair face. What on earth was to be done? Was I to sit down by the roadside and bemoan my fate, and the still worse uncertain fate of my torn away infant. No, such a course would have been unworthy of a man born beyond the Tweed—of a man who had had the courage to transport himself. I carried the younger of my two little ones under my right arm, led the other by my left, and how I managed the 'Manton' I really cannot tell, but if I remember right it was in several ways. At one time carried by the side of the younger child I supported it across my arm; at another with a portion of the fingers of my right hand while I led the elder with the others. If the gun was not loaded I unquestionably was, and to all appearance with destruction too. The weight which Æneas escaped with from the flames of Troy was quite light compared with mine; for after a few steps accomplished in this manner, my anxiety to get to the summit of the hill, from whence I thought I might at least see the direction the carts were taking, or perhaps discover some stranger, though only an aboriginal, who would run after them, induced me to carry my eldest born also in my right arm—and now the difficulty of the 'Manton' was greater than ever. It is almost as impracticable for me to recollect how I did it as it was then to carry it. To the best of my memory, I contrived to support it in the loop of my shot belt, stuffed, as the latter was, as full of heavy shot as it could hold, while I balanced the other end under my arm-pit or my chin. I was pacing it along all the time, however, as fast as my legs could carry me. I perspired at every pore—my strength was tried to the utmost."

Surmounting the rise at last, however, he found the drays upset, and the nursemaid in a state of unwonted hilarity. This lady was a convict, and had but one eye. She consigned all the settlers in the colony to a place which Ross suggestively hints is "warmer than Siberia." This handmaiden—like a transported Miriam—burst into jubilee. "Free men," she vowed, "had no business in Van Diemen's Land. It was not meant for them. It belonged, ay, and should belong, to prisoners only! It was their country, and their country it should be. Ducks and green peas for ever! Hurrah!" This sudden outburst somewhat astonished the good doctor, and the behaviour of the nymph was still more astonishing. "As she spoke, her hands followed the direction that her animated eye pointed to in the joyous regions above—she did not certainly wave her hat, because she had not one to wave, and her Dunstable bonnet had just received a new shape from the impression of the cart wheel under which it had fallen. But she waved her hand in the joy of her heart, and would have sent my then only son and heir to perdition, never to inherit the noble estate on the romantic banks of the Shannon, had not his mother happily caught him by the clothes, while the rump of my newly bought gigantic bullock 'Strawberry' saved his little head from dashing on the ground."

The cause was soon apparent. A bottle of rum which Ross had, "for his stomach's sake," conserved in the bottom of the dray, had been espied by the single eye of his Hobart Town exportation, and she had drank it silently alone. *Hinc illæ lacrymæ!*

There is no need to expatiate upon the "assignment system." Suffice to say, that its main feature was the employment of the abilities of convicts in that groove in which they were best fitted to run. Any free settler who desired a servant could, by complying with certain conditions, hire a well-conducted convict from the superintendent's office. The master clothed and fed his man, and the man worked without pay for the master. Unluckily, it often happened that, to speak metaphorically—the round man got into the square hole. Cooks were hired as wood-cutters, poachers as cooks. Petty thieves, whose soft hands had touched nothing harder than a handkerchief or a watch chain, were sent to grub roots and drive bullocks; while the accomplished valet whose skill in hairdressing was the boast of Portman Square, and whose adroitness in assisting at the compound fracture of the seventh commandment rivalled that of Leporello himself, was too often condemned to hew wood and draw water for the use of some commonplace person who never had intrigued with another man's wife in the whole course of his plebeian existence. Hobart Town society was composed at that period of but three classes, free settlers and that male and female creation which are proverbially said to have populated Yorkshire. The "condition of things" was the most primitive in the world. Literature, as might be expected, was at a discount.

"It will appear strange," interjects Ross, "but it is no less true, the *Hobart Town Gazette* and *Van Diemen's Land General Advertiser*, printed once a fortnight on one leaf, sometimes of white sometimes of coloured paper, as Mr. Bent happened to get it, was at that time the only species of periodical literature which the colony could boast. It contained, however, a very full and circumstantial account of the goods for sale in the town, and the various articles that had arrived from England or elsewhere, and afforded me considerable assistance. It detailed the measures of Government, the appointments of public officers, general notices and regulations, agricultural meetings, and indeed almost everything which a settler required or wished to know. Nevertheless it had no more claim to compete with the newspapers of the present day than Tom Thumb has with Tom Paine. Up to the time I am speaking of, and some years after, there was not a word of slander or defamation put in print in the colony, unless, indeed, the announcements of the Provost-Marshal or Sheriff of that period, injurious as they sometimes were to people's credit, could be called so. The 'free press,' or great fourth estate—the palladium of Englishmen and Van Diemen's Land men too, as it is justly and proudly called—had scarcely come into being in the colony, when a fifth power, 'the abuse of the press,' paramount of all others, such is the rapidity of advancement in new countries, was almost simultaneously created."

Good Doctor Ross, I may observe, in parenthesis, is a little warm on this point. Governor Arthur having been handsomely abused by Mr. Melville, took away from that too out-spoken writer the Government printing, and gave it to our author. Ross being Government publisher, and a Scotchman, had more sense than to risk his position. He "went with the tide," and supported the Government of the day by taking occasion now and then to give poor Melville a sly dig in the editorial ribs. As thus:—

"By the sanction of one of the slanderous journals with which this literary colony now abounds, you may enter the house of the most retired individual—you may turn his dwelling inside out—you may fill it with anything you like, or strip it to the bare walls—you may backbite himself, his wife, and his children, make his servants insult instead of serving him—give him a large nose or no nose at all, just as it suits your convenience—his castle shall or shall not be his castle, agreeably to your will and pleasure. Never on earth was power more supreme or despotic—the Imperial Parliament must submit and give way to its domination, and even Majesty itself must bend if you choose to write home with the consent and concurrence of this glorious, this tremendous autocratic, political association press!"

At the time at which he first landed, however, the "Press" was not in existence. That great engine for the blowing off of private steam not being yet established, the residents of the city were forced to vent their private malice in manuscript. "These were the days of 'pipes.' Certain supposed home truths or lively descriptions were indited in clear and legible letters on a piece of paper, which was then rolled up in the form of a pipe, and being held together by twisting at one end, was found at the door of the person intended to be instructed on its first opening in the morning."

Nor was the expression of private opinion confined to personalities. A considerable dislike towards the country itself was manifested. Sydney was the place, and nothing but Sydney. Any person who settled in Van Diemen's Land was looked upon as but little better than a madman. The same objections were urged by the same class of people who urge similar objections now.

"Sydney was the only place. Why don't you go on to Sydney, sir! There is nothing but oppression here. The colony is ruined, sir. There is not even a drop of good water in the whole island, sir. It is all alum; you will be poisoned if you stop here, sir."

An additional inducement to leave Tasmania was at that time held out by the establishment of the South Australian Company. Ross ridicules the notion of a "South Australia," and gives the names of the projectors of the scheme with a satirical emphasis that circumstances have since rendered amusing:—

"Neither Swan River nor King George's Sound, much less the recent hobby of 'a new colony in South Australia,' was then thought of. Mr. Gouger, whose brilliant conceptions gave the first spark to this great invention, was then, as far as I know, carrying on his trade of stockbroking within the legitimate bounds of that profession. But his ideas, it appears, were too large and spreading to rest quiet within the narrow confines of the Stock Exchange. After hovering some time like a restless bird of prey over the Canadas and other parts of North America, he took a new flight towards these Australasiatic countries, and as the leader of some species of geese described by Cicero and other natural philosophers, drew in his wake a whole flock duly arranged, until having launched them fairly and irremediably in their course he shifts to the rear, while the others fly ahead to destruction. So long and important a flight could not, of course, be undertaken without the sanction of Parliament, and an Act accordingly has been passed 'to empower His Majesty to erect South Australia into a British province or provinces, and to provide for the colonization and government thereof.' The principal birds that compose the flock are, we learn from their own notes and announcements: Colonel Torrens, F.R.S., chairman; George Fife Angas, Esq.; William Hutt, Esq., M.P.; John George Shaw Lefevre, Esq.; William Alexander Mackinnon, Esq., M.P.; Samuel Mills, Esq.; Jacob Montefiore, Esq.; George Palmer, jun., Esq.; John Wright, Esq.; George Barnes, Esq., treasurer; James Freshfield, jun., Esq., solicitor; Rowland Hill, Esq., secretary (not the late reverend preacher in Blackfriars Road); the said Robert Gouger, Esq, Broker, Commission Agent, and prompter, behind the curtain, and all the emigrants with any cash in their pockets, able-bodied mechanics and labourers whom they may be able to draw in their train." Residents in Adelaide can afford to smile at this exhibition of spleen.

Having crossed the solitary vale of Bagdad, and camped at Constitution Hill, bogged his bullocks and lost them, Ross at last reached the "desolate spot" on which his future home was to be built. His preparations for permanent residence were rapid. He cut down some poles and made a "wigwam," and, dwelling in this wigwam for some weeks, set boldly to work to construct a "slab hut," in the midst of a landscape which he thought would have afforded scope for the employment of the pencil of Morland, and "does now, I trust," says he, "to the equally immortal one of my friend Mr. Glover."

The "hut" was built after the following manner:—

"Having first erected a snug hut for my men, with a good sleeping-loft above, which was very easily done by making the frame proportionately higher, and laying a floor of thinly split logs neatly across the joists—I added a very good kitchen, with a fireplace almost as big as a small room behind, a storeroom, a bedroom for my children, with two pretty little four-pane windows looking on the river, a study with a long bench or desk, which served as a library, a workshop, a schoolroom, and spare bedroom by turns (this place had three little windows to it, was lined with shelves all round stuffed full of old books), a small apartment for my nursemaid and youngest child, and a verandah with a porch in the centre, supported on four real Doric columns, formed of equal sized barrels of trees set upright with flutes and other carving of bark as nature gave them. They were, though I say it myself, very pretty, and gave my cottage, with very little trouble, an unassuming, but comfortable, rural appearance. I lathed the whole inside and out; and with the help of the sand and loam which I found at my door, mixed with chopped grass, I gave it two coats of plaster, that hardened and stuck, and sticks to this day, for aught I know, as well as any stucco. My two principal rooms were, moreover, nicely ceiled up to the rafters in the roof, giving them a lofty and arched appearance. They were fourteen or fifteen feet high in the centre, and the arching had this advantage, that it lessened the downward pressure, and saved it from falling, as I have known ceilings in houses of far higher pretensions often do—and especially at the most inopportune times, when the fumes of the dinner on the table informed the treacherous though blind mortar that the guests were assembled below. There was a very beautiful grass plot or lawn, of two or three acres in extent, a little to the right in front of my cottage, and elevated not more than two yards above the margin of the river. I took a great deal of pains with this little spot. I fenced it very carefully round, in connection with my garden and lawn that fronted my cottage, with good six-feet paling on all sides, except towards the river, which of itself was a sufficient fence, besides that the opposite side overhung the stream, as I have said, with beautiful, basaltic perpendicular rocks, with here and there a tuft of flowering shrubs growing out from the crevices. A long, straight path, of four yards in width, stretched from end to end, on the borders of which grew several English flowers, from seeds I had brought with me, intermixed with indigenous ones collected from the bush."

But the settler's life was not a bed of roses. Bushrangers and blacks swarmed about him, and the immigrant was often shot dead on the threshold of that home which he had but just snatched from the wilderness. Yet, if the blacks were well treated, they were not invariably treacherous. Ross says, having *began* with kindness, he found that good feeling continued, and that confidence once inspired, the natives behaved with civility. "They never once committed the smallest trespass or annoyance on my farm, and during the five or six years that elapsed between their final removal by Mr. G. A. Robinson to Flinders Island, and the time of my own removal with my own family to Hobart Town, while the most dreadful outrages were committed by them all round, they never once attacked my farm, or anyone belonging to it."

But the bushrangers were of a different nature. John Cook, Ross's assigned servant, is a good example of the class. This fellow was surly, drunken, and obstructive, and after enduring his ill-humours for some time, poor Ross returned him to the hands of the Government. Three days after he was with his new employer he absconded, and was strongly suspected of being concerned in a murder and robbery perpetrated in the neighbourhood. Some weeks after this Ross missed a gun, ammunition, and an iron pot from his hut, and two days afterwards, on visiting his shepherd's, saw Cook, armed with the stolen weapon, sneak out of the back door. Ten days afterwards, a party of the 48th who were out "bushranger-hunting" caught sight of him, and then he disappeared. "I never more heard of him alive," says Ross, "but about a year after, a skeleton, which some articles of dress, especially the kangaroo jacket, with the iron pot and tin pot he had stolen from me, identified as the remains of poor Cook, and a gun shot entering under his left blade bone, showed clearly how he met his death. The gun and shot-belt were taken away and his miserable bones had been picked bare by the wretched crows, the self-same, I doubt not, whose fore-boding croaking had been so ultimately disregarded both by him and me in the gum trees, while we lay beside our swamped cart before dawn on the banks of the Fat Doe river. I learned from very good, though confidential, authority sometime after that this poor misguided man having on one or two occasions for a small reward aided and assisted a sheep-stealer who possessed some pasture land between the Shannon and the Clyde, and was acquainted with his deliquencies, had subsequently shown some little symptoms of disapprobation of a small sheep robbery committed by the same individual, being a neighbour, on my own flock, and in consequence a schism or quarrel ensued. The sheep-stealer then became uneasy from the fear of Cook on some future occasion coming forward or being called on, should detection and a trial ensue, to give evidence against him. He and another associate had resolved, as they had already 'put aside,' as it is colonially called, one poor man similarly circumstanced as to a knowledge of their doings, to join him once more in the bush under a cloak of friendship, and by sending him unawares and unprepared out of the world, to deprive him of all power to give evidence against them in a witness box."

The "name and fame" of Cook continued, however, for several years afterwards, and existed in 1836 in the "Runaway list," published in Hobart Town and Bow Street.

*Apropos* of the death of Cook, Ross tells a story of the untimely end of a friend of his, which, as an illustration of the "manners of the age," is curious enough. Riding over one day to this man's house, the doctor was surprised to find him "salting down the carcases of six sheep, which he had just killed. He said it was a very convenient plan, as it saved time, and obviated the necessity of bringing home the flock, to kill one every second day for the use of the family. Besides, he added, the six sheep's heads and plucks served his people for more than a day, as though they would throw away one head or give it to the dogs, they could not have the face to waste a whole half-dozen at a time. I was simple and unsuspecting enough to believe there was some convenience in his plan, though it was not great enough to induce me ever to adopt it. The same individual, however, was afterwards tried for stealing a whole flock of about 400 sheep, convicted, and executed with several other bad characters and bushrangers at Hobart Town. I stood at the bottom of the ladder as he mounted to the scaffold. He had his arms pinioned behind his back, and after stooping his head to suck a Sydney orange, which he was unable otherwise to reach to his mouth, he placed it by a rose which he held in his other hand, and shaking hands with me, he wished me farewell, saying, as he looked in my face with a most altered countenance, which I shall never forget, 'Oh, sir! this is the happiest day I ever had in my life.'"

Amid such scenes did the first ten years of our "pioneer's settlement pass. Each day, however, brought an increase of civilisation, and, says happy Ross, "I now saw my way fair before me. My flocks and herds were rapidly increasing—I could readily sell the former at a pound a head, and the latter from £8 to £10. Every day was adding something to the value of my estate, and the efforts which the Government was making to put down the aggressions of both the black and white invaders of life and property, although yet abortive, I looked forward with every hope to be at last, as they have since proved, triumphantly successful."

# JORGENSON: KING OF ADVENTURERS.

IN *Ross's Van Diemen's Land Annual for* 1835, appears the first part of a "Shred of Autobiography, containing various anecdotes, personal and historical, connected with these colonies." This autobiography is anonymous, and was written by a manumitted convict. The second part appeared in the *Annual* for 1838, after Dr. Ross's death. The writer's name was Jorgenson, and the story of his life reads more like a romance than a record of fact. He was seaman, explorer, traveller, adventurer, gambler, spy, man of letters, man of fortune, political prisoner, dispensing chemist, and King of Iceland, and was transported for illegally pawning the property of a lodging-house keeper in Tottenham Court Road. His "autobiography" is written in a vain and egotistical strain, with much affectation of classical knowledge, and is rambling and disconnected. It occupies 195 closely-printed pages of the *Annual*, and readers who prefer their information at first hand cannot do better than procure the volumes and read for themselves. My apology to the shade of the author must be that, as the publication in which his lucubrations appeared is long since out of print, and copies are extremely rare, it is just possible that such a course of action would—on the part of a few thousand readers—be absolutely impossible. I propose, however, to stick as closely to the narrative as I can, and to give Jorgenson's own language wherever practicable.

"Who is so able to write a man's life as the living man himself?" cries Captain Jorgenson. "The age of intellect has merged into the autobiographical. A Homer is no longer wanted to immortalize an Agamemnon. For where is now the man not qualified to sing his own praise? to sound the trumpet of his own exploits? or who, like myself, would suffer the sad but instructive vicissitudes of his fate to pass by unwept and unrecorded, or as Horace says—*illacrymabiles?* No; having been promised a niche in *Ross's Van Diemen's Land Annual*, the only sanctuary and safe retreat of great names, the sole Westminster Abbey which these Australian regions can yet boast—I hasten to fill it up before a greater man steps in to occupy the ground." After this peroration—repeated in the second part as a gem too bright to be lost—Captain Jorgenson proceeds to recount his birth and early adventures.

He was born in Copenhagen in the year 1780, and was the son of a mathematical instrument maker. He received a good education; but though his parents appear to have been in easy circumstances, and would have started him in business, the boy must needs "go to sea." "When I saw a Dutch Indiaman set sail, with its officers on deck dressed out in their fine uniforms, my heart burned with envy to be like them." Old Jorgenson, however, did not approve of his son's notions, and with a view to sicken him of a seafaring life, bound him apprentice to an English collier, and kept him on board her for four years. He was then eighteen, and "beginning to think for myself (for we in Denmark are of age at sixteen)." He quitted the collier, and shipped on board the "Fanny," a South Sea whaler, bound with stores to the Cape of Good Hope. At the Cape he made another engagement with Captain Black, of the "Harbinger," bound for Algoa Bay. Black had obtained his appointment for services rendered on board the "Jane Shore" (prison ship). The prisoners and soldiers concerted a plan of mutiny, and seizing the vessel took her to Buenos Ayres. Black escaped the carnage, and, with 180 others (among whom was the famous pickpocket and swindler, Major Sempill, who refused to join the mutineers) was put into an open boat, and after much hardship got to the West Indies. The "Harbinger" had a narrow escape of being taken by a French ship of forty-four guns (this was in the year 1798), but beat off her enemy and accomplished her voyage without mishap.

Returning to the Cape, young Jorgenson joined a brig of sixty-five tons. This was the "Lady Nelson," commanded by Lieutenant Grant, and was sent as a tender to the "Investigator," commanded by Captain Flinders, on a surveying voyage round the Australian coast. Dr. Bass, originally surgeon of H.M.S. "Reliance," had got down to Western Port from Sydney in a whale boat, and gave it as his opinion that "some strait" must exist in that latitude. Captain Flinders set out from Sydney to ascertain this point, but before the result of his expedition was known in England, the "Lady Nelson" was despatched on the same errand. She was built expressly for the voyage, and was admirably fitted. Jorgenson says she had "a remarkable sliding keel, the invention of Commissioner Shanks, of the Navy Board, which answered so well that I have often wondered it did not come into more general use. It was composed of three parts or broad planks, fitted into corresponding sockets or openings, which went completely through the vessel, from the deck to the keel. These planks could be let down or drawn up at pleasure, to a depth of eight feet, according as the vessel went into deep or shallow water, or in sailing against the wind to obviate the leeway.

Lieutenant Grant received orders to shape his course for the western extremity of what was then believed to be the peninsula of Van Diemen's Land. The first point he made was King's Island (named after Captain King, third Governor of New South Wales). From King's Island they went to Sydney, and then returned and completed the survey of Port Phillip, Western Port, Port Dalrymple, and the Derwent. The "strait" was named after the doctor, and Bass's Straits are a sufficiently credible witness that Van Diemen's Land is *not* part of New Holland.

On her return to Sydney, the "Lady Nelson" was ordered to accompany Flinders in his expedition to the north; but at the Northumberland Island she lost "all her cables and anchors on the coral reefs, and was obliged to steer for the main island of the chain," and eventually returned to Sydney. The "Investigator" went on, and circumnavigated the continent. She had on board Messrs. Brown and Kelly, botanists (the latter sent out at the expense of Sir Joseph Banks), M. Bauer, and Westall the landscape painter. The account of the voyage is well known, as it is written at length in the chronicles of the early explorers, but some particulars given by Jorgenson may find a place here. Having accomplished her task, the "Investigator" was condemned as unseaworthy—a condemnation which Jorgenson disputes—cut down, and sent home under the charge of Captain Kent, nephew (by marriage) to Hunter, the late Governor of New South Wales. Flinders placed his crew and himself on board the "Porpoise" man-of-war, and was wrecked in Torres Straits in company with the "Cato" and the "Bridgewater," "extra East India ships." The "Bridgewater" escaped, and seems to have left her consorts to their fate. The crew of the "Porpoise" got on to the reef, but all on board the "Cato" were lost except three. Flinders took the intelligence to Sydney in the ship's boat, leaving the survivors "building a schooner of the wreck." They were ultimately saved, but the botanical collection of "unknown Australian plants" was lost. Nothing daunted by his mischances, Flinders, being anxious to complete the survey of the continent, and to take the news of his discoveries to England, induced King to place at his disposal the "Cumberland," a small craft of thirty tons burden. Running short of provisions, and relying on his passport, he sailed for the Mauritius, and was detained by the French Government under suspicion of being a "spy." His charts and papers were never more heard of, and poor Flinders was kept a prisoner for six years. "He was at last liberated," says Jorgenson, "by the peremptory order of Napoleon, and died on the 14th July, 1814, the very day that the *Account of a Voyage to Terra Australia* was published."

Dr. Bass met with even a worse fate. That worthy, having completed his survey of the "strait," returned home, but, being unable to rest quietly came out again as supercargo and part owner of the brig "Venus," Captain Bishop, intending to trade to Sydney and Spanish America. On his arrival at Sydney, Bishop went mad, and Bass, "who, though a surgeon and physician, was a skilful navigator," took command of the ship. He went to Valparaiso, and endeavoured to "force a trade." That is to say, "Either buy my goods, or I storm the place." Such amenities of commerce were not unusual in those days. The Spaniards consented, but Bass and his crew being on shore, "relaxing from the fatigues of the voyage," and drinking rum and lime juice, the wily scoundrels seized the "Venus" and cargo, and capturing Bass and his men after a desperate resistance, sent them to the quicksilver mines, from whence they never returned. I fancy that this little episode in the life of the discoverer of "Bass's Straits" is but little known to the many good folks who sail across them. There were some things done in those days not unworthy of Salvation Yeo and the dogs of Devon.

Sydney was a tolerably strange place. It was a sort of South Sea city of refuge, and the French war gave a good excuse for gallant gentlemen with more blood than guineas to exchange the one for the other. The Spanish coast was the great place for gold and glory, and many a sly privateer of the "Venus" class sailed from Sydney Harbour. Jorgenson mentions two — a "Captain M'Clarence, of the brig 'Dart,'" who met with death or the mines at Coquimbo; and "Captain Campbell, of the East India brig 'Harrington.'" Campbell being in Sydney during the year 1803, got news of the peace of Amiens. Being a calculating, long-headed fellow, he guessed that a rupture would soon take place, and prepared to take advantage of the temporary calm. Getting together a crew of desperadoes like himself, he sailed for the Spanish American coast. Entering the wealthiest ports, he brought his guns to bear upon the town, and landing sword in hand, at the head of his men, he plundered, burnt, and ravished, despoiling "even the churches, and bringing back with him an immense treasure." On his return to Sydney, however, contrary to his expectation, news of war had not yet arrived, and, fearful of Governor King's wrath, he buried his plunder in one of the many islands of the straits. His fears were not unfounded. Stern old King—he was an eccentric, homely, honest man—ordered him and his officers into arrest, where they remained for some time in fear and trembling. But Campbell's shrewd Scot's head had not deceived him. When the English news arrived it was discovered that war had been already declared with Spain, and that "Captain Campbell" had but served his country, and was honourably set free.

Jorgenson does not mention if he dug his treasure up again. If he did not, perhaps some lucky fellow may yet stumble upon it. But it is more than probable that a good deal of it found its way into the pockets of Sydney taverners. These gentry must have made large sums. Owing to the frequent failure of supplies from England provisions were very dear. "It was no uncommon thing," says Jorgenson, "to give ten guineas for a gallon of rum. Tobacco was proportionately dear, and tea was never under a guinea a pound. Money itself sympathized with the general rise. The common penny pieces passed for two pence, and half pence for pence. A large quantity of copper was in consequence brought out by the masters of vessels, who thus realised a profit of 100 per cent. The colony was ultimately most inconveniently overloaded with copper money. It was worse than the days of Wood's half-pence, which Dean Swift so ably put down; and Governor King, in like manner, was compelled to put his veto on the further introduction of such money, and speedily settled the point by reducing pence and half-pence to the proper value."

In 1803 the "Lady Nelson" set sail from Sydney with Captain Bowen, R.N., to form a settlement at the Derwent. "The late Dr. Mountgarrett and two ladies" whose names Captain Jorgenson has still the pleasure to "enrol among his friends," accompanied the expedition They were disembarked on the "north bank of the Derwent at Risdon," and then went on to Port Phillip where Collins had endeavoured to form a settlement. During their absence the station at Risdon was abandoned, and the tents pitched on the present site of Hobart Town.

Having completed the settlement of Hobart Town, the "Lady Nelson" returned to Sydney, and, after refitting, went down to the entrance of the Tamar, and reported upon a fit place for a settlement at "Georgetown." She then took a survey trip to King's Island, Kent's group, and the straits, and, finally, took the "establishment for the new settlement at Newcastle, seventy miles north of Sydney, a place rich with cedar, fish, and coals."

Tired of His Majesty's service, Jorgenson now took charge of a small vessel going on a sealing voyage to New Zealand, and then shipped as chief officer of a whaler. They sailed for the Derwent, and our author "can boast of having stuck the first whale in that river." From the Derwent they went to New Zealand, and having cruised for some time in those seas, bore up for London, having on board two New Zealanders and two Otaheitans, whom Jorgenson introduced to Sir Joseph Banks. Sir Joseph took charge of them, paid their expenses, and placed them under the care of the Rev. Joseph Hardcastle, "in order that by initiating them in the truths of the Christian religion, they might be able to confer a similar boon on their own countrymen." The poor fellows died in twelve months.

Jorgenson now went back to Copenhagen, which he found bombarded by the English, and, having seen his friends, was welcomed with great rejoicings. He seems to have become quite a "lion," for the next year (1807), we find him in a position of some importance. By dint of stories about the Australias and the Spanish Main, he, like Mr. Oxhenham, would appear to have fired the hearts of the honest Copenhagen burghers. Old Jorgenson and seven other merchants of Copenhagen, "touched with a spirit of reprisal against the English," subscribed to purchase a small vessel, armed with twenty-eight guns, and presented her to the Crown. She was armed, commissioned, and manned by the Government, and our hero placed in command. Now begins a new epoch in his life.

Our hero's vessel, manned by eighty-three men, and carrying twenty-eight guns, cut through the ice a month before it was expected that any vessel could get out," and coming unawares among the English traders, captured several ships.

Encouraged by this success, and relying on his knowledge of the coast, Jorgenson stood over to England. His courage, however, outran his prudence, and off Flamborough Head he came plump upon two sloops of war, the "Sappho" and the "Clio." The former, commanded by Captain Longford, instantly bore down upon him, and finding that flight was impossible, the Danish privateer determined to put a bold face on it and give battle. Notwithstanding that the "Sappho" had 120 men, he kept her at bay for three-quarters of an hour, making shift to fire seventeen broadsides. At last, his powder being spent, and his "masts, rigging, and sails all shot to pieces," he was compelled to surrender, and was taken in triumph to Yarmouth. That the action was a pretty severe one, is confirmed by the fact that Longford was made a post-captain for his "services" on the occasion.

It would appear that Jorgenson had, like a wise man, secured a retreat. When at Copenhagen the year before, he had "chanced to obtain an interview" with a "public officer connected with the British Ministry," and this individual sent for him to London, where Jorgenson delicately hints at an offer of secret service employment. Fairly established in the city, and introduced to "several of the high official characters of that eventful period," Jorgenson suggested a scheme for the relief of Iceland. That island being in the very midst of the Danish and English combatants, came rather badly off. The inhabitants derived their means of support chiefly from the export trade of wool and fish, and trade being prohibited, and "British supplies" cut off by the Danish ships, the place was in a state of famine. The miseries of the islanders had attracted the attention of English merchants, who—doubtless with a shrewd eye to the main chance—cast about for some daring fellow willing to run the blockade. Jorgenson called upon his old acquaintance, Sir Joseph Banks, and represented his own good qualities strongly. Permission was obtained from the British Government to freight a ship with provisions, and Jorgenson, taking the command, sailed from Liverpool on the 29th of December.

Many predictions were made as to the failure of the expedition, the danger being increased by inclement weather and the winter season. Though the vessel was but 350 tons burden, the insurance cost the benevolent speculators 1000 guineas, for, says Jorgenson, "the enterprise was considered almost desperate," and it was held "madness to attempt such a voyage, which, from the high latitude of the country, must necessarily be made at that season of the year almost in the dark." The bold fellow, however, arrived in safety, and found "the hours of the night brighter than those of the day, owing to the brilliant reflection of the 'Northern Light.'" Finding that matters turned out well, he left the provisions in charge of the supercargo, and hastened back to Liverpool, in order to bring out another cargo.

He speedily loaded two vessels, one with flour and another with provisions, and started again for the north. During his absence, however, the governor, Count von Tramp, had issued a proclamation prohibiting all communication with the English. It would seem that Count von Tramp did not disdain to trade a little himself, for a Danish vessel was in the habit of running small cargoes of rye, which were sold—as Jorgenson hints, to the advantage of the authorities—at 40s. per 200lbs.

Here was a dilemma. The two vessels, anchored in the port with their flour and provisions aboard, were ordered to go away again, full as they came. Jorgenson, like Captain Hiram Hudson in *Foul Play* "knew his duty to his employers," and vowed he would land his cargo at all hazards. He feigned submission, but the next day being Sunday, and the "people at church"—good souls—he landed with twelve of his men and making straight to the

Governor's residence, stationed six men at the front, and six at the back, with orders to fire on any one who should interrupt him. Then, with a brace of pistols in his belt, he walked into the Count's chamber, and informed him that he might consider himself deposed. The Count, "who was reposing on a sofa," made an attempt at resistance, but as there was no one in the house but the cook, one or two domestics, and "a Danish lady," he was speedily overpowered, carried down to the beach, and placed under hatches in Jorgenson's ship. The new king lost no time in "securing the iron chest," and when the people came out of church they found that a revolution had taken place.

"I am not aware," says Jorgenson, "unless some more deep-read historian than myself can cite an instance, that any revolution in the annals of nations was ever more adroitly, more harmlessly, or more decisively effected than this. The whole government of the island was changed in a moment. I was well aware of the sentiments of the people before I planned my scheme, and I knew I was safe."

The next day he issued a proclamation stating that the people, tired of Danish oppression, had called him to the head of the Government. This proclamation seemed to satisfy everybody. The few English on the island imagined that Jorgenson had concerted the plot with the Icelanders, and the Danes believed that he was supported by the English Government. Having thus secured his position, our hero issued laws, all "of course of a popular description." He relieved the people of half the taxes, ingeniously supplying their place by a duty levied on the "British goods" which he had himself imported. He released all people from debts due to the Crown of Denmark, compelled public defaulters to make up deficiencies from their private estates, and advanced moneys for the benefit of public schools and fisheries. He established trial by jury and "free representative government," and with true judgment augmented the salaries of the clergy. Some of these gentry had but £12 a year to live upon, and as the acute Jorgenson expected, "they were not wanting in gratitude, for they all preached resignation and contentment under the present order of things." Having thus provided for wants temporal and spiritual, he erected a fort of six guns, raised a troop of cavalry, and hoisted the ancient and independent flag of Iceland.

The inhabitants appeared to enjoy this novel condition of things, and when the king made a tour of his dominions, received him with acclamations. Indeed, it was but prudent that they should do so, for one contumacious fellow, a magistrate or head-man of one of the northern villages, some 150 miles from Reykavig, refusing to do homage and "surrender the iron chest," the monarch piled brushwood round his front door and fired it, "upon which he immediately submitted." One advantage in primitive government is—despatch. When at Liverpool, Jorgenson had written to New York requesting that a ship might be sent to Iceland with tobacco, and soon after his return to the capital he had the satisfaction of seeing a vessel enter the harbour "with a valuable cargo from New York," which cargo he received in exchange for his (taxed) British manufactures. This commercial enterprise proving so successful, Jorgenson, secure in his own impudence, resolved to visit London and "enter into an amicable treaty with Great Britain in order to permit vessels with British licenses to import grain," and set sail with a fleet of two ships, one the vessel which had brought him from London, and the other a Danish ship belonging to the deposed Von Tramp.

Unluckily, the Danish ship caught fire, and though every effort was made to save her, she burnt to the water's edge with all her cargo. "The firing of the ten guns, with the flames blazing along the shrouds and sails, had," says the king, "a sublimely grand effect upon the water; and when the hold and cargo took fire, the latter consisting of wool, feathers, oil, tallow, and tar, the effect was truly grand, the copper bottom continuing to float like an immense copper cauldron, long after the shades of night had come on." Indeed, in that latitude and in those seas, one might not have inaptly called to mind the celebrated story of the old Viking and his floating funeral-pyre.

This accident compelled them to return to Iceland for provisions; and, putting the passengers on board H.M. "Talbot," then in harbour, Jorgenson made all haste for Liverpool, which he reached in eight days. Fearing that the representations of the English captain might do him injury, he hurried up to London, and saw Sir Joseph Banks. That gentleman, however, justly incensed at the extraordinary breach of trust of which his privateer captain had been guilty, refused to have anything to do with him. And the "Talbot" having meanwhile got into port, the captain made a statement of the "Iceland affair" to the Government. He said that King Jorgenson had "established a republican government in Iceland, for the purpose of making that island a nest for all the disaffected persons in Europe," and added "that he was highly unqualified to hold the command of a kingdom, because he had been an apprentice on board an English collier, and had served as midshipman in an English ship of war."

Hearing of this statement, and fearing the consequences, the king went into hiding for a week or so, but one day, while dining at the "Spread Eagle" in Gracechurch Street, he was arrested and taken before the Lord Mayor, charged with being "an alien to an enemy at large without the King's licence, and with having broken his parole." In vain he pleaded that he was really acting in the interest of England; the Lord Mayor had no taste for romance, and the poor king was put into Tothill Fields prison, there to console himself by the recollections of other monarchs who had been placed in similar positions. Had Voltaire been alive, he might have given him a seat at the supper-table in *Candide*.

After five weeks in Tothill Fields, where he "met with persons the effect of whose intimacy steeped his future life in misery"— notably Count Dillon, then a political prisoner—he was removed to the hulk appointed for the reception of Danish prisoners, and kept there for nearly twelve months, at the end of which time he was permitted to reside at Reading on his parole. Here he cultivated literary tastes, and wrote a little work, entitled *The Copenhagen Expedition Traced to other Causes than the Treaty of Tilsit*. I have no doubt he knew as much about the subject as most people. After a ten months' residence at Reading he received a permission to return to London, and was "soon picked up by my Tothill Fields acquaintance." How he lived at this epoch it is not difficult to conjecture. He says himself: "I was thoroughly initiated into all the horrors and enticements of the gaming-table." He appears to have lived his fair share of life in Bohemia, being now rich, now poor, now strolling in the parks, now lurking in a garret. At last, stripped of every penny, "including a sixteenth share of a £20,000 prize in the State lottery," he took his passage in a vessel bound for Lisbon. Even here his ill-fortune pursued him. Just before the vessel sailed, Bellingham had just assassinated Mr. Perceval in the lobby of the House of Commons, and meddlesome Jorgenson must needs be the first to convey the intelligence to the British Consulate. That worthy, however, disbelieved the story, and as Jorgenson could give no very good account of himself, sent him back to England. Determined to go to Spain—doubtless, like ancient Pistol, with a view to the plunder obtainable at the seat of war—he engaged as mate of a merchant vessel, was discharged at Lisbon, passed through the lines, and visited Madrid. Unable to keep from play, however, he was again robbed of his gains, and selling his clothes, and retaining only a jacket and trousers, entered as seamen in a gunboat which was "going home with the mail." Unluckily the packet-boat hove in sight, and took the mails, while the gunboat was sent to cruise off Cape St. Vincent.

Here Jorgenson assisted in the capture of several privateers, and gained promotion. On arriving at Gibralter he "malingered," and was placed in the hospital, and finally invalided in the "Dromedary" (afterwards sent as store and prison ship to Van Diemen's Land). Arriving at Portsmouth in 1813, he was placed on board the "Gladiator," fifty guns, stationed as an invalid hulk. The berthing of the invalids would not appear to be conducive to their recovery. "Between 700 and 800 persons," says Jorgenson, "were collected in this horribly pent-up place, which could not have afforded moderate accommodation for half of them, even had they been in good health; as it was, they were obliged to remain on deck and below alternately night and day, a most trying vicissitude, which occasioned the death of many." Jorgenson, not liking his position, wrote a letter to the Admiral requesting to be allowed to go ashore. But this coming to the ears of the captain and the doctor, they were indignant, the doctor vowing that the patient was "shamming," and the captain swearing that he would "teach him to apply to the Admiral instead of to him." Upon this Jorgenson reflected—the small vanity of the captain was hurt at his authority being slighted. What would move one man would move another. Jorgenson wrote to the Admiral apologizing for his former letter, and regretting that "he did not know that the captain was only responsible to the Lords of the Admiralty and not to him." This touched the Admiral on a sore point. He ordered the captain and the patient both before him, and to assert his dignity, dismissed Jorgenson and reprimanded the captain.

Getting back to London, Jorgenson seems to have subsisted by writing for patronage, and spying for the Government. In his leisure moments he wrote an account of the Icelandic revolution, which he presented to Sir Joseph Banks. He seems to have become quite a "lion" among the curious at this period. His "tempter," as he calls it, overtook him again, and going up to town he "launched into extravagance," and soon became little better than a sharper.

He tells here a curious anecdote. Being one day at a coffeehouse in the Strand, he met Count Dillon, whose acquaintance he had made in Tothill Fields Prison. Dillon, thinking him an "enemy of England," began to talk freely, and Jorgenson, always ready to turn an honest penny, did not scruple to draw him out with a view to giving information to the Government. Dillon told him of a plot then concerted between the Americans and the French, "to send out an armed expedition" to take possession of the Australias.

This idea originated from the reports given by Boudin, Commodore of the "Geographe" and the "Naturaliste," who had visited the colonies in 1801. Jorgenson had met this adventurer in Sydney, but had at that time no suspicions of his intentions. He recalls, however, that "on the occasion of his making an exploring tour into the interior of New South Wales, I was induced to accompany him, and all his ambition was to advance further than any Englishman had ever been before. We had travelled about a hundred miles from Sydney, and had ascended the Hawkesbury a considerable way, some marked tree or remains of a temporary hut giving constant indications that a European had been there at some former period. I had become so impatient at his incessant reasons, thus continually discovered, for penetrating further, with so futile an object as that of returning to Paris and boasting that he had been where no traveller had been before him, that, espying a large white rock projecting from a little eminence, I ran forward, and standing upon it, called out to him with a show of exultation, that that was the point beyond which no white had been. Boudin then marched about twenty paces further, and returned quite satisfied."

The expedition was to consist of two armed French and American vessels, which, meeting at a certain *rendezvous*, were to sail together into the South Seas, and "participate in the plunder of the colonies." Immediately on hearing this, Jorgenson posted to the Colonial Office, and laid his intelligence before a "gentleman high in office." The information was, however, disregarded, the Government considering it a "wild scheme," and unlikely to be carried into effect "while the whole energies of Europe were drawn to a vortex in the Continental contest." Jorgenson says, moreover, that the "gentleman" remarked, that "even should the attempt be successful, England would lose little or nothing. These colonies are not worth keeping, for they already cost the Government £100,000 a year!

The expedition, however, sailed in 1813, but the two French ships under Count Dillon were wrecked off Cadiz. The Americans proceeded, and captured and burned seventeen whalers. The deficiency thus created in the London market sent sperm oil up to an enormous price. Upon this circumstance, and the indifference of the British Government to the smaller dependencies, Jorgenson remarks— "It is indeed much to be regretted that the navigation, fisheries, and trade of these seas has so long been looked over by the authorities at home. The immense archipelago of the Pacific is studded with islands, and inhabited by millions of friendly disposed people, ready and anxious to exchange their commodities for British manufactures. The benign influence of the Christian religion, which is rapidly extending itself by the aid of our Gospel missionaries, is doing much to raise these people in the scale of civilized society; and although the Americans are hourly taking advantage of our comparative supineness, the approach of an English flag is always, and we trust ever will be, hailed with superior satisfaction. The pearl fishery is said to be more profitable and less hazardous than that of the sperm whale, and the sandal-wood and *bíche-de-la-mer*, which are produced so abundantly on the northern coasts of our New Holland, are known to yield the Dutch, through the medium of the Malays, an immense revenue. Nothing surprised Captain Flinders more, in the course of his navigation of these countries, than the immense fleets of Malay proas extensively engaged in this traffic which he met with in the Gulf of Carpentaria." During the present discussion concerning Fiji and New Hebrides, these remarks will be read with interest.

Just at this time the adviser of the Government was arrested and sent to the Fleet for two years, and when the intelligence of the destruction of the British whaling ships was brought, did not fail to remind His Majesty's Ministers of the services he had rendered. He was supplied with money to pay his debts; but so inveterate was his passion for the gaming-table, that instead of discharging his liabilities, he went to a hazard-table and lost every penny.

Being now securely locked up without hope of release, Jorgenson "amused himself" by writing histories, pamphlets, and stories. Sending these, "neatly written in manuscript," to several persons of rank, he made enough money to live upon, and too little to allow him to gamble. He enjoyed the "liberties of the Fleet," and became a sort of "patron," a Danish Dorrit, a "father of his people." This Arcadian life, however, was somewhat strangely interrupted. One day he was sent for from the Foreign Office, and "had the pleasure to be engaged on a foreign mission to the seat of war," in other words, he took service as a "spy."

Amply supplied with money for his present expenses, and provided with an order to "draw on London," for any funds he might require while travelling, it would appear that Jorgenson had fallen on good days. He had a "career," such as it was, before him, and could have at once left London and the Fleet Prison with credit. His propensity for gambling was, however, too much for him, and instead of going to Dover, he went to a "silver hell," and lost, not only his money, but the very clothes he had provided for his journey.

Totally destitute of the means of living, and ashamed to apply to "the gentleman in the Foreign Office" who had given him his place as spy, and who naturally concluded that his *protégé* was already in Paris, our poor hero was at his wits' end. But with a determination and impudence worthy of Lazarillo de Tormes or the more famous Gil Blas of Santillane, Jorgenson resolved to seize his chance of advancement with his naked hands. Repairing to the friend of debtors, vagabonds, thieves, and adventurers,—the old-clothes man, that great "dresser" for the Beggar's Opera—he exchanged his only suit for a sailor's jacket and trousers, walked to Gravesend, and embarked on board a transport bound for Ostend. At Ostend he met an officer who knew him, and testified to his identity, and an "order" was cashed without difficulty. Of his business on the Continent our friend speaks little—as becomes him. He says vaguely that he was "sent to ascertain what effect the subjugation of Napoleon was likely to have on British commerce," but, as he arrived in Ghent some weeks before the Battle of Waterloo, his explanation is not as satisfactory as it might be, and though we admire his delicacy, we can but regret his reticence. He was at Brussels when the celebrated stampede took place, and may have witnessed Mrs. Crawley's triumph and Jos. Sedley's flight (*relictâ non bene parmulâ*—his moustache ingloriously left behind). He was a "silent spectator of the three days," and wandering over the field of Waterloo after the battle, may perhaps have seen M. Thénardier (like Diogenes with his lantern), seeking for a man honest enough to be worth robbing. How the father of Eponine, and the saviour of the Baron Pontmercy would have fraternized with such a comrade!

The life of a spy in those days was not an unpleasant one. Jorgenson went to Paris with the stream, and found that "the business he had to perform brought him in contact with several celebrated names of that day," and in particular he had "the pleasure to form an acquaintance with a French general, a great favourite of Bonaparte, and now a Marshall of France," and being liberally supplied with money by his employers, enjoyed himself much. Paris at that time was a kaleidoscope of uniforms—Germans, English, French, and Russians, all fraternized and fought. Jorgenson had for six months ample opportunities to study human nature. He could attend the balls of Madame Roni (*née* Rooney); comment on the conduct of Captain Gronow's ferocious duellist; gaze at a distance on Madame Firmiani, or lend the natural vigour of his arm to the assistance of Arthur O'Leary, Esq., beleaguered in the gaming-house of the "Palais Royal." This last conjecture is not without foundation. He rushed to the gambling-houses with eagerness, and played with desperation. Mr. Blunt (the friend of Mr. Sala) did not beggar himself with greater *bonhomie*. Notwithstanding that he was ordered on a special mission to Warsaw, he played until he had nothing to sell but his shirt, and disposing of that garment for seven francs to a sergeant, he buttoned up his coat, and leaving Paris by the east gate, set out along the north road on foot.

It was the month of December, and bitterly cold. Arriving at Joncherie, 120 miles from the capital, Jorgenson found himself worn out with fatigue and reduced to the last sou of the seven francs. He dare not draw upon the F.O. until he reached Poland, and knew no one on the road. Rendered desperate by circumstances, he did just exactly what little Con Cregan did in Dublin—walked boldly into the best hotel, and ordered the best dinner they could give him. The hotel was a *cabaret* of mean pretensions, and the dinner bacon and eggs. Jorgenson turned up his nose with the air of a prince, and determined to make the best of it. As he was very hungry this was not so difficult. Meanwhile the news of the illustrious stranger in the buttoned-up coat had gone the rounds of the village, and the Mayor called to see the stranger's passport. In the course of a lofty conversation with the host, Jorgenson had learned that the Mayor was "Bourbonniste," and in pulling his passport from his pocket, pulled with it a letter from the Duchess d'Angoulême. The Mayor picked it up. "Ha!—oh, a letter!" From my friend the Duchess d'Angoulême. "Thirty thousand pardons, Monsieur," cries the polite Mayor, "but we officials have our duties, you know." Jorgenson finished the bacon, and graciously forgave the impertinence of M. le Maire's enquiries. He was an Irishman going to the Holy Land—poor, like many of his countrymen, but of excellent family, like all of them. "Then," cries the Mayor, "you must see our Baroness D'Este, who will be most glad to receive any person going on such a mission!" Jorgenson visited the baroness—some pious woman without much brains—and not only talked her into paying his expenses at the inn, but got from her several coins to deposit, with her blessing, at the sacred shrine. With this aid our adventurer contrived to get as far as Rheims, and there resolved to make a bold stroke for fortune. "The politics of this ancient city," says he, "were of a very opposite description from those of my last resting place." The prefect was a zealous Bonapartist, and Jorgenson, who, like St. Paul, seems to have been "all things to all men," avowed himself a zealous adherent of that banished potentate, and further informed the prefect of a plot formed by the English to rob the commissariat. The plot was not discovered, but the letter procured a personal interview, and the prefect was so charmed with the stranger that he not only gave him a supply of money, but a fine horse, and a "billet," which entitled him to a certain sum per mile to defray expenses. Armed with these useful evidences of the prefect's political sentiments, Jorgenson reached Frankfort in twenty-two days, not without adventures. At Metz, the Mayor could not speak French, and refused to assist the traveller. "Though," remarks Jorgenson, with a degree of self-complacency only equalled by that of the bashful Plumper, "I have always found it an uphill sort of thing for myself to get over; I have found almost on all occasions, both in the old world and the new, that a certain degree of 'modest' assurance was a great help to a man in getting through life."

Acting on this notion, he put the "billet" (written in French) into the surly mayor's hand, and remarked with a low bow, "You will see, Sir, by that document with what you are to supply me." The excellent man, rather than admit his inability to read, at once gave the modestly-assured Jorgenson all he wished. Another mayor, however, received a specimen of what Frank Smedley called "Oakland's quiet manner," he refused to do anything, and told the bearer of the "billet" that he was a lazy vagabond." Jorgenson, whose Icelandic experiences had taught him to mingle the *fortiter in re* with the *suaviter in modo*, promptly knocked him down, seized a horse, and galloped off amid a demonstration of pitchforks from the inhabitants.

Arrived in Frankfort in a storm of rain, he began to wonder how he should get on, and meeting an apparently charitable Jew, told him his story. The Jew, however, remarked that he had taken him for a rich Polish merchant, and waggishly laying a finger along his nose, departed. The recollection of his good fortune at Joncherie now came upon Jorgenson, and "entering a good inn," he ordered "a sumptuous meal, and went to bed." In the morning he sent for the landlord, told him that he had no money, but expected some in the course of the day; but that if he would permit him to go out he would leave his "waistcoat" as security. The landlord accepted, and once more buttoned up, Jorgenson roamed the town in the hopes of meeting with a friend. But Frankfort was large, and friends were few and far between. From the scanning the faces of passers-by, he at last took—like Balzac—to studying shop-fronts, and, also like Balzac, was at last rewarded by a name which "embodied his idea." This name, however, was not Z. Marcas but Frazer, and its owner was not a cobbler, but a watchmaker. In goes Jorgenson. "Good morning. My name is Jorgenson; that chronometer there was made by my father in Denmark." The honest Frazer looked. Sure enough it was so. A conversation began which ended by the watchmaker taking the waistcoatless son of his fellow tradesman to the house of Lord Clancarty, the British Minister. He sent in his name, "on secret service." The servants stared at his shabby attire. What if he were come to murder his lordship! His fate hung in the balance, when a side door opened, and "a gentleman attached to the Foreign Office" came out, like Horace's god out of the go-cart, and recognised him. All was now put right. He was supplied with money, redeemed his waistcoat, and paid for his dinner.

Mr. Frazer who seems to have been a man of intelligence and position, gave him a letter to the secretary of the Duke of Hesse-Darmstadt, and on presenting it, Jorgenson had "some interesting conversation with his Highness with regard to what I had seen in these colonies" (Tasmania and New South Wales), and spent some time in admiring the ducal gallery of paintings. When he took his departure, the Duke made him a handsome present. Encouraged by these compliments, Jorgenson began to take his proper position, and travelled in a carriage to Berlin, calling on all the celebrities as he passed. He was mistaken by some for an English milord. At

Saxe-Weimar he was introduced to Goethe. "I saw him in the library of the Duke—a magnificent collection of books, containing upwards of 700,000 volumes. Goethe was a member of the privy council, as well as filling the office of librarian to the Duke, a situation more congenial to his literary habits. Though upwards of seventy, he was full of life and spirits. He wore the dress of a privy councillor, a blue coat with gold facings. He was stout and portly in appearance, rather tall, with hazel eyes, remarkably heavy eyebrows, and dark complexion."

At Leipsic our adventurer surveyed the battle-field and like a premature Childe Harold moralized there. In Berlin, the British Minister afforded him "every assistance," and there is little doubt that he held a position of some confidence as a secret agent. He visited Niebhur and Bernstoff (the latter Minister of Foreign Affairs), and appears to have been on terms of acquaintanceship with Prince (then Count) Puckler Muskau. He gives an entertaining description of the Prince's ascent in a balloon, in company with "a female aëronaut, to whom he presented 500 crowns." He played cards with Marshal Blucher, and had the *entrée* to good society. Unluckily, his passion for gambling again beset him, and ultimately proved his ruin. So enthralled was he by the gambling-table, that he never set out for Warsaw at all, but forming an acquaintance with some Poles, "collected from them such information as it was my duty to obtain," and actually wrote several despatches, dated Warsaw, embodying the intelligence thus received.

At last, in November, 1816, he got as far as Dresden, and there his ruin was completely effected. In two days all his money was swallowed up by a "set of sharpers." His false despatches were detected, and, in debt and in disgrace, he determined to retrace his steps to London. His creditors pressing him, he was compelled to leave without a passport, and thus had to "dodge" his way to the seaboard. One instance which he relates will serve as an example of the tricks to which he resorted. One night the gamekeeper at the gate of a small fortified town refused to let him pass. He was cold, hungry, and in despair. The noise of the altercation brought out the gatekeeper's wife. The sex love three things—charity, mystery, and finery. Jorgenson beckoned her aside, and, begging her to intercede in his behalf, pulled from his pocket two silk handkerchiefs, gave her one, and avowed himself a smuggler expecting hourly the arrival of his cart from the frontier. The gatekeeper's wife was mortal, and the gatekeeper was uxorious. The smuggler was asked in to supper, passed a pleasant night, and after a hearty breakfast went out to look after his cart, and "so proceeded on his journey." When he got to London he was paid for his services, and resolved with the money thus acquired to emigrate to Spanish America, the natural home of adventurers like himself. But "venturing a small stake" in hope of adding to the small store he had already with him, he soon lost every penny, and for the next three years of his life was engaged in a "continual whirl of misery and disappointment at the gaming-table."

And now, having sunk lower and lower, he seems to have become something little better than a copper-captain, the swashbuckling bully of the gaming-house. In the year 1820 he was arrested for pawning certain articles of bed-furniture belonging to his landlady in Tottenham Court Road, and was sentenced to seven years' transportation. Pending the execution of his sentence, he was placed under the surgeon of Newgate, Mr. Box, as assistant in the hospital. Here he made desperate efforts to get his sentence commuted, and at last succeeded. Permitted, doubtless, through the influence of his former employers, to retain his post as dispenser for nearly two years, Jorgenson conducted himself with propriety, and getting "favourable notice" from the sheriffs, his case was more minutely inquired into, and it being found that the articles, for the theft of which he had been sentenced, were pawned in the name of one of his fellow-lodgers, he received his pardon, on condition that he should quit the kingdom within a month from the day of his liberation. Unfortunately, however, having a considerable sum in his pockets, the savings of his "gratuities," he again sought the gaming-table, and in the excitement of play overstayed his leave. At last, being several weeks over his allotted time, he resolved to ship on board a man-of-war, and was on his way to the tender in the river, when he fell in with an old acquaintance on Tower Hill who asked him to dinner. This jolly companion had been Jorgenson's predecessor as "assistant" in Newgate, and hearing that he had "outstayed his time," brought in the police, and handed his guest over to the law he had outraged. Jorgenson calls this betrayer of social confidence a "scoundrel," and there are few who will not heartily endorse his opinion. He was tried and sentenced to transportation for life, and though three years in his former situation in the hospital—during which time he revised the account of his Continental tour, and wrote a religious work, *The Religion of Christ the Religion of Nature*,— he was at last sent out to Van Diemen's Land in the "Woodman," which "sailed from Sheerness with 150 convicts and a detachment of military," with their wives and children, in November, 1825.

Some of his experiences of Newgate are curious, as examples of convict discipline of that epoch. He says that "cards were often smuggled in," and that "as there is a standing rule against the admission of any female, unless a prisoner's wife, the majority of prisoners declare themselves married in order to obtain interviews with their former associates. This declaration is, of course, recorded in the books of the gaol, and transmitted in the lists sent to the convict settlement. The trials were conducted with indecent rapidity, and it was a common thing for prisoners to plead guilty "in order to save time." "I well remember," says Jorgenson, "one day when five men were arraigned at the bar, the four most guilty of whom, being asked their plea by the court, answered promptly, and with much *seeming* contrition, 'Guilty, my Lord,' and were sentenced to a few months' imprisonment, while the fifth, sensible of his comparative innocence pleaded not guilty, occupied the time of the court with his defence for three-quarters of an hour, and was sentenced to seven years' transportation."

Capital punishment was frequent, and apparently but little feared. A man named Madden, under sentence of death, "malingered" for hospital comforts in his last moments. "He had fallen fast asleep one evening, when the sheriff came about 11 o'clock to announce to him the awful news that he was to be hanged next Monday morning. The poor creature, raising himself in his bed and thinking I verily believe more of the respect that was due to the sheriff than of his own dreadful situation, touched respectfully with his hand a little tuft of hair that stuck out on his brow from under his nightcap, in lieu of his hat, and bending his head merely said, 'very well, gentlemen,' then laying himself down again and throwing the blankets over his shoulders was asleep and actually snoring in five minutes." At the same time he mentions the case of an old man who was under sentence, and whose wife being in the most destitute condition, often came to the prison vowing that he had money and begging him to give her some—"if it was but a single sixpence." The miser refused, and "actually went to the gallows, and was hanged with nine sovereigns in his trousers pocket." Jorgenson speaks highly of Dr. Box, and cites in support of his assertion of that gentleman's probity, a story to the effect that a gentleman of good family was condemned to death, and as by his decease his relatives would lose a valuable lease of certain Crown lands, his two sons offered Box a bribe of £4000 to declare their father insane. Box would not accept the bribe, but pledged himself to secrecy, and two "eminent physicians," being less scrupulous, the prisoner escaped. He tells also a very strange story of a clerk, in the Transfer Office of the Bank of England, who being committed for forgery attempted to escape through the window of a third storey, but fell, broke his jaw-bone, his hip-bone, and one of his arms. The case was clear, but the accident caused a postponement of the trial until the next sessions, and the prisoner being then brought into court, "carried on a litter and bandaged all round," was again remanded. In the meantime, his friends set vigorously to work, and by dint of high bribery, suborned witnesses, and destroyed vouchers, got an acquittal.

Jorgenson gives as his opinion that convicts were in great terror of "transportation," and regarded it in many instances as a punishment worse than death. "I have known," says he, "several who would have looked upon death as less severe than being torn from their old friends and associates. The very remoteness of the scene and the uncertainty (notwithstanding every representation) of the fate they are to meet with, affects them with a species of horror inconceivable to those who have not been similarly situated. . . . The idea of reforming a person who has been convicted of ever so small an offence at home seems never to be entertained. . . . When in gaol it is a common boast among themselves, and a spirit of emulation exists among them to show who has committed the most numerous and most daring offences, from which they derive a sort of consequence over each other."

Previous to his removal on board the "Woodman," he was placed in the "Justitia" hulk, stationed off Woolwich, and did not appear to like his situation. The hulks were hot-beds of infamy and blackguardism. The authority possessed by the officers was often abused, and the most vicious of the criminal class herded together without proper superintendence, committed the most abominable crimes with comparative impunity. Jorgenson speaks bitterly of his sufferings; and admitting that it is possible that he may exaggerate, one cannot but agree with him when he characterizes the English galleys of that time as "schools of abominable pollution," and avers that "those who have been discharged from them have over-run England and everywhere spread vice and immorality." On board the prison-ship things were but little better. "Each prisoner was supplied with new clothing of the coarsest description," and each, without exception, had a pair of double-irons placed on his legs. . . . Swearing, cursing, wrangling, lamentations, and tears deafened all within hearing, and it appeared as if 10,000 demons had been let loose. . . . By daylight or dark they (the prisoners) did not scruple to steal all that came in their way; boxes and parcels of tea and sugar were torn from those who possessed any, and in case of resistance life was endangered. . . . Those who were most daring and active in these exploits were looked up to with a great deal of respect by their less hardened fellow convicts. . . The thieves easily found receivers, as wearing-apparel and other things were sold to the soldiers and their wives, and the sailors in the half deck." The surgeon-superintendent is described as a good-hearted man, as is also Mr. Leary, a lieutenant in the navy, who commanded the vessel. Jorgenson's description of the voyage is somewhat minute, but too lengthy to quote here. Once fairly in blue water the irons were knocked off and the prisoners sent up on deck in gangs. In the tropics four died of fever, and several were placed in hospital. This "fever"—probably "ship fever"—carried off the surgeon himself, and the "Woodman" was obliged to make the Cape, and take another surgeon on board: Fortunately, the disease did not spread in colder latitudes, and they arrived safely at Hobart Town on the 5th May, 1826; and Jorgenson "remembered sadly," as he contemplated the rising city, that "twenty-three years before he had assisted in forming Rest Down, the first settlement in the island."

The morning after the "Woodman" arrived in Hobart Town, the usual muster of prisoners took place.

The convicts in their prison clothes were landed and marched up to the prisoners' barracks, where they were inspected by the Governor, Colonel Arthur, and in due course "assigned" or sentenced to such further imprisonment as their conduct during the voyage had rendered desirable. Jorgenson had "letters of recommendation" from two of the directors of the Van Diemen's Land Company to their principal agent, Mr. Edward Curr. Unluckily, however, our hero had been enthralled by the representations of a Mr. Rolla O'Farrell, "a gentleman of fashionable appearance who spoke a little French," and had made application to be placed in his office on Government service. This application was granted, and Jorgenson found that he had committed a great error, the Government pay being small and the work arduous. "A prisoner clerk," he says, "received only 6d. a day and 1d. for rations; the former paid quarterly, and the latter every month." He had hoped that the Government would have extended some mercy towards him, not only on account of his period of imprisonment in Newgate, but because of his services on board the "Woodman." But he was disappointed. Strange rumours concerning him were afloat. Some said he was a political pamphleteer, imprisoned for having written against the Government; others, that he had been a political spy, employed against the British Crown. These reports Jorgenson stigmatises as "devoid of truth," adding with some tolerable degree of that modest self-assurance which he alleges is so needful to success in life, that "a system of *espionage* is of so abominable a character, that no man possessed of the least particle of honour would engage in it."

At last, however, he succeeded in getting an exchange into the company's service, and was for some time employed in the office at Hobart Town, as a copying clerk.

Later on there was found for him an employment more suited to his ambition than that of copying letters in a Government office. A party had been formed to explore the company's land, and to trace a road from the River Shannon to Circular Head, and he was placed in command. It was the early part of September, and the rivers were much swollen with recent heavy rains. Each man had with him six weeks' provisions, slung swagwise on his back, (no small weight to carry), and the journey was most laborious. The settlers, however, received them with much kindness, and until they arrived at the Big Lake, north-west of the ford of the Shannon, they got on well enough. At the River Ouse, which runs parallel with the Big Lake, however, their difficulties commenced. No ford was to be found, and for more than thirty miles Jorgenson followed the course of the stream searching in vain for a crossing-place. Being now nearly fifty years of age, and in nowise re-invigorated by his travels and dissipations, Jorgenson was becoming knocked up, and meditated a retreat. Reaching, however, a "cataract pouring down between perpendicular and impracticable rocks," the parties were brought to a ford by the accident of their dogs pursuing a kangaroo, which "led them through an opening" in the cliffs. They crossed the river some miles farther down, but the provisions being nearly expended, were compelled to fall back to Dr. Ross's farm, situated on the confluence of the Ouse and Shannon. From this place Jorgenson despatched a man to Hobart Town with letters for Mr. Curr, and himself explored the country round, "armed with a ponderous sword given him by Dr. Ross."

The messenger having returned after an absence of some weeks, the adventurers made another more successful attempt to pursue their journey. Retracing their steps they penetrated to the source of the Derwent, and ascending the mountains—foot-deep with snow—had hopes of reaching Circular Head, when the desperate nature of the country again barred their progress. The hills were rifted with chasms, and gored with *cañons* and ravines. It was impossible to go on, and the floods which had risen since their setting forth forbade them to go back. Provisions fell short and death stared them in the face. In this plight Jorgenson avowed his ability to lead his companions to a stock hut, and to his astonishment succeeded in doing so. Descending from the hills and keeping between the river beds, the party found themselves in a country of a different aspect, and traversing some broad cattle-tracks leading down a series of gentle slopes, arrived at the banks of Lake Echo. A distinct view of the Table Mountain on the Clyde now cheered their spirits, and by the afternoon of the next day they reached "Mr. Skene's stock hut."

The stockmen observing the tattered clothes, long beards, and portentous firearms of the travellers, took them for bushrangers, and until Jorgenson produced his maps, compass, journal, and letters from Curr, refused to give them shelter. Bushrangers swarmed at that time in the country districts, and the fear of the good folks was not without warrant. Jorgenson's good fortune—now bringing him in contact with a scholar, and now with a "shipmate"—protected him until he reached Hobart Town. It was lucky indeed that he had not succeeded in making Circular Head, for the provisions which were to have been buried there had missed carriage, and had the explorers reached the Bluff they must all have died of starvation.

In the early part of January, 1827, he was again employed by the Company on a like service. It was decided to send a party along the western coast of the island from Circular Head to the Shannon. Proceeding to Circular Head, Jorgenson did good service in "talking over" some of the most dissatisfied of the convicts,—a mutiny had just been put down by force of arms—and with three others, including Mr. Lorymer, one of the Company's surveyors, set out from Cape Cameron to Pieman's River. This expedition was a more disastrous one than the first. The coast was barren and flinty. In various resting-places on their weary journey they fell in with wrecks of beached vessels—melancholy memorials of former visitors. The sand-hills rivalled those of Jutland—"in one place," says Jorgenson, "a mountain of sand had been reared which, after ascending with great difficulty, measured on the top seven miles in length." Timber was scarce, it was even difficult to find a cross pole for their tent. Climbing at last with immense toil the almost perpendicular banks of Pieman's River, a scene of appalling desolation burst upon them. "It was as though some mighty convulsion had rent the earth asunder and sported with trees of enormous length and circumference tearing them up by the roots—trees nearly coeval with centuries back." Beyond this wild stretch of mountain land towered the Frenchman's Cap and the Traveller's Guide, the two landmarks of that dreary spot, Macquarie Harbour. Descending the gullies, with the hope of finding a road through what seemed to be a huge plain stretching away to the westward, they found themselves in a desert of six-wire scrub, so dense that they could not cut their way through it quicker than at the rate of 200 yards a day. This was the "desert" where so many runaways from "Hell's Gates" settlement had been lost, and Jorgenson, finding that his two best dogs had died from hunger, and that the provisions were reduced to two bags of flour, determined to retreat to Circular Head.

Arriving at Cape Cameron, danger thickens upon them They could not find water. They were nearly swallowed by the quicksands on the seashore. They made a raft, and poor Lorymer was drowned in attempting to cross the Duck River. Wet, exhausted, and fainting from want of food, the three survivors at last came upon "the tail of a dog-fish, at which the crows and gulls were greedily picking," and saw in this "savoury morsel a new lease of life." Concealing their firearms in the scrub, and flinging away all unnecessary burden of accoutrements, they pushed on with the energy of desperation, and at last reached Circular Head in safety. Jorgenson lay between life and death for four days, and at last recovered. This was his last expedition on the part of the Van Diemen's Land Company. Arrived at Hobart Town once more, he received his ticket-of-leave, and occupied himself in assisting in editing a colonial newspaper, "being glad," he says, "to employ myself in any way in which I could obtain an honest subsistence." He did not long fill the editorial chair, finding the "proprietor of the paper" not at all to his taste. This worthy man, it appears, "kept him starving," and also, after a fashion which has been found uncongenial to men of letters in every age, "insisted that every one in the house should attend prayers three times a day, and as these prayers were unusually long, and delivered in a tone and dialect extremely disagreeable," Jorgenson was "glad to get rid of the connection."

A new field for enterprise awaited him. The country at that time (1827-29), was infested with desperadoes, who, escaped from the various prison gangs on the island, had taken to the bush. The most daring robberies were committed in open day, and the authorities set completely at defiance. The day before Jorgenson had reached Dr. Ross's house on the occasion of his first expedition to the Big Lake, the place had been "visited by Dunn," a notorious ruffian, whose name yet lives in prison story. This gentleman was a mate of the more infamous wretch Brady, and was the terror of the district. He is reported to have shot down alike aborigines and settlers. Jorgenson tells how he cut off the head of a native and tied it round the neck of a lubra as a token of esteem; on this occasion he merely made one of the stockmen tie up the other two and then fry him some chops.

He was caught and hung not long after, and the compiler of the *Bushrangers* states that he appeared on the scaffold in "a long white muslin robe, with a huge black cross marked thereon before and behind." Such monsters as these were numerous, and "a formidable gang, consisting of upwards of sixty, in different parts of the colony, acted in concert" in stealing sheep, cattle and horses. "If any person accidentally came near where the offenders were killing or driving stock he was instantly put to death, and one was even wrapped up in a green bullock hide and roasted alive by a large fire." The Government had determined to put down these villains with a strong hand. Up to that time it had been the custom to punish with death all captured runaways, but it was found that such a policy did not answer. It was resolved to offer pardon to approvers, and the instant this was done crime began to decrease. When a man had no chance of escape from the gallows whatever he confessed, he not unwisely held his tongue and confessed nothing; but when hope of mercy was held out, many betrayed their associates. As go-betweens of the Crown and the convict, some few daring and trusted agents were employed, and Jorgenson was chosen one of these. Given a letter from the Colonial Secretary to Mr. Thomas Anstey, of Anstey Barton, Police-Magistrate in the Oatlands District, he proceeded to that gentleman's house, and was soon installed as constable of the field police and assistant-constable to the Police-Magistrate. His duties were arduous. The circumference of the Oatlands District alone is more than 150 miles, and "bushrangers harrassing the settlers, and the hostile aboriginal tribes committing many murders and depredations, the situation of a constable was not without its difficulties and dangers." Jorgenson was obliged to visit all the farms and stock-huts in the Districts of Oatlands, Clyde, Campbell Town, the great and little Swan Ports, and sometimes the Richmond District, and slept out among such suggestive names as those of "Murderer's Plains," "Murderer's Tier," "Deadman's Point," "Killman's Point," "Hell's Corner," "Four-square Gallows," "Dunn's Look-out," "Brady's Look-out," and the like. In the record of his life at this epoch, he mentions several names now almost household words in Tasmania, out of which I may cite—Simpson, Anstey, Hepburn, Amos, Robertson, Gatenby, Mulgrave, and Meredith.

After two years of this life, during which he several times narrowly escaped death from bullet or starvation, Jorgenson took part in the celebrated war of extermination against the blacks. The aboriginals had for a long time harrassed the settlers, reprisals took place, and a mutual distrust was engendered. At this time things had arrived at the pass that natives speared white men wherever they found them, and white men shot down natives wholesale in return. In the year 1827, 121 outrages by natives were committed in the Oatlands District alone, and no less than twenty-eight inquests were held by one coroner on the bodies of people murdered by aboriginals. As an instance of the sort of amusement that had been going on for the previous eight years, Jorgenson cites an official report made by a settler named Robert Jones, "residing at Pleasant Place, near Poole's Marsh on the River Jordan, in the District of the Upper Clyde." This report gives so vivid a picture of "squatting" life at that period of Tasmanian history that I proceed to quote it nearly at length.

"On the evening of the 17th and 18th of March, in the year 1819," says Mr. Jones, "I resided in a stock-hut under a stony sugar-loaf, about two miles to the westward of the Macquarie River, then called the Relief River. There were three inmates, of whom one went out on the Relief Plains to look after the sheep. Towards the evening this man came running to the hut, seemingly in a very exhausted state. He said that the natives were spearing the sheep on the plains, and when they saw him they pursued him until he came in sight of the hut. We seized our firearms, consisting of two muskets, and went in pursuit, but they were in so bad a state as to be almost useless. After proceeding about 200 yards, we observed several natives lurking behind the trees. We attempted to get up with them, but they ran up into a high tier, where they were joined by a great number of others. They did not offer to disperse, but on the contrary, some of the most daring came up to us quivering their spears, and making a hideous noise. We presented our pieces with an idea of frightening them, but they heeded us not; and what was worse, the man who carried the ammunition had unfortunately lost it. We now commenced our retreat, in which we found little difficulty, as it was by this time quite dark.

"The following morning, at dawn of day, I went down on the plains, about a quarter of a mile from the hut; I heard a kind of gibberish, and on looking round I saw a great number going towards the hut. I might have made my escape, for they seemed to take no notice of me; however, I ran with all speed to the hut, for I guessed it to be their intention to set fire to it, which might have been easily accomplished, as the inmates were still in bed. I succeeded in rousing them, and we prepared ourselves against an attack. They made a most formidable appearance; some were making along a valley at the back of the hut with lighted bark in their hands, whilst a far greater number took up a position on the side of the hill, whence they could safely throw spears, waddies, and stones at us. They now gave a great shout, and commenced operations, so we were obliged to take shelter under the far end of the hut. They continued to assail us for a length of time; and finding that our pieces would not go off, they made signs for us to quit the place, which we were unwilling to do. I could perceive, as they approached closer, that they were smeared all over with red ochre; and I have since been informed, that when so daubed, it is a sure sign of hostile determination. The whole strength of the tribe present could not have been less than 200 in number. I observed one of a portly stature, who appeared to stand six feet in height. He was smeared all over with red ochre, carrying a spear of peculiar make, different to those of the rest, and much longer; he had no other sort of weapon; and even of that he made no use; he stood aloof from the rest, and issued his orders with great calmness, and was implicitly obeyed. They now formed themselves into a half-moon ring, and attacked us with great vigour. We placed ourselves in the best posture of defence that we could. One of our men stood at the door of the hut with a waddy in his hand, while myself and the third man armed ourselves with shovels, and, in a state of desperation almost, attacked the two wings. This made a momentary impression on them, and they retreated up the hill, being closely pursued by us. On a sudden they made a halt, and again commenced darting their spears, waddies, and stones; one of our men received a spear-wound on the shin bone. We endeavoured to ward off their spears, thinking they would at last be expended. They now rushed down in a most furious manner, so we were obliged to make our retreat towards the plains, having first secured our firearms. We ran down a small valley, with a small rise on each side. I observed a wild cow running with a spear in her, and several kangaroo-dogs were also speared. We were now completely surrounded, and in a very disadvantageous situation. We were obliged to stop; I received three spear-wounds at the same moment; one through my right cheek, another through the muscle of my right arm, and a third in my right side. I endeavoured to pull out the spears, but could not succeed, and one of my comrades came to my assistance. This man himself now received a spear-wound in the back, whilst the third, who was as much exposed as we were, escaped unhurt. I bled most profusely; we kept snapping our pieces, but to no purpose; our caps were knocked off several times, our trousers were full of spear-holes, and the blacks now came rushing down within a few yards with uplifted waddies to knock out our brains. We had now been engaged about six or seven hours, and were greatly exhausted; I stood in utter stupefaction, and we gave up all hopes of escape. At that moment a most fortunate accident occurred, which I have ever considered as an act of Providence. One of the pieces, which would not for a length of time go off, now happily did execution, and the chief, the portly man spoken of above, received a ball, which killed him on the spot. The natives gave way on all sides; they endeavoured to make the chief stand on his legs, made a frightful noise, looked up to heaven, and smote their breasts. With the help of my comrades we made towards the plains, when about forty blacks, forming themselves into two divisions, pursued us until we reached them, when they abandoned further pursuit. A man now came up with a gun in his hand, who asked us what was the matter. He conducted us to a fire by the river-side, and gave us some warm tea. I became very faint, my comrades disincumbered me of my jacket, and sprinkled me over with cold water. We had now upwards of ten miles to travel before we could obtain any assistance, and we were compelled to course down the river, as I was obliged to lie down very frequently. At length we reached the stock-hut of Mr. Rowland Walpole Loane, where we were received with much kindness; after which, suffering severely from my wounds, I was with difficulty conveyed to Hobart Town.

"A party afterwards went in quest of the hostile tribe, and found that they had burned the hut down, after having taken out a bag of sugar, sheep-shears, a tomahawk, a hat, and jacket. All these things they had scattered about in every direction."

This is not the only narrow escape Mr. Jones had from the blacks. In another part of his report, he says:—" In November, 1826, I was attacked by a numerous tribe of the aborigines, at my residence at Pleasant Place, in the parish of Rutland, in the county of Monmouth. On a Thursday morning, I left my wife and family at home, proceeding myself in search of some sheep, and returned about 10 o'clock of the forenoon. I had scarcely entered my dwelling when my little boy came in, saying to his mother that the blacks were about. I seized my musket and went out, and saw two. I pursued them; but when I had got half-way up to the tier, I saw about twenty natives in ambush amongst some wattle-trees. My wife was at the time standing at our door, with a loaded pistol in her hand, and called to me to come down, which I did. The natives followed, swearing at me in good English. They now extended themselves, and as the trees were at that time standing close to the house, they simply skulked behind them. I was on the alert, for I observed one man on one side, and another man on the other side, with lighted bark in their hands; the women and children were up in the tier. I was much perplexed, for I was obliged constantly to run forwards and backwards. The centre of them worked down when they saw an opportunity. It had been a high flood the day before, and the water had scarcely left the marshes, so we were hemmed in on all sides, the river behind, and the blacks before us. Mrs. Jones had several times prevented the men from coming to the house, by presenting her pistol to them, which so exasperated them, that he who was taller than the rest, and seemed to be their chief, exclaimed in a great passion, in English—'As for you ma-am—as for you ma-am—I will put you in the b——y river, ma-am,' and then he cut a number of capers. We had then with us a courageous and faithful little girl, who proposed to go upon a scrubby hill about a mile distant, to tell the sawyers who were at work there, the dangers to which we were exposed; but we would not allow it, fearing she might be speared. Shortly after the girl was missing; it appeared afterwards that she had crawled along the fences, and succeeded in getting up to the sawyers. Guessing that she had proceeded thither, in about half-an-hour after we *cooeed*, and were speedily answered by the men. The native women on the tier gave out a signal, and the blacks all fled. We pursued them, and I got very close to one, when he stooped under the boughs of a fallen tree, and I could see no more of him. We came up to a spot where we found a fire, with some kangaroo half-roasted, and some dogs which ran away. We then observed the blacks ascending the second tier, and we quitted further pursuit, as it would not have been safe to leave the house and family unprotected. This engagement with the natives lasted about four hours."

This statement of Mr. Jones gives a very accurate notion of the condition of affairs in the colony. Jorgenson quotes it with expressions of resentment against the aboriginals which need not be repeated here. There can be but little doubt but that there existed faults on both sides. The colonists, rude, hot-tempered, and blood-thirsty, as many of them were—often made unprovoked attacks upon the natives, and the blood shed in these encounters was bitterly avenged on the first opportunity. "The career of the blacks in Van Diemen's Land," says Jorgenson, "has been ever marked with ingratitude towards those who treated them with kindness, and in their attacks on the whites they pursued them with indiscriminate slaughter, not sparing any who had even vindicated their cause and fed them."

In consequence of repeated outrages of this nature, the Government resolved to bestir itself, but as yet apparently unwilling to commence hostile operations on a "grand scale," contented itself by forming a committee of deliberation, which should take into consideration the whole question. Among the names of the gentlemen constituting this committee, Jorgenson mentions those of the Rev. William Bedford, Senior Chaplain of the Colony, Mr. Roderick O'Connor, Mr. P. A. Mulgrave, and several others.

The sitting of this committee resulted in the establishment of an armed band—a sort of land privateer force—in each district. Mr. Gilbert Robertson, the chief-constable of the Richmond District, had in November, 1828, been sent in pursuit of an aggressive tribe, and had captured six of them without injury to his own men. Upon the strength of this exploit the Government engaged him to go in quest of the blacks for twelve months on a salary of £150 per annum, and in case of success he was to receive a grant of 2000 acres of land. Robertson does not appear to have been particularly successful, for in the spring of 1829 Mr. Anstey received a commission from Colonel Arthur to undertake the superintendence of all the roving parties. Four bands were thereupon sent out, and the direction of these guerillas was assigned to Jorgenson. Mr. Batman had twelve men under his control; Nicholas, in the Campbell Town district, six; Sherwin, in the Clyde district, and Doran, in the New Norfolk district, five apiece. The duty of these bands was to range the country, and, while executing vengeance for outrage committed, to keep the natives within their assigned limits. A bounty of £5 was given for every one of the aborigines taken alive. The settlers round about meantime did yeoman service. Mr. George Anstey, "then a mere youth," headed a party of his father's servants and captured a small tribe; and Mr. Howell, of the Shannon, captured another, and, forwarding them to head-quarters, received a grant of 1000 acres of land. The blacks, however, were bold and united. Arranging their plans of action, they would creep through the country by twos and threes, and suddenly uniting at a given spot, would slaughter women and children and fire homesteads. The settlers in those days never went out to plough without "placing their firearms against a stump in the field."

The nature of the country favoured these sudden attacks. Mr. Frankland, the Surveyor-General, in a report prepared for the express purpose of assisting Colonel Arthur in a campaign which he was then meditating against the natives, says :—"The most lofty mountains rise in basaltic order in all parts of the territory, piercing in their upheaval the more recent formations, and leaving round their bases the various strata of sandstones and fossiliferous rocks. Independent of these great ranges, the whole country is broken into a sea of minor elevations, sometimes extending in long ridges called by the colonists 'tiers,' sometimes in unconnected hills." The nature of the ground thus rendered anything like concerted action of a disciplined body almost impossible, and the guerillas dodged the blacks from gully to rock, from hill to plain, silently tracking their footsteps like Indian warriors on a war-trail.

As might not unreasonably be looked for, Mr. Robertson quarrelled with Jorgenson. The convict performed the work more satisfactorily than the constable, and Robertson sent privately a series of charges against him "to the Governor." Colonel Arthur, however, was not the man to be taken in by any specious misrepresentation of facts. He wrote to Mr. Anstey and ordered a full inquiry, upon which Robertson despatched another missive disclaiming all notion of injuring Jorgenson, and shielding himself under the pitiful pretence that his letter was a private one. Unfortunately, Mr. Anstey had been ordered to furnish monthly reports to Colonel Arthur of the work done by the scouting parties; Robertson had neglected to furnish his report, and as it was clear that he had captured no natives, the inquiry resulted only in a repudiation of his claims upon the Treasury. Mr. Alfred Stephen, the Solicitor-General, however, took up the case, and finally the Governor bestowed on Robertson 1000 acres of land.

The conduct of the scouting parties, however, was so far unsatisfactory that Colonel Arthur determined to put into practice a notion which had been long simmering in his brain,—he would draw a *cordon* round the recalcitrant blacks, and drive them into one corner of the island. The natives, irritated rather than cowed by the constant pursuit of the armed force, had committed some daring reprisals. Watching until their enemies had been betrayed by a false alarm into some fruitless errand, they would in broad daylight sally forth upon the unprotected farms and massacre the inhabitants. So bold had they grown that in one case—a peculiarly atrocious one—six of them climbed the fence of a settler's house, and entering by the back door killed the housewife and three children, while the father and his servants were at work but fifty yards away in the field with firearms at hand. Popular indignation was excited to the highest pitch, and upon the proposition of Colonel Arthur being mooted an extraordinary demonstration took place.

By a Government order issued from the Colonial Secretary's Office on the 9th September, 1830, the whole population of the island was called to arms. "The Lieutenant-Governor calls upon every settler, whether residing on his farm or in a town, who is not prevented by some overruling necessity, cheerfully to render his assistance, and place himself under the direction of the police-magistrate of that district in which his farm is situated, or any other district he may prefer." The whole military force in the colony was to be stationed at those points where the natives were most likely to be encountered. The north side of the island was placed under the care of Captain Donaldson, of the 57th Regiment. Captain Wellman, of the same corps, commanded from "Ross, north-east to St. Patrick's Head, and north-west to Auburn and Lake River." The Bothwell district was occupied by Captain Wentworth, of the

63rd, whose *cordon* extended north-west to the lakes, and south-west to Hamilton Township. The Lower Clyde, from Hamilton Township, south-east to New Norfolk, was under the charge of Captain Vicary, 63rd Regiment. The force at Crossmarsh, and the borders of the Oatlands, Richmond, and Bothwell districts, was commanded by Captain Mahon, 63rd Regiment. Lieutenant Barrow, 63rd, commanded the force in the district of Richmond, "extending north to Jerusalem, north-east to Prosser's Plains, and east to the coast; and Lieutenant Aubin, of the 63rd, commanded the force in the district of Oyster Bay, extending south to Little Swan Port, north to the head of the Swan River, and west to Eastern Marshes, while the whole body thus employed was placed under the general charge of Major Douglas, 63rd, who was stationed at Oatlands. Volunteers from Hobart Town were urged to join the force in the districts of New Norfolk, the Clyde, or Richmond, and those from Launceston were directed to close in with the police to the westward of Norfolk Plains, or in the country between Ben Lomond and George Town, "while," says the *Gazette*, "still more desirable service will be given by any parties who will ascend to the parts round the Lakes and Western Bluff, so as to intercept the natives if driven into that part of the country; and any enterprising young men, who may have been accustomed to make excursions into the interior, and to endure the fatigues of the bush, will most beneficially promote the common cause by joining the small military parties at the out-stations, and in making patrol expeditions with them, and the services of all such will be readily accepted by the military officers in command of the several stations."

The roving parties were to be further increased by every possible method, to which end the Governor desired that "all prisoners holding tickets-of-leave, who are capable of bearing arms, report themselves to the police-magistrate of the district in which they reside, in order that they may be enrolled, either in the regular roving parties, or otherwise employed in the public service under the instructions of their respective employers."

This announcement once made, operations were pushed forward with vigour. Colonel Arthur placed himself at the head of the forces; the "peace" of Hobart Town and Launceston was left to the care of the principal inhabitants, who could not attend the line. Captains Wentworth, Mahon, Bayley, Vicary, Wellman, Macpherson, and Lieutenants Aubin, Croly, Pedder, Champ, and Murray, placed themselves at the head of their respective divisions. The whole field police, all ticket-of-leave men, and "a multitude of convicts, either in assigned service or otherwise at the disposal of Government," were ordered to join the line; and this immense force, consisting of more than 2000 armed men, moved slowly across the island, driving the natives before them. A glance at the map of Tasmania will show the effect of this manœuvre. The blacks were to be "driven" like deer into the south-east corner of the island, to be forced over that narrow strip of sand known as East Bay Neck, connecting Forestier's Peninsula with the mainland, and then—driven across the second isthmus, "corralled," in what is now the penal settlement of Port Arthur. Nature had made for Colonel Arthur an immense stockyard, with two natural gates. The *cordon* drawn across County Pembroke was complete from Sorell Town to Spring Bay. Huge Fires were lighted at night, and guards posted constantly by day. Constantly reinforced, supplied with an ample commissariat, the terrible line closed in as it were inch by inch, and the natives, entrapped in the point of land that runs out between Pittwater and Marion Bay, were compelled to retreat towards East Bay Neck—the first gate of the stockyard. From East Bay Neck it was proposed to drive them still further south, across the terrible Eaglehawk Neck—yet seen in dreams by many a manumitted convict—down to the last point of dry land, the basalt cliffs at whose jagged base breaks unchecked the fury of the Southern Sea. It was as though the blacks, like rats driven to the utmost extremity of a quay, should be compelled to take to the water.

Colonel Arthur, however, did not push matters to this extremity. Having closed in upon East Bay Neck, and driven the natives into the stockyard, he broke up his forces and gave the volunteers leave to return to their homes "to prepare for a second series of operations," which ultimately resulted in something very like the complete destruction of the native race. The disarmed convicts, strange to say, returned quietly to their stations, though Jorgenson hints that several promising conspiracies were nipped in the bud, and the Van Diemonians, in a fever of joy, presented a congratulatory address to the Governor. It was reported that the natives had broken the *cordon*, and papers of the day hint that the expedition was a failure. There is no doubt that, when we take into consideration the state of the country, the feeling of the population, and the fact that a large body of the vilest scoundrels were entrusted with arms, which at any moment they might have turned against their leaders, the undertaking was a brilliant success. But the second expedition was even more wonderful than the first, and the story of Mr. Robinson, the "apostle of the blacks," who, unarmed and alone, went into the midst of them, and by dint of argument brought whole tribes into submission, is in itself a romance. Jorgenson wanders from his own history to relate some of the exploits of this extraordinary man, but as the history of the final subjugation of the native race and the labours of their missionary is worthy of a place to itself, I will reserve further account of them. [Since writing the above, a full account of the aborigines and their extermination has been given by Mr. Bonwick in his *Last of the Tasmanians*.]

But Jorgenson's adventures were drawing to a close. One afternoon at Anstey Barton, in turning over the leaves of the *Gazette* just brought by the mail-boy, Jorgenson observed his own name. He had obtained his pardon! One would think that this intelligence would have filled him with joy; but, if we are to believe his own account, he felt rather miserable than otherwise. He had become used to his chain, and freedom was strange to him.

Moreover, he was in a worse plight free than as a bondsman, for he had to keep himself. The roving bands, of which he was leader, were broken up in the spring (1831), and he was left without employment. He received a grant of 100 acres of land, but with a touch of his old extravagance, he "sold it almost immediately," and, in all probability, gambled away the proceeds. There was no occupation for a swash-buckler like himself, and even had there been some exploring expedition to join, or bushranger to capture, his altered condition had brought with it altered feelings. When a convict, Jorgenson was fearless to desperation; as a freeman he could appreciate the value of life:—" Prior to my receiving a pardon I had fearlessly plunged into rapid rivers, up to the armpits, with a knapsack on my back, containing a weight of 6olbs. to 7olbs When in quest of the blacks, I spent one night at Mr. Kemp's farm at the Cross Marsh; the next morning I proceeded to Mr. George Espie's farm, on the Jordan, to cross the river, as the floods were down. Here, across the Jordan, is a post and rail-fence, where persons may cross, although it is not without danger, the fence trembling from the heavy pressure of the current. I went down, and although I had often crossed when the fence was completely under water, and that there was now a clear rail, I would not venture to cross. Mr. Espie expressed some surprise at my backwardness, as he had formerly seen me cross without any apprehension. I replied, 'Yes, Mr. Espie, I was then a prisoner, and life of little matter, but now that I am *free*, I must take more care of myself.'"

The month after he got his pardon he took up his abode in Hobart Town, but "was sadly put to it to make both ends meet." He seems to have got married also, and speaks of his wife, "who volunteered to take charge of a dairy farm," but as Jorgenson knew nothing about farming, and confounded seedtime with harvest, the pair were speedily discharged. In this dilemma, the king, sailor, spy, courtier, gambler, convict, constable, and explorer, bethought himself of a ninth profession—letters. He had lived in London on his writings : he would try to do the same in Hobart Town. No sooner thought than achieved, and by-and-bye our hero calmly publishes "a tolerably large pamphlet on the Funding System," which brought him in more than 100 guineas. This easily-earned money was soon spent, and he was again destitute, when fortune, which had buffeted him long, landed him safely at last. A letter from the Danish envoy in London to Lord Glenelg was enclosed by that nobleman to Colonel Arthur with an intimation that the "mother of J. Jorgenson, a prisoner of the Crown," was dead, and that he had come into a comfortable little fortune. The curtain falls upon him petitioning the Government for a further grant of land, in consideration of his services in 1829-30-31. Here is one of the "testimonials" out of many he gives as having been attached to the document:—

"These are to certify that memorialist has been well known to me during the last nine years. He was some years under my orders when I was Police-Magistrate of the Oatlands district, during which period he acted successively as my Assistant-Clerk, Constable of the Field-Police, leader of several roving bands in quest of the aborigines, and one of the directors of the Oatland Volunteers, in the *levy en masse* against the aborigines. In all those capacities memorialist discharged honestly and fearlessly the arduous duties which were entrusted to him.

"(Signed) THOS. ANSTEY, M.C.L., J.P.

"Anstey Barton, 10th December, 1836."

Whether he ever got his grant or not I do not know, as his story breaks off abruptly:—" I have," says he, "now come to the conclusion of the second part of my autobiography. It is not for me to speculate upon whether I shall ever be able to write a third portion. This must be left to the will of that Being who rules man's destiny. I have had my full share of days! Little is there in this world to care for. The joys of human life are fleeting and transient; they may be likened to two friends meeting each other on a hasty journey, who ask a few questions, and then part, perhaps for ever, leaving nothing behind but a tender regret. Such is it with the joyous hours of our transitory existence. These pages had probably never appeared, had I merely consulted the state of my own feelings; for I am not, like Jean Jacques Rousseau, fond of thrusting myself on the public with unnecessary confessions,—I have been swayed by motives of a higher character. My youthful readers may derive a lesson from the history of my life. All human wisdom is vanity if not regulated by prudence. One error leads to another, and every deviation from the straight path is sure to entangle the strayed sheep in the mazes of a labyrinth."

Poor strayed sheep! I can fancy worthy Doctor Ross saying, "Jorgenson, you must have had a strange life of it. Can't you jot down some of those yarns you are always spinning for the *Annual?*" and see the wily smile with which the "Captain" replies as he shifts his pipe from one side of his mouth to the other.

*Write* romances! Why, this poor old convict, who has been resting in his nameless grave these twenty years, has *lived* one beside which the "story of Cambuscan bold," the *Adventures of Gil Blas*, or the doings of that prince of scoundrels, Mr. Barry Lyndon himself, dwindle into insignificance. All the raven-haired, hot-headed, supple-wristed soldiers of fortune that ever diced, drank, duelled, kissed, and escaladed their way through three volumes octavo, never had such an experience. Think over his story, from his birth in Denmark to his death in Van Diemen's Land, and imagine from what he *has* told us, how much more he has been compelled to leave unrelated.

# MICHAEL HOWE, THE DEMON BUSHRANGER.

IN the year 1820, a writer in the *Quarterly*, speaking of a book given him to review, says : " It is the greatest literary curiosity that has come before us—the first child of the press of a State only fifteen years old. It would, of course, be reprinted here, but our copy, *pene-nos*, is a genuine Caxton. This little book would assuredly be the *Reynarde Foxe* of Australian bibliomaniacs.

A copy of this wonderful work is now lying before me. It is a ragged and dirty little pamphlet of thirty-six pages. The paper is old and yellow, the letterpress in some places illegible, and several leaves are missing. It is printed in the year 1818, by Mr. Bent, and is called *Michael Howe, the Last and Worst of the Bushrangers*. The popularity of the volume is unquestionable. It is quoted by Mr. West in his *History of Tasmania*, and is extracted bodily into a *History of Van Diemen's Land*, by one Syme, who was a settler there in 1846. Mr. Bonwick, writing in 1856, calls Syme the "historian of Howe;" Syme, however, merely reprinted Bent's pamphlet as an appendix to his own book. The *Sydney Gazettes*, quoted by Wentworth and West, Commissioner Bigge's *Reports*, and a pleasant collection of stories called *The Military Sketch-book*, written by "An Officer of the Line," and published by Colburn in 1827, also contain particulars concerning the bushranger, and have been used by me to supplement the curiosity of the " *Quarterly* Reviewer."

From the year 1813—the year in which Colonel Davey arrived as Lieutenant-Governor—to 1825 the Colony of Van Diemen's Land was overrun with bushrangers. The severe punishment of lash and chain urged the convicts to escape, the paucity of the military force assisted them in their attempts, and the mountainous nature of the country aided to baffle efforts at recapture. In those days the "settler" would till his fields with pistols in his belt, and smoke his evening pipe with rifle placed ready to his hand. Bands of escaped convicts ranged the mountains, descending from their rocky fastnesses to plunder, murder and ravish. They rode about in gangs, they held councils of war, they posted sentries, and took oaths of secrecy. They attacked the gaol, and liberated their companions ; they even issued proclamations, and dictated terms to the Governor himself. Indeed the condition of affairs in Hobart Town was not encouraging to the settler. The convict element was uppermost. Felons were to freemen in the proportion of ten to one.

Concubinage with convict women was customary. The very ships that brought a mingled herd of male and female criminals were the scenes of unbridled license. Each sailor or soldier was permitted to ally himself to a female, and the connection often terminated in a marriage, which manumitted the convict. "The madams on board," says Macarthur, "occupy the few days which elapse before landing in preparing the most dazzling effect in their descent upon the Australian shore. With rich dresses, bonnets *a là mode*, ear pendants, brooches, long gorgeous shawls and splendid veils, silk stockings, kid gloves, and parasols in hand, dispensing sweet odours from their profusely perfumed forms, they are assigned as servants. The settler expected a servant, but receives a "princess." The children of these rakings of the London *bagnios* were not unworthy of their race. Their paramours vied with each other in villany and distinction. Blunt Davey himself was not too curious as to the morals of his domestics, and gentlemen in Hobart Town witnessed some curious scenes. "Society as it then existed," says Mr. West, "nourished every species of crime. Tattered promissory notes, of small amount and doubtful parentage, fluttered about the colony. . . . Plate, stolen by bushrangers and burglars, was melted down and disposed of. . . . They burnt the implements of husbandry for the iron, they robbed the gibbet of the chains, they even wrenched the plate from the coffin of an opulent merchant, and stripped him of his shroud."

In addition to the cheerful condition of affairs at home, armed bandits, mounted on stolen horses, rode abroad, and defied all attempts at capture. Of these gentry, the most noted was Michael Howe.

In the year 1812, the convict ship "Indefatigable," Captain Cross, arrived at Hobart Town; and among the many poor devils whom she carried was one Michael Howe, a native of Pontefract, transported for seven years for robbing a miller on the king's highway. The robber seemed tractable and goodnatured, though cursed with a most pernicious love of liberty. He attempted to escape before the vessel left the docks, jumping overboard, and swimming some distance before he was retaken. On arrival in Van Diemen's Land he was assigned to a Mr. Ingle, a storekeeper, but the life did not appear to suit him. He had been a sailor, had served on board a man-of-war, and owned (according to Mr. West) a small collier. A man of determined character and somewhat romantic notions, he resolved to escape and take to the bush. At that time a scoundrel named Whitehead, with a band of twenty-seven desperadoes, ranged the country; to these worthies Howe made his way, and was received with acclamations by the troop. The first exploit of the gang was to attack New Norfolk—then a small but flourishing township—and to plunder the inhabitants of all their portable property. From New Norfolk they proceeded to Pittwater, and burnt the wheat-stacks, barns, and out-houses of Mr. Humphrey, the Police-Magistrate, affixing to the gate of the ruined barn a paper, on which was drawn—in the same spirit as the coffin and cross-bones of the Irish rent receipts—a gun firing a gigantic bullet at the head of a man.

Mr. Humphrey appears to have taken his loss quietly, but on the ruffians plundering the house of Mr. Carlisle, the settlers thought it time to bestir themselves.

A neighbour of Carlisle's, a Mr. McCarthy, who owned a schooner, the "Geordy," then lying in the river, determined to make a push for a general capture of the gang.

Howe, when a servant at Ingle's, had gained the affections of a native girl, and had induced her to accompany him to the bush. This young woman was only seventeen years of age, and is described as being of some personal attractions. She was accustomed to wait upon her lover, and to assist him in his escapes from justice. On the night when Whitehead fired Mr. Humphrey's house, Black Mary and Howe were encamped with some of the gang on the heights above the plain. According to the girl's statement, the bushranger, in high glee, filled a "goblet" (probably a pannikin), and, as the twilight closed, cried to his comrade Collier, "Collier, we want light! Here's success to the hand that will give it us!" Practical Mary, eager to please her lord, rose to get a firestick from the embers; but Howe laughed loudly, and seizing her by the arm exclaimed, "Sit down, girl! Whitehead's lighting a match for us!" Presently "a tremendous flame arose from two different points below, which threw a glare over all the plain." "There!" cried Howe; "these fires have cost a pretty penny. Here's success to the bushman's tinder-box, and a blazing fire to his enemies!" Mary relates that Howe was kind to her—after the manner of his sex—whenever things went right with him, but if anything "crossed his temper he was like a tiger." He was very jealous of her, she says; and when Edwards, one of his gang, gave her a shawl which he had stolen from Captain Tonnson, Howe pistolled him on the spot.

McCarthy organised a party, consisting of some eleven men, among whom were Carlisle, O'Birne, the master of the schooner, and an old convict of sixty years of age, named Worral. This old man had been one of the mutineers of the "Nore," and though he vows in his narrative (given in the *Military Sketch Book*) that the only part he took in the proceedings was the writing "in a fair hand" several papers for the mutineers, he was transported for life to Van Diemen's Land. This party, armed to the teeth, and guided by a native, set out upon the track of the bushrangers. By-and-by they heard the report of a musket-shot, and creeping stealthily up behind a huge hollowed log, came upon the bandits pleasantly encamped. The scene, as described by Worral, must have been a picturesque one. "Some were cooking pieces of mutton; others lolling on the grass, smoking and drinking; and a pretty, interesting-looking native girl sat playing with the long and bushy black ringlets of a stout, wicked-looking man seated by her. He had pistols in his belt, wore a fustain jacket, a kangaroo-skin cap and waistcoat, with leather gaiters and dirty velveteen breeches." This was Michael Howe. Whitehead, the leader—"a tall ill-looking villain"—was asleep on the grass. McCarthy directed his men to cock their pieces, and called upon the bushrangers to surrender. Instantly the gang were on their feet.

But before a shot was fired, Whitehead called a parley. "We don't want to shed blood," said he ; "go home." McCarthy still held firm, and was further expostulating, when Howe roared, "Slap at the beggars !" and a tearing volley from guns and pistols rattled among the branches. Five of the attacking party fell, and, "keeping up a brisk hedge-firing," they were forced to retreat, leaving one of their number—a man named Murphy—dead on the grass. Mr. Carlisle and O'Birne were mortally wounded. Carlisle died on the way home; O'Birne, who was shot through the jaws, lingered for four days in extreme agony.

McCarthy knew that his unsuccessful attempt would bring upon him speedy vengeance, and applied for military protection. A detachment of the 73rd Regiment were sent out to scour the country, and McCarthy's homestead was garrisoned by a party of the 46th. The bushrangers, unwitting of the ambush, attacked the farm, and a sort of siege commenced. The soldiers, however, gained the day, and a shot from Worral mortally wounded Whitehead. The dying man ran back towards his comrades, crying to Howe, "Take my watch—the villains have shot me." The soldiers ran round the house to take their assailants in the rear, and Worral, reloading his piece, observed Howe bend over the corpse of his captain as if to comply with his request. He ran towards him, but when he reached the spot the miscreant had disappeared, and there lay on the ground the mutilated trunk of Whitehead. In pursuance of an agreement made between them, Howe had hacked off his comrade's head with his clasp-knife, to prevent any person claiming the reward that was offered for it. The gang got clear away to the mountains. The body of Whitehead was gibbeted on Hunter's Island, and Howe became the leader of the troop. The atrocity and daring of the scoundrel now almost surpasses belief. His headquarters were about fifteen miles west of Oatlands, in a place yet known as "Michael Howe's Marsh." He instituted there a sort of rude court of justice, and would subject such of his band as displeased him to punishment. Says Mr. West, "The tone assumed by this robber was that of an independent chief, and in the management of his men he attempted the discipline of war. He professed the piety of the quarter-deck, and read to them the Scriptures." His style and title was "Governor of the Ranges," and he addressed the King's representative as "Governor of the Town." He punished his men with blows and hard labour if they disobeyed him ; and when one day a man named Bowles fired a blank shot over his head in jest, the chief tied him hand and foot, and blew his brains out. He compelled his adherents to take an oath of fidelity upon a (stolen) Bible, and sent insolent messages to the authorities. In a journal called the *Bengal Hurkaru* occurs the following :—"John Yorke, being duly sworn, states : About five o'clock in the evening of November 27th (1816), I fell in with a party of bushrangers—about fourteen men and two women. Michael Howe and Geary were the only two of the gang I knew personally. I met them on Scantling's Plains. I was on horseback. They desired me to stop, which I accordingly did on the high road ; it was

Geary that stopped me; he said he wanted to see every man sworn to abide by the contents of a letter. I observed a thick man writing, as I suppose, to the Lieutenant-Governor. Geary was the man who administered the oath on a prayer-book, calling each man for the purpose regularly. They did not inform me of the contents of the letter. Michael Howe and Geary directed me to state when I came home the whole I had seen; and to inform Mr. Humphrey, the Magistrate, and Mr. Wade, the Chief Constable, to take care of themselves, as they were resolved to have their lives, and to prevent them keeping stock or grain, unless something was done for them; that Mr. Humphrey might rear what grain he liked, but they would thrash more in one night than he could reap in one year. They said they would set the whole country on fire with one stick. I was detained about three-quarters of an hour, during which time they charged me to be strict in making known what they said to me and what I had seen. On my return from Port Dalrymple, I called at a hut occupied by Joseph Wright, Scantling's Plains. Williams and a youth were there, who told me the bushrangers had been there a few days before, and forced them to a place called Murderer's Plains, which the bushrangers called the Tallow-chandler's Shop, where they made them remain three days for the purpose of rendering down a large quantity of beef-fat, which Williams understood was taken from cattle belonging to Stynes and Troy." The poorer settlers were in league with the daring robbers, and were wont to supply them with information. Howe affected to be a sort of Robin Hood—indeed it is probable that the marauder of Sherwood Forest was just such another greasy ruffian. In another hundred years the "light that never was on land or sea, the consecration and the poet's dream"—the consecration of that lecherous butcher, Henry the Eighth—the poet's dream of that beer-swilling termagant, Virgin Elizabeth—the light that gilds the shameless robberies of the glorious Reformation—may shine upon Michael Howe in the character of a romantic outlaw. The people certainly admired him; and though a reward of 100 guineas and a free passage to England was set upon his head, he was accustomed to visit Hobart Town in perfect security. Worral—who had set his heart upon seeing England again, and was always on the watch to capture the bandit—came very near taking him on one occasion. The old sailor was buying some powder and shot in the store of one Stevens, when a man dressed like a gentleman entered. The moment Worral heard him speak he recognised the voice of the fellow "who had cut off the head of Whitehead," and grappled with him. A furious struggle took place, and just as poor Worral thought his 100 guineas and free passage were safe, he received a violent blow on the back of the head, and fell senseless. When he recovered, Stevens, the storekeeper, was holding a pannikin of rum to his lips, and Howe had gone. Stevens swore that "a strange man had rushed into the store and knocked Worral down with a bludgeon." The bethumped old fellow had his suspicions, but like a wise man said nothing, until one day Stevens was detected in "receiving" plunder, and previous to swinging on the Hunter Island gibbet, confessed that he himself had struck the blow—"I wish I'd killed him," he added. A regular campaign was now commenced against the freebooters, and one day a party of the 46th, among whom, as a volunteer, was the indefatigable Worral, stumbled upon a hut on the banks of the Shannon. The bushrangers had chosen their camping-ground with an eye to the picturesque. "It was a flat piece of green land, covered with wild-flowers, and overlooking the most beautiful country that can be imagined: a precipice in our front, from which we hurled a stone that rolled over half-a-mile of steep hill down to a river, all studded with islands and ornamented by the most delightfully displayed foliage on its banks; plain over plain and wood over wood, was to be seen for twenty miles distance, and the blue mountains far away gave one the idea of an earthly paradise, yet no human being ever claimed it—none ever trod over this fair country but a few lawless brigands." Remaining in ambush for some time at the spot, they at last perceived four men approaching, of whom one was Howe. The native girl before mentioned was with him, clad in a dress of skins, feathers, and white calico. The instinct of the savage detected the trap: she pointed, gesticulated, seized Howe's arm, and ran back. The soldiers dashed out, and allowing the less valuable prey to escape, followed Howe. The bushranger, closely followed by the girl, gained the summit of a hill, turned round and fired, but missed, and ran on. For more than a mile the chase continued, the bushranger gaining on his pursuers at every stride, when the girl's strength began to fail her, and she lagged behind. Howe pressed and urged her to further exertion. The pursuers set up a great shout at this, and redoubled their efforts. The girl fell, and Howe in vain commanded her to rise. The soldiers were within five hundred yards of him, and gnashing his teeth with rage, the monster drew his remaining pistol, and, taking deliberate aim at the exhausted girl, fired. He then turned and plunged into a ravine, "where pursuit was hopeless." Howe doubtless hoped that his bullet had taken fatal effect, and that Mary would be unable to speak concerning him. He was doubly deceived. The girl was but slightly wounded, and justly incensed at the brutality of her lover. She volunteered to aid her rescuers to track him to his hiding-place. After a march of three hours, the party arrived at some huts on the Shannon bank. These were deserted, but on the opposite side of the river stood Geary—the lieutenant of the gang—with levelled musket. He fired, missed, and made off. The girl now led them to another place, and as they "arrived at a high rock which overhung the waters of the creek," a shot was heard; a wild figure burst out of the bush, and darted past them. The cliff was steep, but two soldiers, dropping down its hinder side, ran round and cut off the outlaw's retreat. It was Hillier, the most brutal of the band. He turned and faced them for an instant, and then, seeing their numbers, flung away his empty gun with an oath, and sprang head-first from the rock into the river. The drop was a hundred feet, and all thought him a dead man. He rose to the surface, however, and swam for the opposite bank. The two soldiers quickly ran to a narrow ravine formed by the overhanging rocks, and, daringly leaping it, met him as he landed. He took to the water again, but on reaching the middle of the creek, and seeing musket muzzles menacing him on all sides, cried out that he would surrender, and, if they would spare his life, turn approver. The sergeant who commanded the party would make no terms, vowing to shoot him unless he surrendered instantly. So he came ashore, and was bound. Now a very horrible discovery was made. Guided by the native girl, they reached the hut, in which lay a body with the head nearly severed from the trunk. "Ay," says Hillier: "that's poor Peter Septon; he often said he'd cut his own throat, and now he's done it completely." "No man ever cut his throat in that manner," cries Worral. "*You* did it, you villain!" Hillier protested innocence, but a few paces further the party came upon another bleeding wretch, with his hand shattered by a bullet, and his throat partially severed. This was Collier, another bandit. "Villain!" cries he to Hillier, "you would have murdered me as you murdered Septon." The black girl at this moment, seeing that the murderer was inevitably doomed, says: "Hillier, you killed my sister, too!" Hillier, finding it useless to dissemble, confessed. The soldiers brought their prisoners to New Norfolk, making Hillier carry Septon's head tied round his neck. The two men who had escaped with Howe were soon afterwards retaken at Kangaroo Point, and the four were gibbeted together on Hunter's Island, beside the whistling bones of Whitehead. Howe was now reduced to despair. The capture of the huts had deprived him of his ammunition and his dogs —the two sources of life in the bush. He resolved to surrender himself, offering, if his life was spared, to assist the Government in capturing the remnant of his own band. Such was the state of the country, and the terror his deeds had inspired, that Governor Sorrell, who had succeeded Davey, accepted the offer made him, and despatched Captain Nairns, of the 46th, as an ambassador to the bushranger. Howe was brought to Hobart Town, and lodged in gaol, from which he was soon rashly released, and permitted to walk about the city attended only by a single constable. In the meantime the robbers received reinforcements of several escaped convicts, for whom large rewards were offered by the Crown; and notwithstanding that Geary was shot in an affray in the Tea-Tree Bush, the plundering and burning continued. Twenty men were thought to be at large. They seized the boat which carried provisions between Georgetown and Launceston, they sent messages of defiance to the Government, and openly offered an asylum to all escaped convicts. Encouraged by these successes, or perhaps weary of civilisation, Howe eluded his guardian constable, and, having received arms and provisions, made for his old haunts. This was too much for human patience. The Governor made a personal appeal to the settlers, and troops of volunteers were despatched in all directions. Convicts and freemen took part in these excursions, and such exertions were made that of the twenty only three remained at large—Howe, Watts, and Browne. For these miscreants the following rewards were offered :—For Howe, one hundred guineas and a free pardon; for Watts, eighty guineas and a free pardon; for Browne, fifty guineas and a free pardon. Browne surrendered, but Howe was not to be taken. A convict named Drewe, otherwise called Slambow, was shepherding for a Mr. Williams, and determined to make a push for the reward. This Drewe had, it appears, with the majority of the convict storekeepers, often assisted Howe in his escapes from justice. Falling in with Watts, he pointed out the advantages of freedom, and suggested that the two together might easily overcome the brigand. Watts assented, and proposed to Howe that they should send a message to Hobart Town through Slambow. Howe agreed, and the three met at dawn, at a place called Longbottom, on the banks of the Derwent. Howe ordered Watts to shake the priming from his gun, and did the same himself, Drewe had been advised to leave his gun, and was unarmed. The bushranger then lighted a fire, and busied himself in preparing a breakfast for his guest. Watts seized a favourable moment, and, leaping upon him, secured him. Howe witnessed the treacherous scoundrels eat their breakfast in silence, busying himself the while with straining at his bonds. After breakfast the captors started in high glee for Hobart Town, Watts going first with the loaded gun, the bound bushranger in the middle, and Drewe bringing up the rear. They had gone about eight miles, and Drewe, eager for the reward, had refused assistance from his master, when Howe, watching a favourable moment, slipped his hands from the loosened cords, drew a concealed knife, and stabbed Watts in the back. Drewe was clambering up a bank, and saw nothing; but, when he reached the top, Howe coolly presented Watt's gun, and shot him dead. Watts cried, " Have you shot Slambow ? " " Yes," says Howe, " and will shoot you as soon as I can load the piece." Upon this, Watts, though bleeding from the wound in his back, made shift to get upon his feet, and ran some two hundred yards. Howe, doubtless fearing an alarm from the shot, did not wait to complete his work, but made off into the bush. Watt's got to a settler's house, and being sent to Sydney, three days after arrival, died of his wounds. Villain as Howe was, one cannot but admit that his cowardly assailants met with their desserts. The double murder, however, caused a proclamation from Government, offering, in addition to the reward and pardon, a free passage to England, for any one who should bring in the dreaded bushranger, dead or alive. Our old friend Worral determined to make a final effort. Alone in the wilderness, Howe seems to have lived for some time the victim of a despairing conscience. His nature was never without a touch of rude romance, and the recollection of his crimes went far to turn his brain. In his solitary wanderings among the mountains he saw visions. Spirits appeared to him, and promised him happiness. The ghosts of his victims arose, and threatened despair. He kept a journal of his dreams— a journal written with blood, on kangaroo-skin. It is possible that, in a land of fruits and game, he might have lived a hermit and died a penitent. But the barren beauty of the bush afforded no sustenance.

He was compelled to descend from his hut—an eyrie built on the brink of a cataract, and surrounded by some of the sublimest scenery of the Tasmanian mountains—to plunder the farms for food and ammunition. Armed bands, incited by the hope of the reward, lay in wait for him at every turn. Mr. Bonwick describes the condition of the man in the following picturesque passage:—"Clad in kangaroo skins, and with a long, shaggy, black beard, he had a very Orson-like aspect. Badgered on all sides, he chose a retreat among the mountain-fastnesses of the Upper Shannon—a dreary solitude of cloudland—the rocky home of hermit eagles. On this elevated *plateau*, contiguous to the almost bottomless lakes from whose crater-formed recesses in ancient days torrents of liquid fire poured forth upon the plains of Tasmania, or rose uplifted basaltic masses, like frowning Wellington, within sight of lofty hills of snow, having the peak of Teneriffe to the south, Frenchman's Cap and Byron to the west, Miller's Bluff to the east, and the serrated crest of the western tier to the north; entrenched in dense woods, with surrounding forests of dead poles, through whose leafless passages the wind harshly whistled in a storm—thus situated amidst some of the sublimest scenes of nature, away from suffering and degraded humanity, the lonely bushranger was confronted with his God and his own conscience." To capture this hunted outlaw was the task and the fortune of Worral. He allied himself with a man named Warburton, a kangaroo-hunter and confidant of Howe's, and one Pugh, a soldier of the 48th. The three proceeded to Warburton's hut, situated in a lonely spot on the Shannon bank; and Worral and Pugh sat down with their guns across their knees, while Warburton went out to seek Howe. At last, the sun striking a tier of the opposite hills showed two figures approaching the hut. An hour passed, and Worral in despair crept cautiously out. The bushranger was standing within a hundred yards of him talking to the traitor. He drew back, and presently Howe slowly entered the hut, with his gun presented and cocked. He saw the trap at once. "Is that your game?" he cried, and fired. Pugh knocked up the gun, and, says Worral with almost poetic imagery, "Howe ran off like a wolf." I give the story of the capture in the sailor's own words: "I fired, but missed; Pugh then halted and took aim at him, but also missed. I immediately flung away the gun, and ran after Howe; Pugh also pursued; Warburton was a considerable distance away. I ran very fast, so did Howe, and if he had not fallen down an unexpected bank I should not have been fleet enough for him. This fall, however, brought me up with him. He was on his legs, and preparing to climb a broken bank, which would have given him a free run into a wood, when I presented my pistol at him, and desired him to stand. He drew forth another, but did not level it at me. We were about fifteen yards from each other, the bank he fell from being between us. He stared at me with astonishment, and to tell you the truth I was a little astonished at him, for he was covered with patches of kangaroo skin, and wore a long black beard, a haversack and powder-horn slung across his shoulders. I wore my beard also—as I do now—and a curious pair we looked like. After a moment's pause, he cried out, 'Blackbeard aginst Greybeard for a million!' and fired. I slapped at him, and I believe hit him, for he staggered, but rallied again, and was clearing the bank between him and me when Pugh ran up, and with the butt end of his firelock knocked him down again, jumped after him, and battered his brains out, just as he was opening a clasp-knife to defend himself."

Such was the end of Michael Howe. His captors cut off his head and brought it to Hobart Town, terrifying poor Dr. Ross, who, proceeding up country a newly-arrived immigrant, met the ghastly procession. The reward was divided amongst them; the settlers subscribed nearly double the amount, and old Worral was sent "home free, with the thanks of the Governor and the public."

# THE SEIZURE OF THE "CYPRUS."

ON the 9th of August, 1829, the "Cyprus," a vessel which was employed by the Government of Van Diemen's Land to carry prisoners from Hobart Town to Macquarie Harbour, was seized by the convicts and carried into the South Seas.

The story is a romantic one, and if it does not equal in interest the story of the capture of the "Frederick," of which I shall by-and-by have occasion to speak, it is remarkable as showing the condition of convict discipline in the early days of the colony.

Macquarie Harbour—abandoned in 1833—was in those days the Ultima Thule of convict settlement. Established in 1821 by Governor Sorrell as a station for the most irreclaimable of the desperadoes who were sent in shiploads from England until it became a hideous terrorism, which often drove its victims to seek death as a means of escape. The picture of the place as drawn by Mr. Backhouse, the missionary, who visited it in 1832, is most dismal. The scenery is wild and barren, the scrub and undergrowth impenetrable, and from the swampy ground around the settlement arise noisome and death-dealing exhalations. The surf beating with violence on the rocky shore renders approach dangerous, and the westerly winds blowing with fury into the harbour oppose sometimes for days the departure of the convict vessels.

This place was the last home—but one—of the felon. Once sent to "the Hell," as the abode of doom was termed by the prisoners, return was almost hopeless. The ironbound coast, the dismal and impassable swamps, the barren and rugged mountain ranges, combined to render escape impossible. Of the many unfortunates who made the attempt to regain their freedom, all save some eight or nine died or were retaken. The life of a convict at this hideous place of punishment was one continual agony. In those times the notion of reclaiming human creatures by reason and kindness was unknown. Condemned for life to the settlement—often for small offences against discipline—the miserable beings were cut off from the world for ever. The commandant—usually some worthy officer selected from the regiment then in Van Diemen's Land for his severity or strength of will—dealt with the men under his charge as the humour took him. The guard was always under arms, and had orders to fire on any man who attempted to escape. The lash was the punishment most in vogue, but those wretches whose hardened hides the cat had cut into insensibility were marooned on rocks within view of the prison barracks. The work was constant and exhausting. Robbers, murderers, and forgers, told off into gangs, felled the gigantic trees which grew in the neighbourhood of the harbour. Chained together like beasts, and kept in activity by the rarely-idle lash, they bore the logs to the water-side on their backs. Every now and then some feebler ruffian would fall from exhaustion, and the chain would drag him after the main body until he rose again.

A visitor to the place in 1831 says he saw "something which he took for a gigantic centipede, which moved forward through the bush to the clanking of chains and the cracking of the overseer's whip." This was a log borne by a convict gang. Treated like beasts, the men lived the life of beasts. All the atrocities that men could commit were committed there. Suicide was frequent. Men drowned themselves to be rid of the burden of their existence. Three wretches once drew lots as to who should get a sight of Hobart Town. One was to murder the other, and the third was to volunteer his evidence. The lottery was drawn, the doomed man laughed ere his companion beat out his brains, and the two survivors congratulated each other on their holiday on the scaffold at Hobart Town gaol. To this place Lieutenant Carew, with ten soldiers, set out to convey thirty-one prisoners. As not unfrequently happened, the weather proved unfavourable, and the vessel put into Recherche Bay for shelter. The prisoners were all desperate men. Two of them had been before at "Hell's Gates," and detailed the horrors of the place to their companions. In the semi-darkness of the lower deck, where, chained in gangs of four, the miserable wretches speculated on their doom, it was proposed to seize the ship. A prisoner named Fergusson was the ringleader. "At the worst," said he "it is but death; and which of us wishes to live?" But the others were not so bold. Degraded by the chain and the lash, they yet clung to life as the one thing the law had not yet taken from them. There were wooden bars studded with nails fastened across their prison, and two sentinels with loaded arms kept watch at the hatchway. How could they—unarmed, weak, and chained—hope to succeed? But with Fergusson was a man named Walker, who had been a sailor, and he urged them on. "Once free, he could navigate the ship to China!" Six times did the trembling wretches essay the struggle with the soldiers, and six times did their courage fail them. At last a favourable opportunity presented itself. Lying at anchor in the channel, with the land in sight, life on board the ship became tedious even to the officers. Lieutenant Carew, confident in his soldiers and their muskets, thought he would like a little fishing excursion. His wife was on board, but, for some reason or other, refused to accompany him. The surgeon, however, was eager for some amusement, and taking with them a soldier and convict, the two lowered a boat and went into the bay.

It was the custom to bring the men on deck by sixes and sevens for exercise, and it so happened that on this morning it was the turn of Fergusson and Walker's gang. Fergusson, Walker, Pennell, McKan, Jones, and another came up in their double irons, and clanked up and down under the supervision of the loaded muskets. Fergusson saw his chance—if ever he was to get it—had come now.

"Now is your time, lads," he cried; "the captain's away; there are but the two men on deck." Sulkily eyeing the muskets, Pennell and McKan refused, "You have failed me six times," cried Fergusson, with an oath; "If you don't join me now, I'll inform of your former plots." This threat terrified them into compliance. A rush was made. The two soldiers, idly staring over the bulwarks, were knocked down before they could fire their muskets. The hatchway was secured, and, knocking off their irons, the six were masters of the ship. But the captain and soldiers below did not intend to surrender without a struggle. They fired up the hatchway, but without effect, and the other prisoners burst their nailed bars and joined their companions. A parley now ensued, the convicts promising to spare the lives of the soldiers if they gave up their arms. A volley was the only answer, and then two prisoners, by Fergusson's directions, got buckets of boiling water from the galley, and poured them down the hatchway. Panic-stricken by the knowledge that thirty desperate men were at liberty on the deck, and that the seizure of the vessel was only a matter of time, the scalded soldiers surrendered and passed up their arms. Carew and the surgeon heard the firing, and came back with all speed to the vessel. Standing in the stern-sheets, as the two rowers ran the boat alongside, he commanded the mutineers to return to their prison. A gun presented at his head was not the unnatural reply. Fergusson, however, had ordered the priming of the soldiers' pieces to be wetted before they were handed up, and the gun missed fire. Now began another parley. Carew, anxious, doubtless, for the safety of his wife, promised that if the men would give up the ship he would say nothing of their conduct to the authorities at Hell's Gates; but the easily-won liberty was too sweet to be resigned so easily. Confident in his own power, Fergusson told the mutineers that he could navigate the vessel to some foreign port, where they could defy the wrath of the Governor and the Commandant. The prospect of the sheds and the cat, as contrasted with freedom and China, was not too tempting. As might have been expected, they refused,

A muster was now held upon the deck, and Fergusson formally called upon the convicts to join him. All but thirteen consented, and one of the sailors—possibly an ex-convict himself—threw in his lot with the mutineers. Boats were lowered, and the soldiers and the thirteen were landed by the now armed convicts on the barren coast. With a generosity which to those acquainted with convict customs will seem somewhat strange, Mrs. Carew, with her children, was restored to her husband unharmed. Secure of safety, Fergusson ordered rations to be given to his late masters. "The land party," says Mr. Bonwick, "received 60 lbs. of biscuit, 20 lbs. of flour, 20 lbs. of sugar, 4 lbs. of tea, and 6 gals. of rum." The boats were taken back to the ship and hauled on board, and returning to their vessel the mutineers gave three cheers for their bloodless victory. After a hearty supper and a pannikin of rum apiece, the seventeen set to work to organize their future plans. Some were for China, some for India, and two men proposed to go to one of the islands of the South Seas, sink the ship, and settle among the friendly islanders.

After some talk, however, it was resolved to make for the Friendly Isles, where those who chose could remain.

With provisions for six months for 400 men, arms, ammunition, and a sailor captain, the mutineers felt that fortune had befriended them at last. Amid one knows not what wild thoughts of future liberty, the night passed rapidly away, and at daylight next morning the marooned Carew and his companions saw the "Cyprus" spread her sails and move slowly out of the harbour. Then began the sufferings of the conquered party. They were on a desolate part of the coast; impenetrable scrub and impassable mountain ranges lay, for many a weary mile, between them and Hobart Town. It was impossible to communicate with the settlement at Macquarie Harbour; the country on that side was even more desolate and barren than on the other. Communication between the two places was most rare, and effected by that very ship which was now bearing the escaped party in safety to the South Seas. The only hope was that some passing vessel, either driven by stress of weather or urged by want of water, would put into the channel and take them off. The party in all consisted of more than forty souls, and their slender stock of provisions melted away like snow in the sun. Mr. Carew showed his courage. He apportioned out the victuals in equal shares, keeping the rum as a last resource. The soldiers were divided into watches, and he himself took his turn with the rest. Day after day passed with the same monotony of silence.

The allowance of provisions was decreased, and despair began to sit heavily on their hearts. From east to west, from north to south, their haggard eyes turned in vain,

> "The blaze upon the waters to the east,
> The blaze upon the island overhead,
> The blaze upon the waters to the west,
> Then the great stars that globed themselves in Heaven,
> The hollower-bellowing ocean, and again
> The scarlet shafts of sunrise, but no sail."

At last hunger broke through discipline. Two men set off overland for Hobart Town, but, frightened at the perils before them, and menaced by hostile natives, returned. Five more attempted to head the Huon, and, after coming near to death, were rescued. The others remained waiting for death. Desperate, and with but two days' provisions left, Popjoy, a convict, determined to try and make a boat. Assisted by a man named Morgan, he framed a sort of coracle of young wattle trees, and covered it with sailcloth. Over this a mixture of soap and resin was poured, to keep out the water. After many failures, the thing floated. It was twelve feet long, and propelled by paddles. During the last two days of its construction the party were without food. In this rude craft Carew embarked the remnant of his party, and, hoping against hope, got out to sea. Luckily, at a distance of twenty miles, they fell in with the "Oxelia," and the poor fellows were brought safely to Hobart Town. Carew was tried by court martial and honourably acquitted. Popjoy, who had been transported when eleven years old for stealing a hare, received a free pardon, and returned to England.

In the meantime the "Cyprus" was running for the Friendly Islands. The mutineers had chosen officers for themselves. Walker was captain; Fergusson, "dressed up in Carew's best uniform," lieutenant; and Jones, mate. The days passed quickly by, liberty seemed before them, and all were in high spirits. Getting out of their course, however, they came to Japan. Here, in spite of Fergusson's orders, seven deserted, and cast in their lot with the natives of that lovely spot. Fergusson went on, but seems to have begun to lose his prestige among the men. One, Swallow, a seaman and convict, now appears to have assumed the command.

This fellow seems to have been both powerful and intelligent. He was originally transported from England for rioting, but on the way out saved the ship at the hazard of his life. Allowed to roam the deck and assist the sailors, he contrived to enlist their sympathies, and when the transport arrived in Hobart Town they hid him in the lower deck and the vessel sailed away with him. The crew gave him rations. Despite a rigorous search, he was not found until after some weeks. The captain landed him at Rio, and he was soon again in London. There an old companion "peached" upon him, and he was sent back to Van Diemen's Land. Half way to Hell's Gates, the mutiny restored him once more to freedom. To this man was the charge of the vessel entrusted, and he took her to China. On the way a boat with the name of "Edward" on its stern was seized, and Swallow, knowing that he could not account for the "Cyprus," determined to try a new plan. There was a sextant in the cabin which had on it the name "Waldron," and with that and the boat Swallow laid his plot. Abandoning the vessel, he appeared, with three others, as "shipwrecked sailors." Swallow affected to be Captain Waldron, and exhibited his sextant as a proof of his story. The English merchants in Canton got up a subscription for them, and paid their passage Home. Suspicion, however, was excited by the appearance of four more of the party, who did not know the captain's name, but said "Wilson" for "Waldron." Swallow, trapped again, was at his wit's end. Arrived in London, the party were brought before the Thames Police Court, where a few days before a curious incident occurred. Popjoy, having been landed by the mercy of the Crown in London, was cast upon the streets to find his way to gaol or starvation. Imprisoned from eleven years old, and knowing nothing save how to roll logs and cringe to the lash, the returned convict had taken to begging round about the docks. Begging, like stealing, was a crime, and he was brought before the Thames Police Court. There he told the story of the mutiny and the boat-building. Though there was not criminating evidence, the appearance of "Captain Waldron" was somewhat strange, and the story of poor Popjoy—who had been honoured with several paragraphs in the newspaper *Town Talk*—recurred to the mind of the Bench. The suspected men were remanded. This remand cost three of them their lives. Strangely enough a Mr. Capon, who had been gaoler at Hobart Town, was in

London, and, attracted by the report of the case, he strolled down to the Police Court. One glance was enough; Swallow, Watt, and Davis were detected at once, and the whole party committed for trial. Watt and Davis, tried as pirates and escaped felons, were hung in London. Swallow and the rest were sent back to Hobart Town. One was hung at the gaol, and the rest sent back to Hell's Gates for life. Swallow managed to escape the death penalty, and went back to the chain. Twice more he tried to escape, but in vain. At last the weight of his doom broke his spirit, and he submitted to his fate. He worked in his irons for life, and died—still in yellow livery—at Port Arthur, a melancholy instance of a brave man crushed into brutality by a senseless system of punishment.

Five years later Popjoy died also. He made some endeavour to procure a pension from the Government, and only waited the arrival of documents from Hobart Town, formally attesting his services to Lieutenant Carew, to obtain it. In the meantime he obtained a seaman's berth in a merchant vessel, married, and seems to have lived respectably. Coming from Quebec in a timber ship, however, he was wrecked off Boulogne. Taking to the boats, the crew made for the shore, but the sea was running with great violence, and Popjoy, with another, was washed overboard and drowned; and so never got his "pension" after all.

# THE LAST OF MACQUARIE HARBOUR.

FIVE years after the seizure of the "Cyprus" it was resolved that Macquarie Harbour should be abandoned.

The difficulty of access and the barren nature of the surrounding country combined to render the spot inadequate to the growing necessities of the colony. Prisoners were arriving in shiploads, and it was necessary to find for them some more convenient place of settlement. Moreover, Governor Arthur seemed to have learnt that his officers were too far from his control. Rumours of gross abuse of power among the resident officers were current in Hobart Town, and public attention was particularly excited by the revelations incident upon the execution of two men for the murder of their companion, "in order to get a holiday." The accounts of the conduct of the establishment were perhaps highly coloured, but sufficiently true in the main to cause Arthur's resolutions to be universally applauded.

I have already given some description of the settlement itself: let me here add an account of the voyage to it. In 1832, James Backhouse, the good Quaker missionary, to whose simply-written narrative I have before referred, visited "Hell's Gates" in the Government brig "Tamar." "There were in the cabin," he says—"John Burn, the captain for the voyage, Henry Herberg, the mate, David Hoy, a ship's carpenter, Jno. A. Manton, George W. Walker, and myself. Ten private soldiers and a sergeant, as guard, occupied a portion of the hold, in which there were also provisions for the Penal Settlement, and a flock of sheep. Two soldiers' wives and five children were in the midships. Twelve seamen, several of whom were convicts, formed the crew; and eighteen prisoners under sentence to the Penal Settlement completed the ship's company. The last occupied a gaol, separated from the hold by wooden bars, filled with nails, and accessible only from the deck by a small hatchway. One of the soldiers on guard stood constantly by this hatchway, which was secured by three bolts across the opening; two walked the deck, the one on one side returning with his face toward the prison at the time the other was going in the opposite direction; and two were in the hold, seated in view of the gaol. The prisoners wore chains, and only two of them were allowed to come on deck at a time for air; these were kept before the windlass, and not allowed to converse with the seamen. This was rigidly observed in consequence of two of these men having, at a former period, been parties in the seizure of a vessel named the "Cypress" (*sic*) making the same voyage, which was carried off to the coast of China or Japan. . . . The gaol occupied by these men was not high enough for them to stand erect in, but they could stretch themselves on the floor, on which they slept, being each furnished with a blanket."

When the vessel, after a tedious voyage, had reached the entrance to the harbour the main difficulty of the passage really commenced. The Doom-rock lay within the jaws of a sandy, barren bight, and the "league-long rollers" of the Southern Ocean broke unchecked upon the bar. For some time the "Tamar" stood on and off this dangerous channel, unwilling to risk an entrance. "At length," says the missionary—

"When about to run back for shelter to Port Davey we were descried, and a signal to enter was hoisted. We immediately stood in, and in a few minutes the opportunity to return was past. The pilot put off, knowing better than ourselves our danger; his boat could only be seen now and then above the billows; but he was soon alongside, and ordered all the sails to be squared, so that we might go right before the wind. On coming on board, he commanded the women and children below, and then came to me and advised me to go below also. I replied, that if we were lost I should like to see the last of it, for the sight was awfully grand. Laying hold of a rope at the stern, he said, 'Then, put your arm round this rope and don't speak a word.' To my companion he gave similar instructions, placing him at the opposite quarter. A man was sent into the chains on each side with the sounding lead. The pilot went to the bows, and nothing was now to be heard through the roar of the wind and waves, but his voice calling to the helmsman, the helmsman's answer, and the voices of the men in the chains, counting off the fathoms as the water became shallower. The vessel was cast alternately from one side to the other, to prevent her sticking on the sand, in which case the billows would have run over her, and have driven her upon a sandbank a mile from the shore, on which they were breaking with fury. The fathoms decreased, and the men counted off the feet, of which we drew seven and a-half, and there were but seven in the hollow of the sea, until they called out eleven feet. At this moment a huge billow carried us forward on its raging head into deep water. The pilot's countenance relaxed; he looked like a man reprieved from under the gallows, and coming aft, shook hands with each individual, congratulating them on a safe arrrival in Macquarie Harbour."

Such was the place that it was at last decided to abandon, and in 1834 orders came down to break up the settlement.

The Commandant, Major Baylee, 63rd Regiment, embarked the prisoners in a vessel sent specially for them, and accompanied them to Hobart Town, leaving behind him a man named Taw, who was the pilot at the settlement, to complete the work of demolition, and bring away such matters as might have been overlooked in the hurry of the departure of the main body.

Taw was in command of the "Frederick," a brig that had been built at the settlement, and he had as a crew, Mr. Hoy, the shipwright, and a man named Tate, and ten convicts, together with a guard of three soldiers and a corporal. The names of the ten—as given in their own narrative, written while under sentence of death in Hobart Town—were John Barker, Charles Lyons, James Lesly, James Porter, Benjamin Russen, John Dady, William Cheshire, William Shiers, John Fair, and John Jones. The narrative was printed in William Gore Elliston's *Hobart Town Almanac and Van Diemen's Land Annual* for 1838, and forms the basis of this twice-told tale.

On the 11th of January, 1834, everything of value had been placed on board the brig, and the prisoners received the intelligence that the next day they would weigh anchor, and leave Hell's Gates for ever. One of the prisoners, however, was still "in confinement." His name was Charles Lyons, and he had been imprisoned for insubordination. Two convicts and Taw released him and brought him aboard. That night, in the prisoners' berth, Lyons gave vent to his wrath, and inveighed against the tyranny of Taw. He probably guessed what awaited him in Hobart Town.

The next day was spent in running to the bar and back, the heavy sea outside rendering dangerous any attempt to pass the gates. On the morning of the 12th, at daybreak, Taw ordered out the whaleboat and went "to sound the bar," returning with the news that it was yet dangerous, but that if the tide abated towards evening he would risk it.

Now the evils of forced inaction began to show. The men grumbled. They should have been well on their way to Hobart Town and civilisation. Why keep them still in sight of their dismal prison-house? Doubtless with a view to employing them, Taw gave permission for the men to go ashore and wash their clothes. All went except Hoy's servant, and while on shore a plot was concocted.

At half-past 3 p.m. the men returned, and the corporal, a soldier, and a prisoner took the whaleboat and went fishing, so that besides the nine convicts in the forecastle were only Taw, Hoy, and his servant in the cabin, and Tate and two soldiers on deck. One of the convicts—Porter, the narrator of the story—began to sing, and a soldier came below to listen. While he listened, Lesly, Cheshire, Russen, Fair, and Barker stole up the hatchway.

The mate and soldier were noiselessly seized, and Cheshire going down the aft deck passed up the muskets. The song still continued, and the soldier, with the disaffected Lyons on one side and Dady on the other, listened with increased attention. Suddenly a prisoner came down the hatchway and trod upon the toe of Shiers. This was the signal. Shiers presented his fist in the astonished *dilettante's* face, and Dady and Lyons seized him and "made him fast." Shiers and Lyons then rushed upon deck, leaving the prisoner with Porter and Dady below.

Porter—who by his own account was unwilling to join the mutiny—endeavoured to force up the hatch, but presently it was opened from above, and the other soldier and Tate were sent down bound, and he, Dady, and Jones got upon deck. Fair, who seems to have assumed the command, ordered the hatch to be secured, and placed Porter over it as a guard, while Lesly and Russen armed with the soldiers' muskets, stationed themselves at the companion.

Though accomplished with as little noise as possible, the mutiny had roused Taw and Hoy, and they endeavoured to force their way on deck. Lesly and Russen, however, beat them back, but did not fire. All was silent for awhile until Cheshire, creeping to the skylight, tore it up, crying—

"Here they are! Surrender! Surrender!"

Fair and Barker snatched up their arms, and four muskets were levelled down the skylight.

Crouched out of reach of the muskets, the captain and Hoy gave no reply, and then some one of the mutineers fired.

Shiers rushed to the skylight.

"Are you going to commit murder?" he cried.

"No, No," replied they, "it can be done without."

Shiers then called upon Taw and Hoy to surrender, promising to spare their lives.

"My life be the forfeit if we injure you," said he, "we only want our liberty."

Then the two came on deck.

Hoy asked who was to command the brig.

"I am," says Barker, and with the crew I navigate her round the world!"

Hoy then, as did Carew before, promised to say nothing of the escapade if they would give up the brig.

Barker laughed.

"That isn't likely," said he. "We got her, and we'll keep her—liberty is what we mean to have."

Shiers and Barker then asked the prisoners if they wanted anything from out their boxes, as they were going to put them ashore, and allowed them to go down into the cabin and take what they thought proper, only refusing Hoy his pocket-pistols. They were then put into the jolly-boat, together with the mate and the two soldiers; a bottle of rum was given to Taw, whose hands were tied, and two bottles of wine and a peajacket to Hoy, "as he had been indisposed." Indeed the mutineers seemed to have behaved with much consideration and even generosity, priding themselves on not abusing their newly found liberty.

A musket fired over the stern brought the whaleboat alongside, and the soldiers and the prisoner were ordered out of her into the jolly-boat. The soldiers were then ordered to row the party ashore. Seven mutineers—two pulling, one steering, and four armed with muskets as a guard—accompanied them in the whaleboat. Having landed Taw and the others, the jolly-boat was towed back to the ship, and a watch was set all night to prevent surprise, so great was their dread of the resolute Taw.

Next morning a council of war was held as to the disposition of provisions. Shiers—referring to the seizure of the "Cyprus," which would seem to have made a great impression on the minds of convictism—said, "Don't let this affair be like that one. Do not let us leave them to starve, but share the provisions equally between us all. Then when they reach head-quarters they can't say that we'd used them cruelly."

The notion was deemed a good one, the meat was divided as nearly as possible, also tea, sugar, flour, and biscuit; and Shiers taking with him another pair of shoes and bandages and plaster for Mr. Hoy, who seems to have been a favourite, got out the whaleboat and rowed to the shore.

Hoy and two men received the stores, three of the mutineers standing armed in the stern-sheets to prevent the dreaded Taw from rushing the boat.

Hoy then seems to have thanked them for the provisions, and, while commenting upon the difficulty of the task before them, to have wished them success in their enterprise. This at least is the statement of Porter's narrative, but as that gentleman intersperses his story with frequent addresses to Providence and reflections on the bounty of Heaven unusual to convict minds, we may not unreasonably suppose that his reported conversations are not given *verbatim*, and that a great deal of rude language is omitted Moreover, the poor devil was lying in Hobart Town gaol under sentence of death, and had a chaplain for his amanuensis. Under such circumstances he was likely to restrain the natural vigour of his descriptive powers.

Having been blessed—if we believe our convict—by the pious Hoy, a touching adieu took place, and the mutineers returned to the brig. They passed the morning in throwing overboard the light cargo which was in the hold, and then ran out a small kedge anchor with about 100 fathoms of line. The tide being slack, they kedged along until they came to the Cap and Bonnet, and there observing an old whaleboat ashore they destroyed it, lest it should offer means of pursuit to the terrible Taw. It being calm they towed the "Frederick" in safety over the dangerous bar, and a light breeze springing up from the south-east, took her gaily out to sea.

John Fair being "an experienced mariner," was made mate; but Barker, in consideration of his superior sagacity and a smattering of navigation, received the rank of captain. He, "with what few instruments he had," made preparation to take his departure from Birches Rock, and stating that the course should be E.S.E., ordered the whaleboat to be stove in and cast adrift, as there was no room on board for her. All sail was then made; Fair and Lyons divided the men in watches, parting the seamen with the landsmen, and "at 8 p.m.," says Porter, "we set our first watch."

At half-past 9 that night came a heavy gale from the S.W., which compelled them to run under close-reefed topsails. Shiers, Cheshire, Russen, and Lesly were sea-sick, as was also John Barker, and the heavy sea requiring two men at the helm, the others had their work cut out for them.

The morning dawned upon a raging sea and a cloudy sky. Lesly sounded the well, and found the hold three parts full of water, and all hands were set to the pumps. The gale lasted for two nights and a day, and then moderated. But the convict-built vessel proved leaky, "occasioned principally," says Porter, "by carrying such a press of canvas during the gale," and only one pump could be got to work.

On the 16th, Barker, who still suffered from violent sea-sickness, took a meridian, and altered the course of the vessel to E. by S., desiring to "run to the southward of New Zealand, out of the track of shipping." On the 20th a vast quantity of seaweed appeared, and the men grew frightened, thinking they were running on land. Fair begged Barker to come on deck and take an observation, urging the necessity of keeping the crew in good heart. At first the poor fellow refused, vowing—as many sea-sick mariners have done before and since—that the ship might go to the bottom for all he could stir a hand to save her. By dint of persuasion, however, he was got on deck, supported by two men, and assured his followers that all was well, adding, "I can take you safe to South America even though I had no quadrant aboard, by keeping a dead-reckoning. At noon—still supported by his two assistants, like Moses between the two Israelites—he took an observation, and shortly afterwards sent up to inform the men that he would run to the south of New Zealand, and not sight it, as had been his first intention.

So far so good; but by-and-by—the brig running eleven knots an hour under closely reefed topsails, and the pumps hard at work the whole time—murmurs arose, and Barker not appearing on deck for nine days, a deputation was sent to beg him to consider the position of the vessel.

Roused by this the "captain" came up, and, though sick, made shift to attend to his navigation. The weather, however, prevented him from taking an observation until the 30th January, and on that day he altered the course of the vessel to N. by E., being anxious to "make a landfall between Chili and Valdivia."

The crew were now well-nigh exhausted. The old sailors had to do duty for the raw hands, and, to add to their distress, it came on to blow harder than they had yet experienced it. A white squall threw the brig on her beam ends, and carried away the spanker-boom, but notwithstanding the leaky condition of the craft, Fair persisted in carrying on sail. The more chicken-hearted began to despair of reaching land. They now sighted a French whaler, hull down to windward, and desperate Barker gave orders to get out the arms and make ready to defend the brig, in case the stranger should bear down upon them. His precaution, however, was not needed.

After nine days of rough weather the gale abated, and Fair, giving orders to cross the topgallant yards and make sail, on the 25th of February they made the South American coast, about an hour before dark.

Though all hands swore that there was land ahead, the impostor Barker laughed at them, saying that he had kept the reckoning, and they were at least "500 miles off the coast of Chili." Fair, however, put no faith in his assertions, and gave orders to shorten sail. At daylight they found a rocky shore close under their lee, and hauled off. Now Barker condescended to be convinced, and at twelve o'clock informed the crew that they were between Chili and Valdivia. This was the 26th February, six weeks and a day from the time when the captured "Frederick" left Hell's Gates.

Now arose a discussion as to the best course of action. Some advised landing at once in the launch, others to creep along shore, while the more prudent recommended that the brig should be abandoned, and that they should coast in their boat in search of a landing place. This plan was at last adopted. The launch was a big, seaworthy boat; moreover, she had been raised a plank higher, had been decked after a fashion, and fitted with mast, boom, and a suit of sails, while the bad-weather cloth that Taw had used for the whaleboat would answer the purpose of bulwarks. Putting on board her the scanty remnant of provisions, together with firearms, ammunition, and—notable item—a Government cat that had unconsciously cast in its lot with theirs, four of them got aboard the launch, and the others commenced to batten down the hatches of the brig.

These amateur carpenters had indeed but little time to spare. The pumping being stopped, they found four feet of water in the hold, and hastily flinging over two breakers of water and such provisions as they could scrape together, called the launch alongside and got into her without delay.

It was time, for as the sun went down in a lowering and angry sky, the ill-fated vessel that had brought them to freedom sank to her channel plates, and the exhausted and toil-worn mutineers, hoisting sail in the darkness, turned their backs upon her and speeded towards the wished-for but unknown shore.

The next day the miserable boat's crew, drenched with water and shivering with cold—they had been sitting by turns of four in the stern-sheets all night, with their backs to the sea, to prevent the water from swamping them—reached the coast. At three o'clock in the afternoon they entered a small bay, and at half-past four came to an anchor under the lee of a barren reef. Some went ashore, but met with "no sign of human habitation." They slept there that night, having set a watch of two men in case of attack by wild beasts, and in the morning set to work to gather shell-fish. Having made such a breakfast as this somewhat meagre fare afforded, they again set sail, determining to make for a distant point, in the hope of meeting with human beings. Reaching this point in the afternoon, they found two strange pyramidal-shaped rocks, and running in between them, came upon a stream of fresh water. Near this was a deserted Indian hut, but no "Indian," and so, securing the boat and setting a watch, the castaways passed the second night since the abandonment of the brig.

All the next day they sailed from bay to bay in search of inhabitants, and casting anchor in a little inlet at night, prepared to sup on a seal which they had killed ere they started in the morning, but a heavy swell arising carried their boat violently towards the rocks, and they were compelled to use all exertions to keep her afloat. The next day passed in the same fruitless quest. The wind blew hard, the boat leaked, the coast seemed ironbound, and they held on their dismal course with despairing hearts. Camping that night in a snug nook, the cat which they had brought from the brig, and which had shared with them their scanty provisions, made off into the woods. The next day was the 3rd March—about eight weeks since they had seized the "Frederick"—and they made sure that human habitations were close at hand. Running down the coast all that day with a fresh breeze they weathered a point which John Barker said was "Tweedle-point," and ran for a bluff far down the shore. Half an hour before dark they weathered the bluff, and made for the beach, but not finding boat anchorage coasted along until the sun went down.

Their hearts began now to fail them. They had accomplished an almost unparalleled escape. They had seized a prison ship under the very noses of the guards, and under all disadvantages had carried her out to sea, sailed her successfully through an unknown ocean, made land just as she could no longer be kept afloat, and were now about to perish when their hopes seemed nearest to their fulfilment. The shore was barren and rocky, night was closing in, they had no food, and they were miles from succour. "Suddenly," says Porter, "we heard the bellowing of a bullock on the shore." Did their ears deceive them? All held their breath to hear the sound again. No, it was no deception, they were saved!

With renewed vigour they tugged at the oars, and rounding a low-lying reef that projected into the black water, came in sight of large fires. Against the glare of these fires—which had the appearance of blazing rubbish heaps—gigantic shadows moved. These shadows were men and women. Out of the darkness the escaped convicts hailed the shore, but received for a reply only a confused murmur, which seemed to denote alarm. The full swell of the ocean rolled in upon the rocky shore, and it was impossible to land. So keeping out to sea, but still within sight of the cheering fires, they let go their anchor in nineteen fathoms of water, and lay outside the reefs waiting for the day.

All that night they kept awake, conversing on the chance of safety. Perhaps the people they had seen were cannibals, perhaps pirates. At any rate, they were human. When morning dawned they made all haste to land, and mooring the boat to some seaweed, called to the Indians. These came instantly, running down to the boat. They seem to have been Spanish Indians, and informed Shiers that Valdivia was but three leagues distant. The mutineers prudently refused to beach the boat, but Shiers and four men, taking with them needles and thread and a loaded pistol, jumped ashore, and followed the natives to their huts. In the meantime, the boat was pushed off four lengths from the shore, to guard against any attempt that might be made to seize her. By-and-by Shiers returned, and then the other five landed. They found the Indians very friendly and partly civilised. The chief wore a poncho—a square cloth, with hole for the head in the middle—and a pair of blue worsted trousers. The poncho was embroidered; the fellow carried a large hilted knife (probably a Spanish *machete*), for defensive or offensive purposes. They gave this warrior a hatchet "of which he well knew the use," and he did the honours of the village to them. Porter says that the huts were clean and well built, and the people industrious. He observed a man and boy ploughing with four bullocks yoked by the horns. The ploughshare was of wood hardened in the fire. Both sexes wore their hair long, but the men—having no razors—plucked out their beards by the roots with two shells provided for the purpose. Porter made repeated requests for something to eat, but his conductor either could not or—as he thinks—would not understand him. Having bestowed upon him some buttons, pins, and needles, the rejoicing mutineers set sail for Valdivia. At three o'clock in the afternoon they reached a point of land to which their attention had been drawn, and perceived a flagstaff and 12-gun battery. They had made their port at last.

Valdivia is the chief town of the most southern province of Chili, and is situated nine miles up the river which bears its name. It was founded in 1551, by Pedro de Valdivia—one of the gentlemen adventurers of that stormy time—who gave it his name, and grew rich by working the gold mines in the vicinity. In 1590 it was captured by the natives, but was afterwards rebuilt and strongly fortified by the Spaniards. The harbour—at the mouth of which our convicts were now resting—is one of the most spacious on the coast. Three years after the date of our story—in 1837—it was ruined by an earthquake.

Pulling in under the guns of the battery, Barker harangued his comrades, and enlarged upon his own abilities, which had brought them thus far in safety. It being believed that Spain was hostile to England, they resolved to tell their story, and throw themselves on the mercy of the Governor. Barker then gave each of the men half a sovereign, and divided all the clothing and valuables equally, with the exception of two watches, which he kept for himself. They then pulled for the shore.

The Spaniards received them with humanity, and they stayed that night at the fort. The next day it was agreed that Barker, Shiers, Lesly, Russen, and Cheshire should hire a canoe to go up to the town, and lay their case before the Governor. This was done, and on the next day (March 7th), a party of soldiers came down and took the remaining five up to the city, where they were lodged in prison. Being taken before the judge, they told their story, giving the names they went by in Van Diemen's Land, and he remanded them until the arrival of the Governor.

They remained in prison five days—the mate was allowed a dollar per day, the boatswain half-a-dollar, and the rest a quarter dollar, "and provisions being very cheap," says the narrator, "this was amply sufficient for our support." On the 13th, the Governor arrived, and they were taken before him. He seemed inclined to look favourably upon them, but asked them why they came to that part of the coast. Whereupon Barker, with unblushing effrontery replied—"Because we knew that you were patriots, and had long ago declared your independence, and we throw ourselves under the protection of your flag, relying on your clemency." Upon this the Governor, saying that he believed they had spared life and had committed no murder, promised to use his influence with the President at San Jago to procure them permission to live in Valdivia, but that they must in the meantime return to the prison, and remain there peaceably.

In the meantime a Captain Lawson, their interpreter, "a gentleman" says Porter, "of great respectability," drew up a petition praying for their release, and got the principal inhabitants of the town to sign it. On the following day they were again brought before the Governor, who said that he would liberate them at once were he not fearful that some of their number would make their escape. Upon this the ever ready Barker made a melodramatic speech, begging His Excellency to rather shoot them all dead in the palace square than deliver them up to the British Government. The Governor, who seems to have been a good-humoured fellow, and who had doubtless been regaled with a highly-coloured description of the horrors of Hell's Gates—bad enough, in sober truth, Heaven knows—promised to protect them, vowing that out of respect to their heroic journey he would not give them up. "And," said he, "if you will promise not to escape, should a vessel come to-morrow to demand you, you will find me as good as my word." He then advised them to "beware of intemperance," and to pay back to the Government as soon as possible the money expended in their subsistence while in prison. The ten then took lodgings in the town, and next day assisted in launching a vessel of 100 tons burden—a ceremony which was performed with the aid of a band of music and in the presence of the Governor in person. The owner expressed himself much satisfied with the behaviour and talent of the Englishmen, and declaring—so says Porter—"that he would rather have them than thirty of his own countrymen," "engaged them to fit her out" at fifteen dollars a month and provisions.

The adventurous ten now seemed to have fallen on good days. They were well clothed, well fed, and well liked. Macquarie Harbour and its agonies were forgotten. They cast away the recollection of their past dangers and crimes, and appear to have maintained themselves by honest industry. The Governor took great interest in their well-being, and when on the 25th April, the "Blonde" frigate, Commodore Mason, arrived in port, sent for them and told them to be of good cheer, that he would not deliver them up to bondage, that the dispatches from San Jago having arrived, he could officially receive them as Chilian subjects; and that, if they pleased, they might marry.

Spanish America is noted for the beauty of its women—Chilian ladies are even now the belles of the seaboard, and our adventurers jumped at the offer. The attraction of the gossip by the fountains, the chatter of the quaint old market place, the dances by night under the orange-trees, were too strong to be resisted. The fierce black eyes of the *manolas*—for in those days there were yet *manolas* in Spain and *grisettes* in France—the more golden glory of the Malaguena, transplanted from the sultry seaport of Old Spain two generations back, the sparkling purity of the Andalusian—granddaughter of some brilliant adventurer of Seville—conspired to capture the hearts of the escaped prisoners—all honest English sensualists, I have no doubt. Five of them were immediately married, and at the wedding of that lucky scoundrel, John Barker, the Governor and his lady attended in court costume.

But this felicity was not to last. Nine months after these auspicious events, on the 10th February, 1835, the ten were carried off in the night to the guard-house. In a terrible fright, they speculated on the cause of their arrest, when suddenly the ubiquitous Governor arriving, tells them not to be frightened. "There is an English frigate lying outside the harbour," cries he, "and I was afraid that did you hear the news you would take to the forest, and have been all slain by Indians. Here is a letter that I have just received."

This letter proved to be from Commodore Mason, and stated that its writer, having learned that several Englishmen were in the town, who had come in some "clandestine" manner to the coast, desired them to come on board and give an account of themselves.

The ten upon this fell into great trepidation. "If we go," cried one of them, "we shall never return." "I thought so!" said the Governor (let us remember that this is the statement of a convict under sentence of death). "I will protect you. Should they force their way here, I will send you up the country under escort to an Indian chief of my acquaintance, who will protect you. If the captain of this vessel wishes to speak with you, he shall do so at my palace. You shall *not* go on board."

This worthy man, Don Fernando Martelle, doubtless a Spaniard of mettle, who, having given his word, meant to keep it, proved a true friend; for a cutter from the frigate attempting to pass the battery, the Spaniards fired a 32lb. shot over the heads of the crew, and presently the frigate departed, bearing up in the direction of Valparaiso.

So far, so good, but more evils were in store. On the 2nd May, 1835, the "Achilles," a 21-gun brig of war, arrived with a new Governor. This gentleman was coolly received by the inhabitants, "who," says poor Porter, "had heard but an indifferent account of him," and the refugees began to dread lest a new Pharaoh had arisen who knew not Joseph. The old Governor, however, gave them an excellent character, and Governor Thompson, the *novus homo*, promised to protect them. They soon discovered, however, that his promises were of little value. Don Fernando left on the 20th of May, and as soon as he had gone hostilities were commenced.

The remaining seven (Jones, Fair, and Dady had wisely taken service in a brig, and had got away from the place) were ordered to present themselves at the guard-house every evening, and suffered other small indignities which the narrator does not particularise. It had been previously agreed that no attempt to escape should be made, as the Governor swore that, should any man succeed in getting away from the city, he would hang the others without mercy. This agreement had been hitherto strictly kept—the departure of the fortunate three was permitted by Don Fernando—but in this last extremity Barker broke it. The boat in which the mutineers had made their adventurous voyage had been long moored at the back of Government House; but the old Governor, tempted by an offer of forty dollars, had at last sold her, "masts, oars, sails, and all," to one of the Spanish merchants. In the month of June, Barker, enlarging upon the excellent qualities of the old boat, offered to build one for the Governor. This proposition met with a ready approval, but when the boat was finished, Barker, pretending that she was too small, offered to build a larger one, if the Governor would permit him to get stores, &c., in his name. This was conceded, and in three weeks Barker, Lesly, and Russen completed a three-oared whaleboat, and fitted her with sails and provisions, on the Governor's credit.

All was now ready, and on Saturday night, the 4th July, Barker, Lesly, Russen, and a man named Roberts, "formerly mate of a brig," crept out under cover of the darkness, and slipping down the river, got out to sea. On Monday morning, at 10 o'clock, their flight was discovered, and the Governor, in a furious rage at being outwitted, dispatched six soldiers and a crew, with orders to "bring back the Englishmen, dead or alive." This was easier said than done, and in a week the soldiers returned, without having seen the fugitives.

It is not improbable that the townspeople, among whom the Englishmen were liked and the Governor cordially detested, began to ridicule his Excellency with the proverbial Spanish freedom of popular speech, for he seems to have determined to revenge himself on the luckless four, Porter, Lyons, Cheshire, and Shiers, who remained. In vain did the poor fellows plead their innocence and good conduct. In vain did their black-eyed wives weep, and their tawny kinsfolk remonstrate with justice. The four were ironed together, and thrown into the prison of Valdivia, and the English Consul at Valparaiso having been communicated with, a schooner was sent which brought them to Callao—a port not altogether unknown to several illustrious Victorians in the present day—and here the dreaded Mason got them at last. The "Blonde" took them to Valparaiso, when they were placed on board the "North Star," 28 guns, and sent to England.

Arrived once more in London, they were placed in the "Leviathan" hulk, and then shipped (with a fresh batch of convicts) on board the "Sarah," and sent back to Van Diemen's Land, there to be tried for their lives. One can fancy the pleasant time these poor devils must have enjoyed, speculating on their fate, and imagination does not refuse to suggest the stories of the horrors of Hell's Gates with which they would beguile the time and attention of the convict "new chums." A "prison-ship" in those days was an excellent preparatory school for the gallows. Arrived in Hobart Town on the 29th March, 1837, they were tried before the Chief Justice, for "piratically seizing the brig 'Frederick,'" and were sentenced to be hanged. Their case, however, excited some interest, and they appealed to the "English Judges." These gentlemen were merciful, and commuted the death-penalty to "hard labour for life."

Their perilous journey, their strange adventures, their three years of freedom in the old Spanish town, resulted only in a change of prisons. Port Arthur was substituted for Macquarie Harbour.

Barker, Lesly, and Russen, were never heard of again. Whether they were wrecked on that stormy coast, killed by Indians, picked up by a stray ship, and returned to civilization, or striking on some savage island colonized another Pitcairn, no one can tell. Despite their treachery, their romantic story makes one hope that they got their longed-for liberty at last.

# BUCKLEY, THE ESCAPED CONVICT.

EVERY country can claim for itself a Robinson Crusoe of home manufacture. He of Australia is William Buckley. The story of this gentleman's Selkirkian experiences is in good truth an old one, for not only is his name familiar enough to all Australians, but he was one of the first settlers in the colony of Victoria. As the majority of reading Australians are aware—Victoria, or, as it was originally called, Port Phillip, was twice colonized—first, by Lieutenant-Governor Collins, and, secondly, by Batman and Fawkner. The first was a forced, the second a voluntary colonisation. Governor Collins came in 1803, with convicts. Batman and Fawkner came in 1835, with free men. Buckley belonged to the first expedition, and, the only white man who remained in the country, he lived long enough to see the second. He was one of the convicts brought out by Governor Collins, and succeeded in escaping to the bush and maintaining himself there for thirty-two years. His "picture in little" has been often painted, but as perhaps few persons are familiar with the details of his life and adventures, this sketch (compiled from an account of his wanderings written by himself) may not prove unacceptable.

William Buckley was born in 1780 at Macclesfield, in Cheshire. His parents were poor folk, who cultivated young William upon a little oatmeal. He had two brothers and a sister, but at sixteen years of age he left them, and never saw them more. Apprenticed to a bricklayer he scorned the hod, and longed, like Norval, to "follow to the field some warlike lord." His father objected, but the Norval parallel still holding good, "Heaven soon granted what his sire denied." A sergeant in the Cheshire militia, assisted by ten guineas bounty, proved too much for parental advice, and William enlisted. He was at that time a prize for any recruiting sergeant. His height was gigantic, his strength excessive, and his brain-power feeble. He made a capital soldier. Getting into the King's Own (4th Foot), he was sent to Holland, and fought there, receiving a wound in the hand. On his return to England he obtained leave of absence, and indulged in "riotous habits." His Dutch experiences did not appear to have been of an improving kind. Possibly the army swore as terribly in Flanders in the days of Buckley as it did in those of Captain Tobias Shandy. However, be that as it may, Buckley would seem to have borne rather a bad character; and being, as he neatly puts it, "implicated in an offence that rendered me liable to punishment"—to wit, receiving stolen property—was tried at Chatham, found guilty, and sentenced to the hulks. After six months' work at the fortifications of Woolwich, he was ordered on board the "Calcutta," bound for Australia; and from this date his story, as far as we are concerned with it, may be said to commence.

Lieutenant-Colonel Collins, of the Royal Marines (who had previously been Judge-Advocate to the colony of New South Wales at its establishment by Governor Phillip), had been compensated for loss of legitimate promotion by the governorship of the projected colony of Van Diemen's Land. He was placed in command of the ships "Calcutta" and "Ocean," with instructions to form a convict settlement on the south-east coast of New Holland, and on the 27th April, 1803, left England for that purpose. A journal kept by the Rev. R. Knopwood, chaplain on board the "Calcutta," gives us some particulars of the adventure.

After a somewhat stormy voyage, the expedition sighted Port Phillip Heads at 5 a.m. on the 9th October, and moored in the bay. After some prospecting of the adjoining land, it was resolved to go higher up the bay, and eventually near Point Lonsdale a site was fixed on for the new city, and the stores were disembarked. On the 25th October, at 8 a.m. the British flag was hoisted, and it being the King's birthday into the bargain, some waste of powder was occasioned. The convicts were then divided into gangs and put to work; and after a skirmish or two with the blacks, the colonists began to shake themselves down. Our hero Buckley was by this time in a position of some importance, and Mr. Knopwood records that on the 2nd November a complaint was made to him by the future Crusoe that "one Robert Cannady had defrauded Buckley, the 'Governor's servant,' of a waistcoat." Hearing the case in his capacity of magistrate, the worthy chaplain upheld Buckley's cause, and ordered the waistcoat to be given up. Notwithstanding his apparently comfortable condition Buckley was discontented. He complained that the rope's-end was a little too freely administered, and that the work was too hard. A magazine and storehouse were the first public buildings erected, and upon these Buckley—in virtue, I suppose, of his early lessons under the Cheshire bricklayer—was employed. He had been brickmaking or bricklaying for about three months when he resolved to attempt his escape. Such attempts were frequent.

There seems to have been some wild notion abroad that California was situated on the other side of the continent, and that Sydney was within easy walking distance. The prisoners were not very closely watched: some of them were employed at some distance from the barracks, and escape was not difficult; but the character of the surrounding country rendered any projected stroll to China or California a serious matter, and in the majority of cases the poor ignorant fellows returned with gaunt frames and hungry faces, begging to be flogged and fed. The Rev. Knopwood's journal is full of attempted escapes, but he usually records one of two results—a return or a death. The soldiers shot at any escaping convict, and if they missed him, the settlement would content itself with the surety, proved by sad experience, that in a few days he would return to the camp, or his dead body would be brought in by some exploring party.

On the 27th of December, one of these "escapes" took place. At 9 p.m. six convicts endeavoured to make their escape, of whom Buckley was one. They were beset by a look-out party, and one man was shot. His name was Charles Shaw. The next night great fires were seen at a distance, and supposed to be lit by the runaways. On the 6th of January a search was made, the worthy chaplain himself armed and assisting, but without any effect. The colony became alarmed. Six men away in the bush was a bad example. The next day the drums beat to arms, and a select body of marines were sent in pursuit of the fugitives, but though they were tracked for fifty miles, they could not be discovered. Believing that the absconders had died in the bush, the commandant was satisfied, and refrained from further exertions. On the 6th of January, one of the party, named M'Allender, came in and surrendered, giving up a gun which he had stolen. He said that all the others had died or been lost in the bush. This intelligence was for the colonists satisfactory, and in four days the occurrence was almost forgotten. Indeed, the Governor and his officers had something more interesting than convicts' escapades to occupy their minds.

From the very first landing the people had grumbled at the situation and the climate. It was the height of summer. The thermometer averaged 110° in the sun. Fires were frequent; once, indeed, the huts of the officers and marines and the marquees themselves were nearly consumed. The soil was sandy and uninviting, the surrounding country barren and grim. Water was not too abundant, and as yet no river of any importance had been discovered. Collins had not the wit or the luck to penetrate to the Yarra, or to coast to the Barwon, and disgusted with the inhospitable soil, he yielded to the entreaties of his officers, and broke up the settlement. The 24th, 25th, and 26th of January were spent in re-embarking the convicts, stores, and soldiers, and by daylight of the 30th Port Phillip was deserted. It had been colonized for the space of three months, and during that time one child had been born. "On the 5th of November," says the chaplain, "Sergeant Thomas's wife was delivered of a boy, the first child of European parents born at Port Phillip." This boy was named Hobart.

The record of the chaplain's experiences, as far as I have been able to follow it, ends at three o'clock on the afternoon of the day of the desertion. "At 3 p.m.," says he, "I dined with the Governor." Perhaps the conversation at that dinner was not without reference to the fate of Buckley and his companions. I can imagine the good chaplain sighing over his glass, and mentally congratulating the repentant M'Allender upon the good sense which induced him to return to bondage. There could be no hope for the runaways now. Even if, by some wild chance, a hardier absconder succeeded in dragging himself back to camp, eager for the lash and loaf, his tardy penitence must come too late. The hot January sun would glare down now but upon deserted and unfinished buildings, bared spaces of ground, and all the melancholy ruin of abandoned habitations. Convict M'Allender himself, snugly disposed in the lower deck of the

"Ocean," might feel not uninclined to plume his ruffled feathers at the good fortune which had preserved him from the hideous fate of his unhappy companions.

Let us see what that fate was.

On the evening of the 27th of December this occurred. At sunset, the hour of returning to the shed, four men—one of whom had possession of a gun obtained from the Governor's garden—sneaked round the partially finished buildings, and took to the bush. A sentry challenged, and receiving no reply, fired, and shot the last of the party. The others ran for the best part of four hours, and though pursued, were not re-captured. That night they camped on the bank of a creek, and in the morning pushed on again with redoubled vigour. They had some bread and meat, sundry tin pots, the gun before mentioned, and an iron kettle. It was resolved to head for Sydney; and in happy ignorance of the whereabouts of that city, the adventurers set their backs directly against it, and made straight towards the present site of Melbourne.

They crossed the Yarra, and reached the Yawang hills on the third day's journey. Here the last particle of the treasured bread and meat was consumed, Sydney was distant, and starvation imminent. Buckley, who by virtue of his size and courage was elected leader of the party, ordered a retreat to the sea-coast, where mussels and limpets might keep life in them. With some difficulty they made their way to the beach, and wandered along it for three days, subsisting on gum, fish, and limpets. They broiled their poor fare on the embers, having flung away their kettle on the second day's march, as being too heavy to carry. It was found, Buckley says, thirty-two years afterwards by a ploughing settler. By this time they had made the circuit of the bay, and from their lair could see the "Calcutta" lying at anchor below them. Maddened by hunger, and desperate with dread of death, the grim philosophy of the lash and loaf overtook them. They lighted fires by night to attract the attention of the settlement, and hoisted their ragged garments on trees by day. Once a boat—probably the one with our armed chaplain—was seen to approach, and a rescue was hailed with a sort of dismal delight, but she returned without seeing their signals, and hope vanished.

For six days the miserable wretches starved within sight of their prison home, and at last plucked up courage to make a last effort for life. They told Buckley that they had determined to retrace their steps round the bay to the settlement, and urged him to accompany them. The desperate giant refused. He would have liberty at any hazard. Death in the gloomy swamps, the fantastic underwood, or the barren sand-hills, seemed not so terrible as the death-in-life of the convict sheds. They might go if they pleased, he would remain. They did so, and all but one (M'Allender, who carried the now useless gun) met the fate they dreaded.

Buckley, left to himself, turned his face to the wilderness, and doggedly set out in search of Sydney. "How I could have deceived myself into a belief of reaching it," he says, "is astonishing. . . . . The whole affair was in fact a species of madness." For seven days he travelled, swimming rivers, fording creeks, and plunging through scrub. His hope was to follow the coast-line until he reached his destination. He lived on shell-fish, gum, and the tops of young plants. On the sixth day the climate grew warmer. This added to his distress, for it increased his thirst. He began to have difficulty in finding food, and coming to two rocks that stood close together, flung himself down between them in despair. The rising tide drove him out of his miserable refuge, and climbing to the top, he slept, and hoped to die.

The next morning, however, he found something which cheered him. All through the journey the runaways had seen and heard the natives. Buckley had twice swam a creek to escape from them, and at night the forest was glow-wormed with their fires. The dying wretch—he had been without food for three days and was at the last gasp—came upon a smouldering log. The sight gave him new energies. He tore down some berries, roasted and ate them, and searching a little further found a "great supply of shell-fish." At this place he remained for more than a week, and then coming to a big rock, sheltered by an overhanging cliff, from which a plentiful stream of fresh water continually gushed, he made himself a sort of hut. Here he lived in rude contentment, and feeding on shell-fish and a sort of wild berry, began to experience the delights of freedom.

He was soon disturbed. One day three natives appeared and took possession of his home. They did not seem terrified at his appearance, but ate and drank (crayfish and water) with great gusto. They were dressed in opossum skins, and armed with spears. Buckley, weak with illness and unarmed, made no resistance to their will, and they bore him off to their huts. That night they watched him or he would have escaped. In the morning, after a vain attempt to obtain such remnants of his woollen stockings as time and the shingle had left him, they went away, and he, frightened at the chance of their return, took to the bush. For some months he wandered about, living the life of a wild man, and subsisting on roots, berries, and shell-fish. The weather set in gloomy and tempestuous. He was frequently without fire, food, or shelter, and his sleep was broken by terror of the natives. The physical instinct of life-preservation must have been very strong in the man; a less stolid animal would have got rid of his burden long ago. One day, crawling rather than walking through the scrub, he saw a mound of earth with a spear sticking up out of the top of it, and being in want of a walking-stick, he pulled up the weapon. That spear saved his life.

Having lain down that night under a tree, at grips with his last enemy, and not expecting to see the light of another morning, he was perceived by two lubras, who brought their husbands in great amazement to see the white man. The husbands, with that intelligence which is the privilege of the male sex—saw the state of the case at a glance. A great warrior had been buried at the mound. Great warriors, as all the world knows, change into white men after death. Buckley was a white man; and, moreover, he had in his hand the very spear that had been stuck into the tomb. Nothing could be more satisfactory, and saluting the half-starved convict, by the name of Murrangurk, they bore him off to their huts, with much shouting and demonstrations of joy. Luckily for the restored Murrangurk, this joviality soon took the practical form of gum-water and chrysalids, upon which he dined heartily.

After a terrific corroboree, in which the women beat skin-drums until they fainted, and the men hacked themselves with knives until they bled, Buckley was duly received into the black bosom of the people, and presented with a nephew. This ready-made relative proved attentive, and Buckley accepted his position with grace, reflecting that if his nephew was not very wise, " there was no chance of his uncle having to pay his tailor's or other bills. A consolation," he adds with some humour, "that many uncles would be glad to possess with equal security."

Buckley soon fell in with the customs of his rescuers, and for the next thirty years lived with them as one of themselves, joining in their fights, and taking a prominent part in their councils.

He was married to a charming but faithless woman, who unmindful of the honour done her, eloped with a young warrior of her own race a fortnight after her marriage. Her justly indignant relatives, however, quickly knocked her on the head, and upheld the sanctity of the marriage tie. Despite his ill-success in the matrimonial lottery, Buckley appears to have found considerable favour in the eyes of the lubras. He relates with calm satisfaction many interesting intrigues, and pauses frequently in his narrative to heave a tender sigh at the recollection of the many ladies who were waddied for his sake. He became at last a sort of father of the people, presiding in the council and issuing orders to the senate. The tribe which originally adopted him were almost totally destroyed in battle, and he then found a home among the friends of one of his wives.

His account of his wanderings is not particularly interesting. The Australian black is as far removed from Uncas and Chingachook, as Uncas and Chingachook are from reality. Mr. Buckley's friends had no medicine men, no tents, no Great Spirit, no fawnskin clothes, no mocassins, no calumets, and no buffalo. They were simply a set of repulsive, filthy savages, who daubed themselves with mud, and knew no pleasure save that of gorging. I am afraid that Mr. Buckley's narrative shows the beautiful fallacy of the Native poetic theory. An Australian Romeo would bear his Juliet off with the blow of a club, and Juliet would prepare herself for her bridal by "greasing herself from head to foot with the kidney fat of her lover's rival." Poor Paris!

However, here and there we get amusing hints of primitive innocence. In happy ignorance of cookery, Mr. Buckley's friends eat "all kinds of beasts, fish, fowl, reptile and creeping thing.' They have no notion of mechanical appliance, and a rude dam that Buckley made astonished them greatly. Their arms are spears, clubs and flint-headed tomahawks, and they spear their fish and dig out their wombats. No genius among them had ever invented a net or a snare. They keep count of time by chalk-marks on the arm. They paint themselves for battle or feast. They bury their dead in mounds, or suspend them in trees. They eat their enemies, having previously grilled them between heated stones. Affectionate wives preserve the knee-joints of their dead husbands as relics, and wear them round their necks, locket fashion. Deformed children are instantly brained, and the population is kept within reasonable bounds by judicious weeding of an extensive family. A child every two years is considered enough for every reasonable mother, and should she indulge in more, the indignant father cracks its skull against the nearest tree. [Nothing is new, you see—not even Social Science.] Cannibalism is a luxury, not an ordinary practice; but Buckley mentions a tribe called the Pallidurgbarrans, who eat human flesh whenever they get a chance, and employ human kidney fat, not as a charmed ungent for the increase of their valour, but as a sort of Dundee marmalade, viz., "an excellent substitute for butter at breakfast." These gentlemen are the colour of "light copper, their bodies having tremendously large and protruding bellies." They ate so many natives at last that war was declared, and some inglorious Pellissier drove a few hundred of them into a cave, and setting fire to the surrounding bush, suffocated them with great success.

When a girl is born she is instantly promised in marriage, and from that time neither she herself nor her mother must speak to the intended son-in-law, nor the son-in-law to them. Marriage is quite *à la mode* with these people. The nearest approach, however, that they make to civilization is in popular theology. They believe that the earth is supported on props, which are in charge of an old man who lives at the most remote corner of the earth. Occasionally this old man sends a message to say that unless he gets a supply of tomahawks and rope to cut and tie more props with, the earth will "go by the run, and all hands will be smothered." One of these messages arrived while Buckley was there, and he says that intense excitement prevailed, and tomahawks galore were sent on to the "old man." "Who this knowing old juggling thief is," says Buckley, "I could never make out. However, it is only one of the same sort of robberies which are practised in the other countries of what are called Christendom." Popular theology is accustomed to cry out for "more props."

At last, after thirty-two years of savage life, Buckley met two natives, one of whom carried a flag over his shoulders. He had long given up all hope of meeting with white men; he had forgotten his language and almost his name, but the sight of the flag gave him a strange shock. The natives told him that they had seen a vessel at anchor in Port Phillip Bay, near the Indented Heads, and, all hands having left her on a boat expedition up the river, they had climbed on board and helped themselves. They proposed to Buckley to go back with them and help to decoy the people on shore, when they would kill them and seize the cargo. Now for the first time the hope of escape from the hideous liberty he had sought arose. He pretended to fall in with their views, and going down to the seashore, made every effort to privately attract the attention of the new comers. But he had forgotten the English tongue, and could only make hoarse and unintelligible noises. Twice a boat approached him, and twice, hearing his frantic gibberish and seeing his savage costume, the sailors laughed and pulled off.

While watching the vessel, the natives told him that some years before another vessel had anchored in the same place, and two white men were brought ashore by four or five others, who tied them to trees and shot them, leaving their bodies bound. There were many such mysteries of the sea in those times.

In a few days more the vessel departed, and poor Buckley going to the spot where he had last seen her crew land, found a white man's grave—grim answer to his hopes and prayers. A few months after this he found a boat stranded on the shore, and learned that two sailors had been saved and well-treated by the natives, who wished to bring them to him, but that the castaways, suspicious and ill at ease, had gone off in the direction of the Yarra. There they were savagely murdered. A vessel would seem to have been wrecked somewhere on the coast, for barrels were found. One of these contained what Buckley, who found it, supposed to be beer or wine, but the flavour appeared "horribly offensive" to him, and he staved the cask.

At last his "good time" arrived. One day two young natives met him, and, waving coloured handkerchiefs, informed him that three white and six black men had been landed from a ship which had gone away again, and that they had erected two tents. The natives suggested murder and robbery, and told Buckley that they were in search of another tribe in order to fall upon the white men more effectually. Alarmed by this intelligence, Buckley started for the white camp, and, reaching it next day, sat down at some little distance and made signs to his countrymen. His strange colour, his wild garb, and his gigantic height appeared to alarm them, but they spoke kindly to him. Buckley could neither understand nor reply. At last one man offered him some bread, "calling it by its name," and as he did so, Buckley says, "a cloud appeared to pass from over my brain, and I repeated that and other English words after him." They took him to their tents and gave him biscuit, tea, and meat. He showed them the initials W. B. on one of his arms, and they regarded him as a shipwrecked seaman. Little by little he recovered the use of his tongue, and could speak with them. They told him that the vessel which had landed them would be back from Launceston in a few days with more people and a fresh supply of tools; and that they were about to settle in the country, and had already bought land of the native chiefs. "This," says Buckley, "I knew could not have been, because, unlike other savage communities or people, they have no chiefs claiming or possessing superior right over the soil, theirs being only as heads of families."

The natives now began to assemble in great numbers, and announced to Buckley their intention of killing the new settlers, desiring him to aid them, and threatening him that they would sacrifice him with the weaker party if he refused. Buckley was a little frightened at this, but succeeded in persuading his old friends to wait until the return of the ship, when, he said, the amount of plunder would be increased. The ship not returning as soon as was expected, the natives began to grow impatient, and then Buckley, throwing off all disguise, openly sided with the white men, and, arming himself with a gun, vowed he would shoot through the head the first man who flung a spear. This threat, and a promise of unlimited presents, kept them quiet, and at last the vessel arrived. She brought Batman and his party, and having landed the stores, returned next day to Van Diemen's Land. Buckley now told his story, and Mr. Wedge promised to use his interest with Governor Arthur to get him a free pardon. He was installed in the meantime as interpreter and guide to the expedition. When the vessel returned, Batman went on board and fired off his gun as a signal to Buckley that his pardon had arrived. The next day he received that document, dated 25th August, 1835, exactly thirty-two years from the date of his landing from the ship "Calcutta."

By this vessel instructions were brought to the directors of the company to proceed further up the Yarra, and in three days the site of Melbourne was marked out. The next vessel brought Mr. Gellibrand and a number of settlers, to whom Buckley was engaged as interpreter, at a salary of £50 a year and rations. He accompanied them in an exploring expedition, and assisted Mr. Batman to build the "first habitation regularly formed at Port Phillip," a house on Batman's hill.

The tide of immigration now poured into the new settlement, and Melbourne became a township. Captain Lonsdale (of Buckley's old regiment) came over with a detachment of the 4th to assume the command of the colony, and made Buckley his personal attendant. He was now in clover, was well-dressed, well-fed, and a man of no small importance. He quarrelled with a Mr. Fawkner from Launceston, "who had been an old settler, but had no connection with the company." He acted as constable, and hunted down and apprehended a black-fellow for killing a shepherd. Governor Bourke and several officers of the New South Wales Government visiting the place, Buckley received him at the head of 100 natives "ranked in line, and saluting him by putting their hands to their foreheads" as he directed. The Governor was interested in the "wild white man," and asked him many questions about his wild life. Buckley replied with suitable dignity, and ended by accompanying His Excellency into the interior—about as far as Mordialloc—and showing him the lions. On his return he heard of the loss of Mr. Gellibrand and Mr. Hesse, and volunteered to look for them. The loss of these gentlemen threw the settlement into a great state of consternation. They had attempted to ride from Geelong to Melbourne, and had been lost in the bush. It was generally thought that they were murdered by the blacks, and several natives were shot without the slightest reason. All search for the missing men proved unsuccessful, and Buckley returned. An absconder from Van Diemen's Land being apprehended about this time, Buckley was sent in charge of him to Launceston, and returned in a steam-vessel, having on board Captain Fyans, who had been appointed Resident Magistrate at Geelong.

He now seems to have been discontented with his position, "and finding that some persons were always throwing difficulties in the way of my interests, and not knowing what might be the result, I determined on resigning office, and on leaving a colony where my services were so little known, and so badly appreciated by the principal authorities."

On the 28th December, 1837, Buckley sailed from Melbourne, in the "Yarra Yarra," and landed in Hobart Town on the 10th of January, following. Here he was made much of, public-houses were thrown open to him, and strangers stood treat to him. One gentleman took him to the theatre, and "one of the performers came to ask me if I would like to visit the place again and come upon the stage." Buckley, with that wild desire to go "behind the scenes" which thirty-two years of barbarism had not shaken out of him, said that he would like it much. The next day, however, he discovered the reason of his friend's kindness, he was to be exhibited as the Anglo-Australian giant! "I soon," says he, "gave a denial to any such display, very much to the mortification, as I afterwards understood, of the stage manager, who had publicly notified my appearance." I wonder who was this ingenious dog. He doubtless gauged the public taste accurately—Buckley would have been a "good draw."

Shortly afterwards a Mr. Cutts, one of his old shipmates in the "Calcutta," who had now become a wealthy and respectable settler near Green Ponds, made interest with Sir John Franklin, and Buckley was appointed assistant storekeeper at the Hobart Town Immigrants Home; and when that establishment was broken up, he was transferred to the Female Nursery as gatekeeper.

At the Immigrants Home he "became acquainted with a family consisting of a respectable mechanic, his wife and daughter," and the mechanic being killed by the natives near the Murray River, Buckley proposed for the widow and was accepted. He was married in March, 1840.

Ten years afterwards he was paid off by the Convict Department, with a pension of £12 a year, and on this, and a subscription raised by his friends, he lived until his death, which occurred in February, 1856, when he had attained the age of seventy-six.

# THE SOUTH AUSTRALIAN LAND BUBBLE.

AMONG the many bubbles of speculation that, reflecting in their shining sides prismatic worlds of fortune, have been destined to burst in the most commonplace of soapsuds, it would be unfair to class the speculation-born colony of South Australia. But, though neither so magnificently blown as its prototype of the South Seas, nor reflecting such elegant foolishness as that most glorious bladder blown in the Rue Quincampoix, the South Australian bubble was quite as flimsy and quite as dangerous. Luckily, a fact unsuspected by its blower saved it from bursting—the soapsuds were made with mineral water, the pursuers of the floating globe fell into a quagmire, but found a copper mine.

In the year 1829, Captain Sturt, exploring the Murrumbidgee, came to Lake Alexandrina—a shallow sheet of water, sixty miles long by forty in breadth—and discovered the future province of South Australia. Almost simultaneously with his discovery was published in London a little book entitled, *A Letter from Sydney*, edited by Mr. Robert Gouger, and written by Mr. Gibbon Wakefield.

I have neither the inclination nor the ability to give in this place an exhaustive article upon the immigration question, still less to comment at length upon the system of Mr. Gibbon Wakefield, but a slight sketch of the scheme laid down by that ingenious theorist may not be altogether unacceptable.

The *Letter from Sydney* produced, as it deserved to do, a profound sensation upon speculators in England. Its author was a man of ability, and wrote with taste and elegance. Placing the most audacious misstatements side by side with the most brilliant sketches of place and people, he covered the fallacy of his argument by the brilliance of his wit. The catherine-wheels flashed so dazzlingly that one could not see how slender was the stick on which they turned. The *Letter from Sydney* was written with a purpose. It purported to be from the pen of a gentleman of taste and fortune, who, emigrating to Australia under the impression that his easily-purchased land would prove remunerative, found himself poor for want of the means to develop his riches— for want of men to hew down his magnificent forests of timber, tenants to rent his fat and fertile farm land, and miners to bring to the surface his wealth of iron, coal, and copper. Interspersed with exquisite descriptions of scenery and humorous sketches of colonial discomfort, and colonial society, he draws a succession of pictures of the misery which would befall the landowners whenever the cessation of convict-shipping should leave them dependent on free labour.

Having thus prepared the mind of his reader for some sweeping reform, Mr. Wakefield proposes his modest remedy—to raise the price of land. Cheap land makes dear labour; for the working man who by economy and industry accumulates enough money to purchase a "house and home," will decline to hire himself to reap those fruits which he shall not enjoy. Cheap land makes cheap independence, and cheap independence is fatal to individual wealth. The author of a *Letter from Sydney* pointed out with dismay that in a country where "common" labourers could maintain themselves without seeking hired service, the "gentleman" who desired to sell timber, grain, or coals, must hew, reap, and dig for himself, and such proceedings have been disdained by "gentlemen" in all ages. In this wretched country of Australia Mr. Wakefield found that "intellect and refinement," as he viewed them—that is to say, the reading of purposeless novels and the lettered leisure of the idle wealthy,—were altogether at a discount, and that the "common" folk, such as mechanics, farm labourers, and men who ought to be dying by inches in factories, or starving unmurmuringly in the overpopulated agricultural districts of England, were the only people who could "enjoy" colonial life. Dear labour meant independence to the labourer, cheap labour meant wealth to the capitalist, and the author of *A Letter from Sydney* being a capitalist, desired to increase his capital. He longed for parks and palaces, for gardens, fountains, picture galleries, and preserves—not that the labourers who were to help him to obtain all these fine things might share in the enjoyment of them, but that he himself might become in Australia the monopolist he was too poor to become in England. The method he advised for the accomplishment of the monstrous design was ingenious in its speciousness. Land was to be made so dear that labourers "could not obtain it too soon;" that is to say, a wealthy man could purchase by main force of his wealth, and compel the poor man to hire himself in order to till and reap. A portion of the money thus invested in land by the rich man was to go into a fund for the bringing out of emigrants, who might "further benefit the capitalist," by lowering the price of labour, and who were to consist of healthy young married couples. Thus the rich man would be spared the pain of contributing a moiety of his wealth to support the aged and the sick. A succession of "common" young men and women arriving by a succession of ships would compete with each other for the honour of hewing his trees and drawing his water, and to such young men and women was held out the delightful prospect of earning by an artificially enforced servitude the right to settle on the land which they could obtain now for the mere trouble of tilling it. This system was termed the "sufficient price" system, and as such has been partially adopted in New South Wales and New Zealand.

The book took the public by assault, it was at once so plausible and so pathetic. It touched at once the souls and pockets of men. The rich man saw an easy method of getting richer, the agricultual schemer saw a virgin field for his experiments, the middle-class farmer was enchanted with the notion of rivalling the lord of the manor, and becoming the "squire" of a respectful Australian tenantry, while the philanthropist admitted that to remove the starving population of St. Giles to a greater Britain situated somewhere in the South Seas, was a suggestion of a most excellent character, and that Mr. Wakefield deserved great credit for it. During the agitation caused by the Reform Bill of 1832, public attention was diverted from Mr. Wakefield, and a company formed under the title of the South Australian Land Company failed to float. In 1833, however, a second company was formed which included Grote the historian and Henry Bulwer, and after some changes of constitution the company, under the title of the South Australian Association, was finally established. By an Act passed in 1834 the tract of country discovered by Sturt was created a province, the minimum price of land fixed at 12s. an acre, and the business of colonization deputed to eight members with Colonel Torrens (proprietor of the *Globe*) as chairman.

Thus established, the most strenuous exertions were made by the Association to ensure the popularity of their enterprise. Mr. Gibbon Wakefield, placed virtually in command, attended the rooms of the Association at the Adelphi, and by sheer force of talk caught bishops, mill-owners, and journalists. The rooms were crowded with members of Parliament, mouth-orators, and pamphleteers, all eager to give to the world the realization of Utopia "at a sufficient price." The post of Governor was offered to Colonel Charles James Napier, but he declined the appointment, and Captain Hindmarsh, R.N., accepted the office. Colonel Light was made Surveyor-General, and Mr. Gouger, Colonial Secretary, while Mr. Fisher (better known to colonists as Sir James Hurtle Fisher) received the post of Resident Commissioner.

Colonel Light was despatched in March, 1836, and Captain Hindmarsh in July; while in November the "Africaine" arrived with Mr. Gouger, a banking association, and the *South Australian Gazette*, a paper first published in London, and taken out wholesale to be "continued" in the new colony. Governor Hindmarsh arriving in December, found fault with the site fixed upon by Colonel Light, as the future capital, "Adelaide," was built upon a creek leading out of St. Vincent's Gulf. The port was a mangrove swamp, seven miles from the city, and the piano of Mrs. Hindmarsh was floated ashore through the surf, to a mud bank covered with the *debris* of immigrants' furniture. Hindmarsh having "read his commission under a gum-tree, in the presence of about 200 immigrants and officials," entered upon his duties by attempting to change the site of the city. As the fortunate first-comers had already purchased "eligible town lots" for a price upon which they had hoped to realize large profits, his efforts received determined opposition, and a quarrel arose between Mr. Fisher and His Excellency which ended in His Excellency's recall. The Association now appointed Colonel Gawler, who united in his own person the offices of Governor and Resident Commissioner, and reconciled conflicting parties.

Immigrants now began to arrive wholesale, and a fierce competition ensued for the "town lots." Now the Commissioners had issued what they termed "preliminary orders" at £72 12s. each, which enabled the holder to select one acre of capital and 120 acres of country land. The order of this selection was governed by the chances of a lottery, conducted on the principle of those which recently became so notorious in Victoria. The first-comers having made their selections, the remainder of the 12,000 acres of "city" was put to auction and sold to the highest bidder. The majority of these "orders" were in the hands of the South Australian Company. A gigantic "land swindle" was now inaugurated. Instead of South Sea stock, or John Law's paper-money, the speculators trafficked in blocks of country which should be farms, and stretches of turf which would soon be terraces. Mr. Davenport Dunn's scheme was realized, and the "watering-place" was sold before a hut had been built upon it. It will be easily seen that in this lottery the holders of "preliminary orders" had the best of the game. They held virtual pre-emptive rights, and the speculator never knew but that at the last moment his next door neighbour would produce a "preliminary" order and swoop upon the section he had hoped himself to secure. A traffic took place similar to that which had made and marred the adventurous Scotchman, and raised Mr. Secretary Craggs from the footboard to the Council. The "orders" were sold like scrip, and a class of speculators and enthusiasts, of whom Lord Lytton's "Cousin Jack" may be taken as a favourable type, swarmed in the "nine square miles" of the unbuilt city.

Colonel Gawler arrived just precisely when this land-jobbing was at its height, and when the reports of the colony's prosperity had turned the heads of all the "intending immigrants" in England. Nothing was left undone by the Association to secure the success of their infant country. Mr. Gibbon Wakefield was in his glory. He was the apostle of this new gospel of universal happiness at a "sufficient price," and Members of Parliament bitten with the desire to "do something popular" flocked around him eagerly proclaiming the excellence of his teaching and the purity of his motives. Colonel Torrens himself did not disdain to deliver lectures upon the propriety of emigrating at once to Adelaide, and is reported to have monstrously stated that that city held the same position with regard to the valley of the Murray as New Orleans did to the valley of the Mississippi! There was, however, no one to dispute these assertions, and ship-load after ship-load of gentlemen and ladies left England for this Arcadia in the mangrove swamp at St. Vincent's Gulf. To the new-comer the condition of the infant colony was astonishing. The town was formed of iron huts and wooden shanties, in which well-dressed ladies played upon 100-guinea pianos, and gentlemen in the most correct evening costume entertained their friends with champagne and potted meats. Dandies who six months before were strolling up Pall Mall, or lounging in the stalls of the opera-house, waded in patent-leather boots across the sand to leave cards upon newly-arrived families of distinction who—until their parks and palaces became absolute facts—occupied zinc-roofed cabins and weather-board cottages. While labour was in course of becoming cheap, provisions became dear. 8s. and 10s. were

charged for a coarse meal, and "servants" were not to be had at
any price. But the lottery supplied money as fast as it was needed,
and "young pioneers of civilization" having unpacked their
fashionable coats, pieced together their dog-carts, and got their blood
horses conveyed ashore at a cost that nearly equalled that of the
animals themselves, sold their "preliminary orders," and gave
supper parties to each other at the "Southern Cross Hotel" to
commemorate the fortunate moment when they first undertook to
found an empire. The inexhaustible lottery supplied apparently
inexhaustible funds, and as the bank readily discounted the paper of
notable purchasers, the sellers found their sections transmuted from
barren blocks of unexplored country into cash and credit, both of
which seemed illimitable. Into the current madness Governor
Gawler seemed to fall. He set up public buildings with ruinous
rapidity. He organised a police at a rate of expenditure which
seems altogether incommensurate with the then value of such
a body. He built roads, wharfs, and hospitals, and erected
a Government House at a cost of £20,000. It was so evident
that the colony was going to become a second Carthage, that to do
less would have seemed mean in the eyes of the colonists. Having
done this, he sat down in comfort, guarded by a volunteer corps, and
surrounded by a little Court, consisting of the white-handed
gentlemen and ladies who were to be the aristocracy of this mighty
city of the mangrove swamp.

But this happy state of things was not long to last. Immigration
began to check itself, and the price of land to decrease. Wool-
growing was found to be more profitable in Port Phillip and New
South Wales. The "healthy young married couples," owning to
such preposterous things as home affections and family ties, refused
to be transplanted to the South Australian Canaan, and such
labourers as did come were waiting to be employed by the
"gentlemen farmers" who were gambling in Adelaide. Moreover,
such plebeian commodities as beef and mutton began to grow
scarce, and the Carthaginians felt the pangs of famine. It is probable
that the place would have been abandoned altogether but for
the "overlanders." "Overlanding" was a profitable and, withal,
romantic occupation. Young men of spirit, wearied of the capital,
and prompted by love of gain and adventure, purchased cattle and
sheep in New South Wales, and drove them "overland" to the
"New Orleans" of Colonel Torrens. The journey was not without
its perils. Hostile natives attacked these Australian caravans, and
the hot winds of the North were no insufficient substitute for the
simoom of the Arabian deserts. The scanty streams of the interior
were too often dry, and the adventurers, wandering from the track in
search of water, were lost in the barren wilderness that bordered this
new civilization. Yet "overlanding" had powerful charms. The
life was free and vigorous. The trammels of conventionality slipped
from off the limbs of these wrestlers with the powers of the desert,
and they felt the joy of an almost savage independence. Traversing
the great grey forests, or camped by the edge of some friendly

K

waterhole that, sheltered beneath its solitary clump of trees, at once invited and forbade the journey into the limitless plains ahead of it, the purveying patriarch of this Australian land felt that wonderful and subtle happiness which is born of solitude and silence. Alone, with their flocks and herds in the vast wilderness, they found, for the first time, that individuality which they had lost amid the buzz and roar of the crowded capitals of Europe. There 10,000 items went to swell the sum total of their importance. They were recognised and respected by virtue of a million accidents. Their tailors and bootmakers, married cousins and unmarried uncles, all contributed to make them famous. Even a man who owned the "nattiest groom in London" had a sort of personal reputation, and many a worthy gentleman climbed into notoriety on the shoulders of a cook or a coachman. But in the cattle-yards and the camping-ground such aids to celebrity were unrecognised. Personal prowess and personal intelligence alone availed the ingenuous youth who sought for a place among the "overlanders." Unless he had in him some quality which commanded respect, respect was not accorded to him. But when, after his fatigues, miseries, and regrets, he reined his horse one day on the summit of some mountain-spur, and seeing beneath him the wide waste of the untrodden "bush," awoke suddenly to the consciousness that he was the lord of that wilderness, that in it he could live unmolested and secure, that he could find there a home and a subsistence, with no aid but that of his own hands and his own brains, then for the first time did he discover to what a heritage of power his birthright as a "man" entitled him.

The sleek "Downing Street colonists" of Adelaide were astonished at the arrival of these sons of the wilderness. The "trapper" of the Rocky Mountains found a parallel in the bearded embrowned "overlander," with his keen eye and ragged defiance of formulæ. But with the rags and keenness the parallel stopped. The gentleman stockowner was no more to be compared in social relations to Rube Rawlins than was Rube Rawlins to a gold-stick-in-waiting. Once arrived at Adelaide, the rags and the defiance disappeared, and "new arrivals fortunate enough to be admitted to the evening parties of a lady of 'the highest ton,' were astonished to find, when, to fill up basso in an Italian piece, she called upon a huge man with brown hands, brown face, and a flowing beard, magnificently attired, in whom they recognised the individual they had met the day before in a torn flannel jersey, with a short black pipe in his mouth." Perhaps the life of an overlander was at that time one of the most agreeable in the colony. The force of endurance and intelligence not only received due acknowledgment in the shape of praise and party-giving, but was substantially recognised in current coin of the realm. Such a combination of circumstances is rare. The banditti-like gentlemen, "who rode blood horses, wore broad-brimmed sombreros trimmed with fur and eagle plumes, scarlet flannel shirts, broad belts filled with pistols, knives, and tomahawks," and who were regarded by the Adelaidians with something of the feeling which greeted "the arrival of a party of successful buccaneers in a quiet seaport with a cargo to sell, in old Dampier's time," had not only the gratification of being the cynosure of neighbouring eyes, but of making considerable profits on their original outlay. But in the midst of this picturesque extravagance came the final crash. In order to meet the expenses of Utopia—in the way of buildings, roads, and bridges—Colonel Gawler had drawn bills upon the Treasury, and the Commissioners and Association losing credit, a series of drafts to the amount of £69,000 were dishonoured. As soon as this direful intelligence became known, the bubble burst. A rapid exodus took place. The "working men," poor fellows, finding themselves doubly deceived, threw themselves on the Government for support. The population of the city "diminished in twelve months to the extent of 3000 souls." The price of food, rent, and wages fell 50 per cent. Adelaide was almost deserted, and, like the owls and the bats in the Palace of Palmyra, police horses grazed in the gardens of the Governor.

Gawler was dismissed, and Mr. Gibbon Wakefield and his friends endeavoured to put the burden of disgrace upon his shoulders. That they at the time succeeded in doing this there is not a shadow of doubt, and until very lately Colonel Gawler has been held the scapegoat of South Australian colonization. Lord Stanley, the Colonial Secretary, knocked the last hole in the bottom of this sinking ship. In 1842, that far-seeing statesman brought in and passed two Acts, one of which fixed the minimum price of land at £1 per acre, while the other handed over the colony to the government of the Colonial Office. The effect of these measures was immediate. As a land-speculating colony South Australia was ruined. It was found, moreover, that agriculture could not be carried on at a profit with hired labour, and the only paying pursuit in the country was wool-growing. The despised "interior" was now let in "runs," and to the colonial Melibœi heaven at last vouchsafed that proverbial wealth which springs from well-pressed woolpacks. Yet even this wealth was long in arriving. The Port of Adelaide was deserted, and the visits of the "overlanders" had ceased. The shipment of wool was attended with difficulty and expense, and it seemed as though the bubble having burst, the soap-suds were more alkaline than is usual.

In this plight, an accident restored the colony to something resembling its pristine glory. "The promoters of the colony," says Mr. Samuel Sidney (to whom, together with Mr. Forster, I am indebted for the materials of this sketch), "had placed coals, marble, slate, and precious stones among their probable exports; but copper and lead had not entered into their calculations." Copper and lead, however, existed, and in 1843, Mr. Dutton and Captain Bagot purchased an eighty-acre section, which contained the "Kapunda mine." South Australia was once more famous. Close upon the "Kapunda" followed the "Burra Burra," and Mr. Kingsley has already told the story of the second speculation-mania.

Application was made to the Governor for a special survey of 20,000 acres, at £1 an acre. The application was granted, and a day and hour fixed for the payment of the £20,000 *in cash*. Now, cash was scarce, and local interest began to grow despondent. How could famine-stricken Caanan raise £20,000 in cash? To add to the perplexity, arrived from Sydney a party of speculators well supplied with gold, and announced their intentions of buying up the "survey." A flash of the old gambling spirit reanimated Adelaide. Sydney should *not* thus snatch the prize from the grasp of the colonists. On the last day for payment a desperate struggle was made to obtain the needful amount of gold coin. "On that day," says Mr. Sidney, "many secret hoards were dug out; husbands learned that prudent wives had unknown stores, and old women were even tempted to draw their £1 and £2 from the recesses of old stockings. Almost at the last minute the money was collected, counted, and paid, and the richest copper mine in the world rewarded the long-sufferings of the South Australians."

But the whirligig of time brought in its revenges. The "gentlemen" whose interests were so tenderly cared for by Mr. Gibbon Wakefield, were disgusted to think that the "common" labourers should come between this wind of good fortune and their own dilapidated nobility. Was this to be the end of the "sufficient price" system? Forbid it Torrens!

A lottery was proposed, by which either section of the community should win or lose a chance in the unopened mine. The "common" people won, and picked 10,000 acres, which they called "Burra Burra." The "gentlemen" termed the remaining portion the "Princess Royal." In 1850 the £50 scrip of the "gentlemen's" section was not worth £12, while "Burra Burra" was, as Mr. Sidney called it, "the richest copper mine in the world." Despite Mr. Gibbon Wakefield, the "working-man had won the game after all."

Our bubble, cast in copper, may now be likened to one of those contrivances of the domestic cistern which, let the tap turn as it will, always keeps half its bulk above water.

# THE FIRST QUEENSLAND EXPLORER

ON Friday, the 27th of February, 1846, the barque "Peruvian," bound for China with a cargo of hardwood, left Sydney Harbour. The "Peruvian" was commanded by George Pitkethly, and had a full complement of passengers and crew. The captain's brother was first mate, and the captain's wife was also on board. The names of the other passengers were Mr. and Mrs. Wilmot, child and nurse, and Mr. J. P. Quarry and his little daughter. The breeze was fresh, and all had hopes of a successful passage. On Sunday night, however, the wind increased to a gale, and on Tuesday the "fine weather" sails were blown out of the bolt ropes. On Friday every stitch of canvas was taken off, and the vessel drove under bare poles. On Saturday, however, the weather moderated a little, and that night, during the first watch, the mate made more sail. The captain held consultation with his brother, and calmed the fears of his wife and the lady passengers by telling them the worst of the danger was now over. It seemed, however, that during the gale the ship had been driven out of her course, for Pitkethly said that she was in the neighbourhood of the Horseshoe Reef, and desired the hands to keep a look out for broken water. Thus, having got all things snug, Sunday night passed over. Between three and four o'clock on Monday morning, however, an unexpected calamity happened. A man named James Murrell had been at the helm from twelve to two, and had been relieved by the eldest apprentice. The second mate was officer of the watch, and the brothers Pitkethly were below asleep in their bunks. The night was cloudy, and from out of the dusk ahead of them the second mate saw suddenly rise something that was "either land or a dark cloud." He ran down to the captain and returned as quickly as possible. Just as he reached the deck the vessel struck upon a rock, and a terrific sea sweeping over her stern, carried him overboard, and "he was never seen again." The shock awakened all on board, and the captain and crew ran up in great confusion, many still in their night-dresses. A glance explained the position of the ship. The "Peruvian" was fast on the rock, and the sea running high, nothing could be done but wait for morning. This the shivering wretches, crouched under the lee of the cuddy, resolved to do.

When day broke, the full danger of their position became apparent. No land was in view, but as far as the eye could reach, the points of the rocks pierced the white surf. The "Peruvian" had run upon the very centre of an impassable reef. The captain ordered the boats to be got over the side, and the jolly-boat was hung in the tackles and lowered. The moment she touched the broken water she went to pieces. The long-boat was old and shaky, but she was their only chance. They launched her over the side, intending to keep her there until they could get the women and provisions into her, but the sea ran so high that she was filled as she hung in the tackle. The situation was now indeed desperate, and when the captain, who seemed beside himself with anxiety, ordered some hands to jump in and bale out the water, they refused. The condition of the old and battered boat was such that none would risk their lives in her, except one man—the captain's brother. The younger Pitkethly commenced to bale, but as he lifted the second bucket to the gunwale, the heaving of the sea jerked the stern-post out of the boat, and the fore-tackle getting adrift, she was carried away from the wreck on the next wave. Lines were thrown to the unfortunate man, but none reached him. He saw that his case was hopeless, and bidding good-bye to his brother and his brother's wife, sat down in the bows beside a live sheep that had been penned there and calmly waited for his death. It was not long. In a few minutes the long-boat sank, and he went down in her without a cry.

Upon this—the last chance being gone—the captain called all hands into the cabin and prayed. This course of conduct was productive of good. The spectacle of women and children who needed their aid, calmed and sobered into self-reliance the excited sailors, and the women and children were encouraged by the sight of so many sturdy brave men ready and willing to help them. Going on deck again, the propriety of making a raft was discussed, and though it was gloomily admitted that the chance of being picked up was an extremely remote one, it was resolved to try this last expedient. They cut away the spars, and bound together first the mizzen, then the mainmast—a difficult task, for, says Murrell, "they came down with the sails all flying." Working in imminent peril of his life from every sea that washed over the wreck, Pitkethly at last gave the last blow to the last nail. The masts and spars lashed together, and graced with a sort of platform in the middle, formed a rude raft, and with infinite toil they got the unwieldly thing afloat by middle-day Sunday. All this time the sea was pouring over the torn and mangled bulwarks, and the ship was literally bursting with the water she had swallowed. Each instant it was thought that she would go to pieces.

Provisions had been previously collected for the boats, but when search was now made for them, it was found that the bread had been spoiled by the salt water, and nearly all the preserved meat washed overboard. All that the poor wretches could muster were nine tins of preserved meat, a small keg of water, and a little brandy. This scanty store being stowed in the safest portion of the raft, with the captain's instruments and charts, blankets were spread for the women and children, and the vessel abandoned. There were then on the raft three women—Mrs. Pitkethly (the captain's wife), Mrs. Wilmot, and the nurse-girl. The rest of the crew were Wilmot and Quarry, the captain, the carpenter, the sailmaker, the cook, four able seamen, four apprentices, and two negroes—stowaways who had been detected the night after leaving Sydney Heads. It was intended to hold by the ship for a day or so, and if possible build a boat out of the boat-planks aboard, but in the middle of the first night the strength of the current swept the raft from her moorings and carried her out to sea. When morning broke the deadly reef was just visible on their lee, with the wreck sticking on its back like a slug on a black bough.

Left thus face to face with the ocean and their fate, the little company made a compact among themselves. The stores should be divided equally, and there should be no drawing of lots "to take each other's lives." At first matters seemed rather cheerful. The captain directed the course of the raft, and by the aid of their sail they made forty miles a day. They were in high hopes of reaching land. Three tablespoonfuls of preserved meat a day were served out to each person, and the water was measured in the neck of a glass bottle—four such drams—one in the morning, two in the middle of the day, and the other in the evening—being allowed to each. Occasionally a few birds came on board, and the raw flesh and hot blood were looked upon as delicacies. This lasted for twenty-two days.

Then the usual agony began. On the twenty-third day they saw a sail, which kept in sight for four hours, but finally disappeared. "This," says Murrell, "greatly disappointed us." The preserved meat began to run short. The allowance of water was decreased day by day. The poor women, crouched under the lee of the platform, were told, that in a few days there would be no meat, and no water. These days became hours, and then one morning the last morsel was devoured, and still no land appeared.

Mr. Quarry, who had been a long time ailing, told the man next him that he would die now, and did die next morning. His little daughter was yet alive, and cried over the corpse. Fearfully mindful of their "compact," the survivors stripped the body instantly and threw it overboard. The sharks tore it to pieces before their eyes, and the captain who seems to have been a God-fearing man, read the burial service over the great graveyard on which they floated. That evening they caught a rock-cod fish with a line and hook baited with white rag, and cut it into equal parts. Two more days passed, and they caught a fish each day. Then it rained, but the exhausted creatures seem to have neglected to secure as large a supply of water as they might have done. The two children now died. Mrs. Wilmot's baby went first, then little Miss Quarry, and lastly Mrs. Wilmot herself. Her husband "took off what clothing she had on, which was only a nightdress, and threw her into the sea, but he told us if we were men we would not look at her." The body of this poor lady floated near the raft for more than twenty minutes. During the next day two more men died, and "then," says Murrell, "they dropped off one after the other very rapidly, but I was so exhausted myself that I forget the order of their names."

The condition of the survivors was terrible, yet, true to their promise, they abstained from cannibalism. The captain, however, suggested a method of procuring food that seems to well-dined folks sitting beside cheerful home fires almost as repulsive. The sharks swarmed round the raft; and if they had but a bait they could catch them. There was really bait enough. They cut off the leg of a man who had died and tied it to the end of an oar, while half way up the oar was a running bowline, through which the fish must put his head to take the bait. One man held out this hideous fishing-rod while the other held the bowline. A shark came, and was caught. The carpenter killed him with his axe, and cutting the monster into strips they made a hearty meal of him. This plan was pursued with success for some days. At last they espied shore, and were driven down the coast. Twice they attempted to land, and twice did an adverse breeze drive their unhappy craft out to sea. At last, at midnight, on the forty-second day since they abandoned the wreck of the "Peruvian," they landed on what is now known as the southern point of Cape Cleveland. Of the twenty-two souls who had left the wreck only seven remained—Mr. Wilmot, James Gooley, John Millar (the sailmaker), one of the boys, James Murrell (the narrator), and the captain and Mrs. Pitkethly.

An attempt was made to get water, but it was not successful, and wearied out, the seven lay down on the sand and fell asleep. That astonishing run of good fortune which had followed them during their terrible passage across the sea, and had supplied them with birds and fish, did not yet desert them. It came on to rain in the night, and in the morning, the holes of the rocks were full of fresh water. When the sun got up, the captain took a glass out of a telescope which he had preserved, and lighting by its means a piece of rag, kindled a fire, at which lumps of shark were boiled and greedily devoured. In the course of the day oysters were found by the captain, who appears to have divided them between himself and his wife, for Murrell says, that "the others" were compelled to crawl and get some for themselves. On this desolate rock might was right, and the captain had the axe. In a few days Mr. Wilmot and Gooley gave up the fight. They were too sore and sick to crawl to the oyster bed, "so they lay down by a waterhole and died, nobody being equal to provide for more than themselves."

For five days more this agony continued, and then the captain, "in his rambles," came across a native canoe containing lines and spears. Millar, the sailmaker, determined to go away in this canoe, and try and reach civilisation. In vain did his comrades attempt to dissuade him. He was determined. A quick death in the breakers was preferable to a long torture on the barren reef. He started, and the sea he had defied so long swallowed him up. His body was afterwards found on the shores of the next bay. The little company, now diminished by three, received a still further shock. As Murrell and the captain were crawling over a hill into the adjoining bay, they saw a full-rigged ship running down the inside channel. They had no means of signalising her, and sitting down on the rocks watched her slowly disappear—with what bitterness of spirit one can easily guess. They then came upon the tracks of natives, and followed them as far as they could, but the rain had rendered their footprints illegible to their inexperienced eyes, and after dragging themselves a little farther they returned wearily to camp.

Two days after this poor Mrs. Pitkethly said that she heard the blacks "whistling and jabbering round about her;" but she was in a very low state of health, and her assertion was treated as the hysterical fancy of a nervous woman. She was right, however. It appears that the natives believe that falling stars indicate the presence of a hostile tribe, and over the place where the poor shipwrecked creatures had been fighting with death many stars had appeared to fall. The natives observing this circumstance—the wandering shepherds of old would have called it a "miracle"—came down to the rocks, and one of the boys, who was lamed with boils on his legs, was seen crawling through the shingle. Mrs. Pitkethly persisted in her statement, and at last went out on the rocks to see for herself. On the cliff above them were a number of natives. "Oh, George," cried the poor soul, "we have come to our last now; here are such a lot of wild blacks."

But the intentions of the natives were friendly. They came down holding out their hands in token of amity, and snuffing curiously round the strangers, felt them all over from head to foot. So affectionate did they become, indeed, that ten old men insisted on sleeping in the cave with them. In the morning a further discussion arose. Murrell and the lad were claimed as "jumped-up whitefellows" belonging to a tribe at Mount Elliot, while poor Pitkethly and his wife were similarly claimed by a tribe living at Cape Cleveland. This dispute seemed likely to end in an awkward quarrel, but was ultimately adjusted by a division of the spoil of the raft. The natives—as usual—dressed themselves in the coats, trousers, and other garments saved from the wreck, and some even tore the leaves out of the few books and fastened them in their hair. Having thus seized upon everything of value, they commenced to strip the prisoners, but the boy begging to be permitted to keep his shirt, and endeavouring to impress them by pointing to the sun, that unless he was so allowed he would infallibly be roasted, they graciously gave him back the garment. The captain was, however, stripped completely naked, and it was only with the greatest difficulty that poor Mrs. Pitkethly was allowed to retain her scanty garments.

Some roots, seemingly of the truffle order, were now brought, and the natives signified their desire for the strangers to join with them in a corrobboree. This was impossible, but Murrell, by way of compromise, as gentlemen at evening parties transmute "the singing of a song" into the "telling a story," sang them a hymn—

> "God moves in a mysterious way,
> His wonders to perform"—

at which they were much pleased. The sight of the grinning savages surrounding the four poor shipwrecked creatures singing a hymn about the providence of God must have been a strange one.

Received into the camp, they gradually recovered their strength and learned the language. Immense corrobborees were held over them, and natives crowded from all parts to see them. Murrell expressed a wish to go back to his white friends, and it was agreed that the natives should let him know whenever a ship was seen near the coast. Yet their kindness was rough at times. They seemed to regard their captives as pretty and curious toys to be shown to the best advantage, and the attendance of the "white men" was demanded at every corrobboree. Murrell gives an interesting description of the ceremony of the Boree, or making the lads men, which is too long to quote here. It consists principally in undergoing various torments designed to test courage. Cane rings are put on the arms of the youths, and tightened so as to impede the circulation of the blood. "Their arms swell very much, which puts them in great agony. They are then left in that torture all night. Their cries are terrible to hear. To keep their fingers from contraction and thus deforming them, they sit with their hands and fingers spread out on the ground, with the heels of their feet pressed closely on them. In the morning they are brought out in the presence of their mothers, sisters, and relatives, and just above and below the mark of the cane ring on their arms they make small incisions to let the blood flow"—a curious way of celebrating a coming of age, and, if possible, more unpleasant than the many unpleasant ceremonies practised by all savage tribes. In happy Europe the "heir" only gets drunk.

The Queensland blacks appear to differ but little in their customs from others of like race. They burn their dead and carry the ashes about in a sheet of bark for twelve months, when they throw them into a waterhole. Their religious belief is of the most negative character. They say that their forefathers witnessed a great flood, and all the people in the world were drowned except some half-dozen who went up into a high mountain—Bibbiringda (inland to the north bay of Cape Cleveland). Murrell thinks that this is some dim recollection of the Noachian deluge. It is strange that aboriginals who have no tradition of their many wars, and whose memory is so slight as to tell them nothing about their father's father, should invariably hold the most orthodox recollections of the Noachian deluge. They live on roots, fish, fruits, and birds. The men have several wives, and imitate the example of the sententious Cato in their treatment of them.

For seventen years Murrell lived among these fellows. His companions died. The boy went first and then the Captain. Unhappy Pitkethly could endure his position no longer. He and his wife were there in the midst of savages, almost without clothes, and compelled to conform to the barbarous practices of the country. He seems to have felt more for his unhappy wife than for himself. "Up to this time," says Murrell, speaking of two years from the date of the landing, "she managed, by dint of great difficulty to keep herself partially covered, but he knew it could not last much longer, and the thought of her having to come so low, and her utter helpless condition, was too much for him—he sank under it." Four days afterwards poor Mrs. Pitkethly followed her husband, and both bodies were buried by Murrell's request, in the sand together. Unhappy creatures! It is difficult to imagine a more dreadful death for a carefully-nurtured woman.

The slow years rolled on with Murrell, until, like Buckley, he had all but forgotten his own language, his own name, all save the memory of his native land. At last ships began to appear. A vessel came to the shore while Murrell was absent, and the sailors gave shirts to the natives. Then another ship was seen, and the natives, remembering their companion's wish, attempted to attract the attention of the crew, but the Englishmen, not understanding their wild shoutings and yellings, fired at them and drove them away.

Not long after this a white man with two horses came upon some natives lamenting the death of an old man, and, raising his gun, shot the old man's son who was lying on his father's body. For this act of treachery he was, not unjustly, massacred by the tribe. Murrell says that this man was a Mr. Humphrey, of Port Denison, who was out looking for a "new track." After this several white men were seen, and also tracks of cattle, and Murrell determined to make an effort for liberty. He told the tribe that his countrymen fired at them because they did not understand their language, but that he would go and explain to them. After some demur they consented, and the man who lived with Murrell sent his gin with him to approach a white man's hut which they had discovered some miles down the coast. Getting clear of the scrub, the exile saw the smoke of the chimney, and the sheep feeding on the grass. The sight of these strange animals so terrified the gin that she ran back alone. Murrell went into a waterhole where he washed himself as white as he could, and then "standing on the fence to keep the dogs from biting him," he hailed the hut. There were three men living there, but one, the shepherd, was looking after the sheep. Another one came out, and one cried, " Bill, here's a yellow man standing on the rails, naked. He's not a black man—bring the gun." Poor Murrell, in terror, cries, "Don't shoot. I am a British object, a shipwrecked sailor. Of course," he adds, " I meant subject, but in the excitement of the moment I did not know what I said." The two men, whose names were Hatch and Wilson, received him kindly, and heard his story. They asked him if he knew what day and date it was? He said he did not. "Sunday, the 25th January, 1863. You have been lost seventeen years." He tried to eat bread, but it choked him, and he had lost relish for tea and sugar. By-and-by the shepherd, Creek, came home, and Murrell unfolded his plans. He would go back to the blacks as a sort of ambassador of peace and goodwill. The three white men accepted this conclusion, adding, as a sort of rider to Murrell's original proposition, that if he did *not* come back in the morning, they would put the black trackers on his trail, and shoot him.

Arrived at the camp Murrell did his best for his countrymen, and, by exaggerating their numbers and strength, induced his protectors to promise an "equitable division" of the country. The natives implored him to remain with them, but he reminded them of the threat of the "trackers," and was firm. The parting, as Murrell describes it, was affecting. "When I was coming away, the man I was living with burst out crying, so did his "gin," and several of the other "gins" and men. It was a wild, touching scene. The remembrance of their past kindness came full upon me and quite overpowered me. There was a short struggle between the feeling of love I had for my old friends and companions, and the desire once more to live a civilised life which can be better imagined than described." He returned to the hut, was fed and clothed, and returned to his right mind. At the end of a fortnight he was taken into the newly-made town of Bowen, where a subscription was raised for him. Thus snatched from barbarism, he ran the usual little round of tea parties. People were eager to hear this newly-caught lion roar. From Port Denison he was passed to Rockhampton, and from Rockhampton to Brisbane. At Brisbane a pious Baptist got hold of him, and "publicly baptised him on a profession of faith in Christ." He was received as a "lion" at Government House, and eventually accepted an official crumb in the shape of a keepership of bonded stores. Upon the strength of this appointment he married, and lived comfortably, becoming possessed of freehold property. He was a general favourite with the inhabitants, and was popularly known as "Jemmy." In appearance he was short and thick-set, with sunken eyes and a wide mouth. His teeth were worn down to the gums, "for," says his biographer (Mr. Gregory), "they were his only knife for years." His hardships had told upon his health, and he suffered greatly from rheumatism. Nevertheless, he was active and cheerful, and not without a hankering after his old life. He offered his services to the Leichhardt expedition, but they were not accepted—the *Port Denison Times* thinks to the injury of the expedition. He was born at Heybridge, near Maldon, and was bred to the sea, and his first voyage to the colonies was made in the "Ramales" to Hobart Town. He died at Port Denison on the 30th October, 1863, at the age of forty-one, leaving a wife and one child. His death was considered almost a public calamity, and was thus spoken of by the local press :—

"It is our mournful duty," says the *Port Denison Times*, "to record the death of the pioneer white man in the north—James Murrell—which took place on Monday, 30th October. For some time he had been suffering from a wound received in the knee during his sojourn among the aboriginals, which had been attacked with rheumatism, and ultimately brought on inflammation and fever, which resulted in his death.     .     .     .     .     Jemmy was devotedly attached to his wife and child, and during his late illness, when his mind passed, as in a dream, through the scenes of misery and care of his exile, he always returned to his wife and child, and his only care seemed to be that they should in future be provided for. He was a general favourite throughout the district, and when his death became known in the town on Monday, the whole of the flags at the ships in harbour, and at the various stores throughout the town, were lowered to half-mast. The funeral took place yesterday, and was attended by a large number of mourners, including many of our influential citizens. The men belonging to the Pilot Station had asked and obtained permission to act as bearers to their old comrade's remains. The police also attended, and moved in the procession next the hearse; then came the mayor and the police-magistrate, followed by a long string of vehicles, horsemen, and pedestrians."

Such is the strange story of the first Queensland explorer, and it is given—with details necessarily omitted here—in a pamphlet, edited by Mr. Gregory, and published at the *Courier* Office, Brisbane, in 1865.

# AN AUSTRALIAN CRUSOE.

ON the 22nd of May, 1796, Henry Goodridge, the landlord of the "Crown and Anchor Commercial Inn," in the town of Paignton, near Torbay, in Devon, took an additional horn of ale because that a son was born to him.

The Goodridges are a well-known and respected family in Paignton. Indeed, that village consists, to speak generally, of but three families—the Goodridges, the Hunts, and the Browses—and the three are so intermingled by marriage that there is not a Hunt or a Browse that is not in some way related to a Goodridge. The birth of young Charles, therefore, was the cause of some festivity, and gossips predicted great things of him. The brat, however, did not appear likely to flourish, being "subject to fits and weakness." He squinted terribly, moreover, and Mr. Thompson, the "surgeon of the village," despaired of him. As he grew he gained strength, and, under the tuition of Mistress Lome, the village "school madam," became an expert in the arts of reading, writing, and arithmetic.

Paignton, communicating as it does with Brixham and Dartmouth, was frequently visited by sailors "ashore" for the spending of their pay, and the reckless jollity of these fellows begat in Charles Goodridge a desire for a seafaring life. As Mr. Oldmixon descended with his crew of valiant mariners upon the staid seaport of Bideford, and inflamed the minds of the wandering fishers with tales of glory on the Spanish main, so did the tars from the "fleet" heat the imaginations of the honest men of Devon with their yarns, anent thrashing the "Mounseers," and pouching the prize money. Master Goodridge—despite that his father kept an inn on the Western road, and was a warm man, with his stocking comfortably lined—must needs go to sea, and at the age of thirteen hired himself as cabin-boy on board the "Lord Cochrane," a hired armed brig stationed off Torbay to protect the fishing craft against the French cruisers.

The commander, Lieutenant Joseph Tyndal, agreed to take the lad for "three months on trial," and at the end of that time he was bound apprentice to the owners, Mr. Martin Gibbs and Mr. Bulteel. Fairly entered upon the life he had chosen for himself, Goodridge experienced a fair share of the adventures current at that epoch. He fought a Portingallo with knives, and, to the honour of Devon, thrashed him soundly. He came nigh to losing his life in a storm off the coast of Wexford, and took part in an action with a French privateer. In 1813 he shipped on board the "Trial," Captain Woolcott, of Dartmouth, engaged to transport parts of the 20th and 38th regiments of foot to St. Sebastian, then to fight the French in Portugal and

Spain. Having landed the troops, not without some firing from the forts surrounding the harbour, the "Trial," with six other vessels, was despatched to Bilboa to take home French prisoners, and Goodridge hints darkly of the horrors of the passage. The "Trial" then returned to Spain with medicines and stores for the army, but Goodridge did not sail in her. A fortunate circumstance for him, as she was totally wrecked at St. Andero. The next five years were spent in voyaging in any trader that would ship him, and notwithstanding that he was twice shipwrecked, and once nearly captured by pirates, his ardour for the sea was in no way abated. Being at home in April, 1820, his mother vehemently prayed him to remain, but he—headstrong and hot-blooded—vowed that he would ship for a longer voyage than any he had hitherto attempted, and would not return home for seven years. His vow was fulfilled with interest.

Going to London on the 1st of May, 1820, he found a cutter of seventy-five tons, the "Princess of Wales," commanded by Captain William Veale, about to sail on a sealing trip to the South Seas, and instantly, full of hope of adventure, entered on board of her. The date of this turning-point in his fortune was rendered remarkable by the fact that it was the day on which the Cato Street conspirators were executed, and Goodridge going to witness the brutal ceremony, came nigh being pressed to death in the crowd. The "Princess of Wales" had formerly been a Margate hoy, and was bought by Messrs. Barkworth and Brook, of 80 Old Broad Street, London, specially for this expedition. The crew consisted of the commander, the mate (Mathias Mazora, an Italian), ten mariners, and three boys. The "agreement," signed by owners and crew, was to the effect that the vessel "was to proceed to the South Seas after Oil, Fins, Skins, and Ambergris, each mariner to have as his share one out of every ninety Skins procured, the boys proportionately less, the officers proportionately more." So with a fair wind they sail from Limehouse Hole on the 9th of May, and arrived at Torbay on the 16th. Being weatherbound for three days, Goodridge goes to bid farewell to his family at Paignton, and leaves them with a sorrowful heart, his only sister being ill of consumption, and not expected to recover.

On the 3rd of July the "Princess of Wales" arrives at St. Jago, and having watered, crosses the line on the 19th of July, makes for the banks of Brazil, and meeting the westerly gales, steers for Walwich Bay, on the African coast. Here they explore in search of water, and fall in with "500 savages, all naked, but armed with spears." These gentry, however, being informed that the white men had not come to enslave them—their sad experience of white men—grew friendly, and a barter was begun. Says Goodridge: "For small quantities of iron hoop, bread, and tobacco, we obtained bullocks, goats, and ivory. The iron hoop was termed by the natives *cantabar*, the tobacco, *baccassah*."

They round the Cape in boisterous weather, towards the end of September, and, failing to make the islands of Marsaven and Diana, steer for Prince Edward's Islands (lat. 46° 40′ S., long. 38° 3′ E.), which they sight on the 1st of November. Next day they set to work. The operation of sealing, as pursued by these mariners, is not child's play. There is no harbour for shelter, and it is therefore necessary that one party go ashore provided with provisions, while the remainder of the crew look after the vessel and salt the hides already procured. The wind is violent, and chops perpetually, so that, scarcely having made all snug under the lee of the island, they would be compelled to slip cable and stand out to sea. The land, barren of tree or shrub, affords no shelter for the shore-going party, and their boat, hauled upon shore, serves them for a dwelling-house.* Their provisions are salt pork, bread, coffee, and molasses, and upon this hard fare they are compelled to violent labour in hunting and killing the seals. We can imagine that, cold and wet, cut to the bone by the bleak gales, and soaked by the biting brine, Goodridge and party were not in the most cheerful plight. In addition, moreover, to the physical hardship was the ever-present anxiety that the ship might be driven out to sea by one of the constantly-recurring gales, and that they should see her no more.

The fortune of the party was so dismal that it was resolved to go on to the Crozets, which were made on Christmas Day. The Crozets are about lat. 46° 47' S., long. 46° 50' E., and are seldom visited. They are five in number, and form a sort of irregular triangle, the largest being about twenty-five miles in circumference. Barren of herbage, and almost iron-bound, these rocks of mid-ocean serve only as a home for seals, or a roosting-place for wandering sea-birds. The "rookeries" of the King Penguin and the Booby Bird abound, extending sometimes for half a mile along the shore, while the rocks at low-tide are resorted to by large numbers of sea-elephants—a larger kind of seal. In this wild and desolate spot did Captain Veale hope to make the fortune which should rejoice the eyes of his young wife in Devon. The sight of the seal along the shore, the incessant cry of the flocks of gannets and petrels that darkened the air, and the ludicrous aspect of the penguins waddling affrightedly to their nests, inspirited the crew of the cutter, and they landed with high hope.

On the 5th of February, having already collected about 700 skins, it was resolved by Captain Veale that the eight sealers should proceed to the easternmost island, while the remaining six should, under his command, take the vessel to a bay in the island first touched at, where she would, he thought, ride in safety. The division was made as follows:—

The sealing party.—Mathias Mazora, mate, aged 46, in command, Italian; Dominick Spesinick, aged 50, Italian; Emanuel Petherbridge, aged 24, Dartmouth; John Soper, aged 17, Dartmouth; Richard Millechant, aged 16, Dartmouth; John Norman, aged 24, London; John Piller, aged 25, London; John Walters, aged 46, London. Eight in all. In the vessel.—William

---

* The method of thus turning a boat into a house is called tussicking. The boat is turned bottom upwards, one gunwale is raised three or four feet, by means of a sort of turf wall, leaving an opening sufficiently large for a man to crawl in or out, as a doorway. A fire of sea-elephant blubber is made at this opening, and each man, on retiring, takes his station between the thwarts of the boat, where he usually rows.

Veale, age 28, in command, Dartmouth ; Jarvis Veale, his brother, aged 24, Dartmouth ; Henry Parnell, aged 17 ; William Hooper, aged 28 ; Benjamin Baker, aged 16, London ; John Newbee, aged 24, Hanover ; Charles Goodridge, aged 24, Paignton.  Seven in all.

It was customary for those on the vessel to visit the sealing party every week with provisions, take on board the skins collected, employing themselves in the meantime in salting those already obtained.  The last time such a visit was made was on the 10th of March, in very boisterous weather.

On the 17th, a gale came on from the S.E.  Veale thought it advisable to gain an offing, and the "Princess of Wales" slipped her cable accordingly, and stood out to sea.  Before she had proceeded any distance it fell a dead and ominous calm, the swell still continuing.  It was impossible to launch a boat in that heaving sea, and equally impossible to anchor, for repeated soundings gave no bottom.  The island presented to their view a perpendicular cliff, with numerous jagged rocks projecting into the angry sea, and against this cruel wall they were momentarily drifting.  It was midnight, and moonless.  There was not a breath of air, and the only sound that met their ears was the roar of the surf that was soon to engulf them.  Says Goodridge :—

"The suspense was truly awful ; indeed the horrors we experienced were far more dreadful than I had ever felt or witnessed, even in the most violent storms ; for on such occasions the persevering spirits of Englishmen will struggle with the elements, even to the last blast, or to the last wave that may overwhelm them ; but here there was nothing to combat ; we were led on by an invisible power.  All was calm above us—around us, the surface of the sea, although raised into a mountainous swell, was comparatively smooth ; but the distant sound of its continual crash on the breakers, to which we were drawn by an irresistible force, broke on our ears as our death-knell, and every moment brought us nearer to what appeared inevitable destruction."

[Readers fond of coincidences can compare Poe's account of the storm at the end of " Arthur Gordon Pym."]

At length, at a little after twelve, the cutter struck with great violence, and was instantly ashore, exposed to the full fury of the waves.  Veale desperately got out the boat, and each one flinging into her something he deemed of value, the seven scrambled out of the sinking vessel.  A fine rain was falling, the boat was surrounded by rocks, masses of floating kelp impeded their progress, and the nearest shore was a perpendicular cliff of great height.  To add to the terror of their situation, an enormous whale driven in by the storm rose close to them and began beating the water "within a few yards of the stern of the boat !"  From this strange giant their good fortune preserved them, and by dint of tugging at the oars they succeeded, after four hours' incessant labour, in effecting a landing on the beach.  So great was the violence of the surf, that the boat was swamped and nearly carried out to sea.  All clinging to her at imminent risk of their own lives, they got her on shore and turning her bottom upwards,

L

crept under her, and thus sought sleep, "being all miserably cold, wet, and hungry."

In the morning they held review of their possessions, and found that in addition to the knives, steels, and fire-bags, which each one carried in his belt, they had but a kettle and a frying-pan. The fire-bag, as it is termed, is a necessary to a sealer. It consists of a tinder-box and cotton, secured from the damp in a tarpaulin case. In this lamentable state of affairs they sallied forth to procure food, and speedily despatched a sea-elephant, with whose blubber they kindled a fire by which to cook the more toothsome portions of his carcase.

Thus warmed and fed, an expedition was made over the rocks to the spot where the cutter had foundered the night before, but it was seen at the first glance that all hopes of saving her must be abandoned. She was lying on the rocks on her beam ends, with a large hole gaping in her lower planks, and the still heavy sea breaking over her rendered it impossible that she should hold together much longer. Their endeavours must now be addressed to saving such fragments of wood, nails, bolts, &c., as might be made serviceable to them.

On the following morning (19th March), the boat was launched, and, despite a rough sea, they succeeded in picking up the captain's chest and the mate's chest. The next day they were rejoiced by some crusts of bread, but, as if to mock them, the bread appeared sodden with sea water, and not eatable. They found also on this day the only shred of paper, or printed matter, saved from the sea.

Captain Cox, the agent of the Merchant Seaman's Bible Society, had visited the "Princess of Wales" at Gravesend, and had presented the captain and crew with one of the Bibles provided by the society for distribution. William Hooper, seeing something floating in the water, recognised the gift of good Captain Cox, and crying out lustily, "Pull up! Pull up! Here's our Bible!" the book was secured. "What made this circumstance the more remarkable," says Goodridge, "was that although we had a variety of other books on board, such as our navigation books, journals, log-books, &c., this was the only article of the kind that we found, nor did we discover the smallest shred of paper of any kind except this Bible; and still equally surprising was it, that after we had carefully dried the leaves, it was so little injured that its binding remained in a very serviceable condition, and continued so as long as I had an opportunity of using it."

The Bible, which was afterwards to afford those pious men of Devon much consolation, was the last thing saved from the wreck. The next day nothing remained of her but the topmast, which was entangled with some weeds.

During the next three weeks the weather continued so wet and boisterous that it was as much as they could do to procure food for themselves, but at the end of that time, collecting the materials they had saved, they set about erecting for themselves a sort of hut.

They sank a foundation and rolled fragments of rock together, piling them one upon the other until a rude wall was obtained. This being thatched with grass—let it be remembered that there was not a tree or bush on the whole island—made a tolerable housing-place; and to render it the more snug, Veale recommended that the rafters should be covered, where practicable, with the skins of the sea-elephants, which was done.

The hut was divided into bunks with strips of planks, and one long plank nailed at the foot of these bed-places stood them in lieu of chairs. Their table was the ground. Veale erected for himself a separate sleeping-place at the end of the hut towards the sea.

While this rude cabin was in course of construction, they discovered traces of a party of Americans who were known to have visited the islands some sixteen years before, and to have built a hut and other conveniences, but the sea-elephants had trodden everything into the ground. John Soper, however, searching for eggs, found a pick-axe, which he brought home in great glee. With this pick-axe they dug up the earth around the ruined hut, and found some pieces of timber, together with several nails, and—most glorious discovery—a part of a pitch-pot, which would hold about a gallon. By aid of a piece of hoop, this relic was made to do duty as a frying-pan, and upon finding a "broad axe, a sharpening-stone, a piece of shovel, and an auger," the party considered themselves overburdened with ironmongery. The handle of the old frying-pan, which was worn so thin from constant use that it was nearly worn out, was affixed to a handle, and being ground sharp, made a formidable weapon for the killing of seals.

Let us now consider what productions these islands afforded to these Crusoes. The first and great mainstay of their necessities was the sea-elephant. This creature, which appears from Goodridge's account of it to be a sort of walrus, abounded. The largest elephants were about 25ft. long, and 18ft. in circumference. Their blubber was not unfrequently seven inches thick. One of these huge brutes "boiled down" would yield, according to Goodridge's estimation, nearly a ton of oil. The males made their regular appearance about the middle of August, assembling in great numbers along the beach. Fierce combats took place among them, the which were often witnessed by the castaways, who, recognising the various bulls by notable scars won in past fights, "named them according to their prowess, Nelson, Wellington, Blucher, and Bonaparte." The females have their young early in September, and suckle them for about five weeks. The calves when just born are quite black, having beautiful, glossy skins, found to be, says Goodridge, an excellent material for caps. The females return to the sea in October, having finished nursing their unwieldy infants, but the bulls often proceed inland for two or three miles, and, sometimes to the number of more than a hundred, live amicably together until December. By that time—reduced almost to skeletons by reason of their long fast—they return to the sea. In February they come up again in good condition, and lie huddled together like pigs, occasionally indulging in sham fights, regarded by the seamen as preparatory to the real fights in August.

The sea-elephants served Goodridge and his party for meat, washing, lodging, firing, lamp-light, shoe-leather, sewing-thread, grates, washing-tubs, and tobacco-pipes! For food they used the heart tongue, sweet-bread, snotters (the fleshy proboscis which hangs over the nose, and gives the creature its name), and the flippers. The flesh was not unpalatable, and the flippers boiled into a jelly, together with some eggs and a pigeon or two, made a soup that might not be despised by a *gourmét*. For the "washing tub" they turned the elephant on his back, and having removed the intestines, allowed the blood to flow into the cavity, and washed their linen dipped in the blood, as a washerwoman would in soap suds. After rinsing it two or three times in the running brook close by, the linen was cleansed as well as if they had used the best soap for the purpose. "Grates" were made of the bones placed crosswise, upon which pieces of blubber were laid, and lighted "lamps" were constructed of pieces of rope yarn drawn through lumps of blubber (which could be obtained in masses of a foot square), and it was found that the firm grease melted slowly. "Shoes" were composed of strips of skin cut to the shape of the foot, and drawn round the ankle with thongs, while—great achievement—excellent tobacco pipes were made of the elephants hollowed teeth as bowls, perforated by the wing-bones of the water-fowl as stems. As a substitute for tobacco they smoked dried grass.

Second on their list came seals. These were not plentiful, and their flesh was moreover found to be rank. The dog seals are called Wigs, the female seals Clapmatches, and the young seals Pompeys. Anybody with a taste for research can amuse himself by discovering the origin of these remarkable expressions.

There was no lack of fish or fowl upon the island. Sea-birds frequented the place in vast numbers. Four varieties of penguin are mentioned, to which Goodridge gives the names of King Penguins, Macarooneys, Johnnies, and Rock Hoppers. The last named are described as being somewhat larger than a duck, build their nests among the cliffs and rocks, congregating in numbers of three or four hundred together. The Johnnies and Rock Hoppers suffered themselves to be robbed of their eggs without attempting resistance. The King Penguin, however, is more pugnacious, and uses its winglets as flappers, wherewith to box the ears of the assailant of its nest. Goodridge complains that some of these birds gave him severe blows.

In addition to these were "Nellies"—a sort of goose, albatrosses, petrels, eaglets, divers, teal, and pigeons. The albatrosses build their nests on the plains, and live in clubs of about 200 members. If the ground be at all marshy, they raise their nests about two feet by digging a trench round them and throwing up the earth in the middle. It is to be presumed that none of the castaways had read *Ye Ancient Mariner*, or that if they had they did not share the superstition of that single-speech sailor. "On Sundays," says Goodridge, "our dinner consisted of giblet soup, prepared from the heads, feet, &c., of the albatross, which were first scalded in boiling water, and then cooked in our best style." The pigeons were caught with nooses and baits, as the New Zealanders catch the mallee hen.

The only vegetable on the island was a plant resembling a cabbage in appearance. William Hooper, who had sailed in the South Seas, thought this plant a great prize, having eaten one resembling it when on his whaling trips; but on a first trial of the enticing vegetable it proved bitter and uneatable, and it was not until they boiled it for some hours that they could stomach it.

Fortunately they were able to vary their flesh diet by fish. "Our mode of fishing," says the narrator, "was certainly a novel one. One party used to take long strips of the sea-elephant's blubber, and putting one end close to the water, a fish resembling a gurnet would come and nibble at it, and then by drawing it gently up the sloping rocks, the fish would follow it far enough for another person, watching his opportunity, to strike it a smart blow with a club, and thus knock it sufficiently far up the rock to enable him to secure it. They had, however, in course of time, become so shy, that they were not to be taken in this way, and we were obliged to have recourse to a more scientific method; for this purpose we took out the rings that were attached to our sharpening steels, and having sufficiently heated them in the fire, we bent them into the shape of fishing-hooks, and then gave them good points with the sharpening stone we so fortunately found in digging where the previous visitors to the island had formed their hut. Having now fishing-hooks, our next affair was to manufacture lines, and this we soon managed by untwisting portions of the cordage we had saved from the wreck; and by re-twisting the oakum into small threads, and those again into cord, we were fully equipped to make war on the finny tribe; the blubber also forming a very enticing bait, we had soon a plentiful supply; and fish, flesh, and fowl frequently smoked on our board at one meal. Even an epicure could have found but little fault with a dinner where two of the courses were soup and fish."

Imagining themselves cut off for ever from civilisation, they determined to spend their lives hopefully and with good cheer. Mr. Veale having preserved his watch, they were able to regulate their time with tolerable accuracy, and marked out for themselves a course of life suitable to their condition. They rose at eight in the morning, and breakfasted at nine. After breakfast some of the party went catering for the day's provisions, while others remained "at home" to cook and wash. "We dined at one," says Goodridge, "and took tea about five." "Tea" was simple, consisting of raw eggs beaten up in water. This mess they called "Mocoa." On grand occasions they added to their Mocoa the brain of the sea-elephant, which was very sweet and palatable. A chapter of the Bible having been read by Veale, they retired to rest at ten.

Even in this society of outcasts religious differences found a place. Mathias Mazora, the mate, was a "professed atheist," and set himself to deride and make sport of the religious exercises of his honest comrades. It is gratifying, however, to find that the atheism of Mr. Mazora was promptly snuffed out. The freethinker laboured under the disadvantage of not knowing much English, and therefore, however convincing his arguments may have been, he was unable to deliver them with the force he could have wished. "Being extremely ignorant," says Goodridge, "not being able to read, at least not the English language, and having no one to second him, his conduct did not disturb the general harmony that reigned among us." Moreover, a "marvellous conversion" is related of this atheistical mariner. It is probable that his brain was never very strong, and that solitude and anxiety did not tend to strengthen it. He is either a great liar, or his "atheism"—which one can presume him to have professed as being a less troublesome creed than any with which he was acquainted—turned to "insanity." Through much listening to Scripture he strove to enact the story of Saul of Tarsus in his own person, and forthwith indulged in a "vision" of a most orthodox and gratifying nature. One evening when alone seeking for birds' nests, darkness overtook him before he could reach the hut. The ground round about was full of huge pits of slime made by the sea-elephants, and Mazora, being afraid of tumbling into one of these, sat down despairingly. In this plight, and considering earnestly his desperate needs, he betook himself vigorously to prayer. In a few moments a bright light appeared about him, and he was enabled to reach the hut in safety. To those familiar with such marvellous narrations it is superfluous to add that from that moment Mathias Mazora became a true believer.

Thus with superstition, or imposture, already engendered among them, the little troop ate their elephants, and lived monotonously on for nine months. A fire, which nearly burned their boat-hut, was their only diversion. On the 13th December, however, they were unexpectedly cheered by meeting with their lost companions.

The sealing party—left, it will be remembered, on the 10th of March—had come to the conclusion that the "Princess of Wales" had been wrecked in the storm. Moving from place to place, as the fortune of food compelled them, they had at last determined on visiting the island where their companions had, all unknown to them, found refuge. The meeting was joyous, and the new-comers having, not silver and gold, but a frying-pan, nails, and hammer, the comfort of the little colony was materially increased.

Before the two parties had met, the terror of death in that solitude had seized the marooned men, and they had solemnly marked out a grave-yard, and fixed each upon his own grave. Now life stirred strong within them.

They resolved to build a ship!

This was an arduous undertaking, for save some gigantic trees (upheaved the simple men thought by an earthquake) they had no timber. Their stock of nails was scanty, and they had but their boat sails as canvas. Loth to destroy their boat, they determined to make use of the logs of wood, and after many long consultations, resolved on their course of action.

The vessel should be 29 feet long, of 12 tons burden, and lugger-rigged. They would build her out of the wood used for the huts and the timber left by the American party. They would make sails for her of sealskin. When she was completed, a solemn casting of lots should be had with prayer, and the five thus chosen should put to sea in the hope of falling in with some ship and bringing succour to their companions. Accordingly, early in the year 1822, they set to work. They were divided into two parties, one to obtain provisions, while the other worked. The poor fellows presented a strange appearance. Their clothes had worn out, and they had attempted to make themselves garments of sealskin. These were little more than bags buttoned on, in true bush and sailor fashion, by slips of wood in lieu of buttons. The all-purveying sea-elephant supplied these, as well as oakum for the boat and stores of provisions for the voyage. The topmast of the cutter formed the keel of this wonderful vessel, and her sides were patched with heaven knows what artfulness of planking, cut with iron hoops, burnt out with fire of seal-blubber, nailed with wooden rivets, and caulked with fur run together with tallow.

In nine months, that is to say in January, 1823, the "vessel" was in a fit state for launching. "Such as she was," says Goodridge, "one ship-carpenter, working with ordinary tools might build her in two months."

All hands were now summoned to assist in the launch, when an accident occurred which came near to overturning all their plans. The hunting-party, returning to the huts in their boat, met with a storm which beat in the stern of their craft, and cast them ashore. It was necessary that they should waste more precious time in repairing this damage. Without tools they toiled many days to make the boat sufficiently seaworthy to enable them to rejoin their companions. One day Dominick Spesinick, who was an elderly man, left them to stroll along the shore. In a short time he returned gesticulating with vehemence, but speechless. Rough Veale asks, "What the devil is the foolish fellow at?" and at last comprehends that Spesinick, being on a high point of land, has seen a vessel. The party had been so often deceived by the appearance of large birds, which, sitting on the water, had all the form of a distant ship, that they declined to believe the story, and, afraid of the cruel disappointment, refused to follow Spesinick. His impassioned entreaties, however, at last prevailed, and it was decided that John Soper should go with him, carrying a tinder-box in order that he might make a fire if necessary, and attract the notice of the crew.

The pair started. Night fell, and they did not return. It was suggested that they had seen the vessel, and got aboard her. Others, more charitable in their conclusions, affirmed that the vessel was but the phantom of the old man's brain, and that he would return with his wearied comrade before morning broke. The day dawned, however, upon that sleepless night, and yet no sign of the scouts. "It's all a dream of his," said Veale, "we had better go and look for our food, lest our friends fail to launch the newly-built boat, and we perish here alone."

They had already spread themselves along the shore, when Millechant gives utterance to a wild shout, and runs whooping like a madman along the sand. A boat full of men cheering in English is coming straight to them over the sparkling sea. Down go eggs and blubber, and the rescued mariners stumbling forwards caper and weep in extravagance of joy.

Spesinick and Soper had chased the phantom all night. The old man sank at last overpowered with fatigue at the summit of a cliff, from which they could both see a schooner sailing smartly from the island. Soper tries to kindle a fire, but fails; runs down into a valley, and loses sight of the vessel. Finally fires the fern in despair, and sends up a smoke like Ætna. The schooner lays to, and sends a boat; but sees no one. The sailors go ashore to explore, and on returning find a wild figure clad in skins *clinging* to the sides of the boat. It is old Spesinick.

The schooner is an American, the "Philo," Isaac Perceval, master, bound for the South Seas on a whaling and trading voyage. Perceval receives them all aboard, and the next day they quit the Crozets, leaving their ship still on the stocks.

The captain had some disinclination to taking on board all the party, but eventually consented to do so. It was agreed that the rescued men should be landed on the Isle of France, and that in the meantime they should assist the crew of the "Philo" in seal-fishing. This arrangement having been concluded, the "Philo" set sail for St. Paul's Island (about 1,100 miles to the north-east of the Crozets), and arrived there on the 3rd of February.

The venture of the "Philo" was successful. The coast abounded with fish, and seal were plentiful. They continued at their work until the 1st of April.

Towards the end of March the shipwrecked men began to feel the restraints of such rude civilisation as they had imposed upon themselves. Soper and Newbee, indeed, desired to remain on one of the islands, offering to take their chance of a vessel arriving to rescue them. As Amsterdam Island is situated in the direct track of all vessels going to New South Wales, there was not so much madness in the proposition as might at first be apparent. Captain Perceval agreed, making them first sign a document stating that they were so left by their own expressed desire. The two self-reliant mariners having been then left to their own devices, a dispute arose between the refugees and the crew. Mazora, the whilom mate, declared that the captain did not allow him sufficient clothing, and vowed that he would report the negligence to the authorities of the Isle of France. The captain, justly incensed at this ingratitude, took a severe course; he put Master Mazora ashore. The sympathies of the refugees being with their comrade, nine of them came aft in a body, and said that if Mazora was put ashore they would go with him. The captain would not budge from his determination, and all but the brothers Veale and Petheridge left the schooner.

Thus landed for a second time upon a desert island, the plucky fellows did not despair. There was for them a tolerable house, built by former seal-fishers, and the island was not far out of the usual track of shipping. They hoped to be soon picked up by a passing vessel, and to have in the meantime accumulated as many seal-skins as would pay their passage home. So for two months they lived, eating crayfish, wild hog, and seal. Some former occupant of the place had sown turnips, the tops of which served to flavour their soup.

On the 3rd of June, at daybreak, as seven of them were lying in their hut, John Piller, who lay opposite the door, started up, crying, "A sail! a sail!" They kindled a signal fire, and soon had the satisfaction of seeing the vessel approach the land. The weather was boisterous, and it was not until the next day that a boat came ashore. The vessel was the "Success," a sloop of twenty-eight tons burthen, and was tender to the "King George," Captain Bryant, whaler. It had previously been agreed between the masters of the two vessels, that if they lost each other they should steer for St. Paul's or Amsterdam as a rendezvous. The "Success" having missed her mate, was now fulfilling her part of the contract. Mr. Anderson, the master of the sloop, found upon examination of his provisions, that he could feed but three more mouths, and it was agreed that lots should be drawn by the exiles. Three were away fishing, but the remaining seven cut up pieces of paper, and having marked three of the pieces with the letter P, put them into the bag and drew. The three prize-holders were Goodridge, Barker, and Piller. The two latter, however, feared to embark in so small a craft for so long a voyage, and gave up their chance to Hooper and Walters. Walters was eager to go, recognising in the "Success" a craft which he himself had helped to build in South Georgia some years before.

The "Success" brought news of Soper and Newbee. Soper, who had been a wild fellow in his youth, and had run away to sea, took a notion in his head that his grandmother, who lived at Dartmouth, had died and left him money. Being impressed with this idea, his desire to remain on the island vanished, and the "Success" coming in sight, he and his companion nailed together a few boards, and put off to her. Anderson agreed to take him, but Newbee, unwilling to leave his "skins," refused to go, and after some conversation, Soper resolved not to abandon his companion. The two strangely-mated men shook hands with the crew, and stepped again upon their frail raft with intent to reach the island. Those on board the "Success" watched them until near the shore, and saw a monstrous wave suddenly engulph them. The fury of the surf forbade all attempt at rescue, and the adventurous pair perished.

After a stormy passage, during which provision and fuel ran so short that the eleven mouths had but 4lbs. of pork and raw potato apiece daily, the "Success" arrived at Hobart Town. Hooper recognised a shipmate of his named Richard Sands, who had been transported for smuggling, and asked him for assistance. Sands being in the boat's crew of the port officer, Dr. E. F. Bromley, begged that gentleman to aid the shipwrecked mariners. Dr. Bromley —a good Samaritan—fed and clothed them, and by-and-by the sale of their sealskins placed them in tolerable comfort. Goodridge now began to write a narrative of his adventures, and was in the midst of his work when a curious incident occurred. Mr. Brook, one of the owners of the "Princess of Wales," arrived from England.

Brook was asked to dinner with Dr. Bromley, and happening in the course of conversation to mention that he had lost a vessel in the South Seas, Bromley slapped his fist on the table, and bid a servant call up the men who were below. Goodridge appeared and told his story, "at which," says he, "Mr. Brook was delighted, as it gave him an opportunity to prove the loss of the vessel, and thus recover the insurance."

The captain of the vessel that brought out Brook offered to take the three back to England, but Walters only accepted the offer. Walters had a wife in London, but upon reaching home discovered that she had married again, thinking him dead. The vulgar Enoch Arden did not die. Like a wise man, he returned again to sea, and left the lady in peace with her spouse.

Hooper and Goodridge remained at Dr. Bromley's for two months, when Hooper shipped on a whaling voyage, and Goodridge hired a boat from Mr. Bethune and began trading in firewood. The "Crusoe" had now settled down to earn a civilised livelihood, and his story for seven years is that of an industrious and hard-working man. He entered into the service of Mr. Austin (who kept the "Roseneath Ferry") near New Norfolk, and eventually hired the ferry-boat from him and made money. He became acquainted with Mr. Austin through a man named Davis, who was transported for robbing a dwelling-house at Torbay, and had been employed in Austin's service. Mr. Austin proved a firm friend to Goodridge, who became a sort of retainer of the Austin family, and in the year 1831 went home to England in the same vessel with Mr. Josiah Austin, the nephew of his patron. Goodridge gives some interesting particulars of the kindness and shrewdness of the Austins, and ends by remarking that the nephew of the ferry proprietor had, in 1838, "settled at Port Phillip, New South Wales, where he had flocks of sheep to the amount of 8,000 or 10,000." The gentlemen who talk at public dinners about "pioneers of civilisation" might with propriety study the history of Goodridge's worthy patron.

Little more remains to tell. Arrived in England, Goodridge found his father and mother yet alive, and was received with kindness by them. He married in his native village, but fell into ill-health, and seems to have subsisted by the sale of the book from which I have compiled this paper

The Veales and Petheridge were landed in the "Isle of France," and finally made their way to England. An account of their shipwreck and adventures is given in the *Morning Herald* of November, 1823. The elder Veale went again to sea. A gentleman whom I met the other day told me that some years ago he saw him in a shipping-office in London—"A regular old sea-dog!" Jarvis Veale went to America, where he married. Petheridge, in 1852, was sailing a small craft in and out of Dartmouth. The others, who had been left at Paul's Island, met with some further adventures. They collected sufficient skins in twelve months to freight a vessel that happened to call at the island. In her they proceeded to South America, and with the proceeds of the sale formed a settlement on an island near Japan, and cultivated cotton and rice. It is thought that Millechant eventually became owner of the property, and died a rich man.

So much for the fortune that befel the captain and crew of the "Princess of Wales."

# THE IRISH PATRIOT-CONVICT'S ESCAPE.

AT two o'clock in the afternoon of the 7th April, 1850, the convict ship "Neptune" cast anchor in the Derwent. The fortunes and freight of the "Neptune" were uncommon. She had come from Bermuda to the Cape with convicts, but the inhabitants of Cape Town refused to allow the prisoners to land, refused even to supply food for them, and the "Neptune," after some red-tapery, was compelled to set sail for Van Diemen's Land. On board her rejoicings prevailed. While yet at anchor in Simon's Bay, despatches from Lord Grey were read, which, "in compensation for the hardships of their long voyage and detention," graciously extended to all the prisoners Her Majesty's conditional pardon, "except to the prisoner Mitchel." So on the 8th the prisoners land in high spirits (after an eleven months and seventeen days' cruise in the "Neptune," land of any sort is pleasant), and twelve of the most powerful ruffians are straightway made constables. The "prisoner Mitchel," however, yet remains on board, ignorant whether he will be returned to that solitary confinement that had held him at Bermuda, or clapped into the cells at Maria Island in company with the other prisoner, "William Smith O'Brien."

The sufferings of the "prisoner Mitchel" up to this point are interesting enough, but this is not the place in which to enlarge upon them. Suffice it to say that he was one of those Irish exiles, those "rash and most unfortunate men" who, agonized at the struggles of their unhappy country choking in the red-tape bonds of English misgovernment, attempted to cut the knot with the sword and failed. The Alexander of Ireland had not yet come.

Yet, looking back for a moment upon that most miserable time, I cannot see what else remained to the Young Ireland party. They had carefully planned a revolution of moral force. Ireland was to be regenerated. Irishmen were to be educated out of their prejudices. Ireland was to recover what she had lost by the Union, and claim for herself the right of legislation. The *Nation* (brilliant meteor, now quenched in the blackest of Irish bogs) was the lever by which the world was to be moved. The *Nation* spoke the voice of the leaders of the people, and, conducted with surprising ability, made itself a power almost before men were aware of its existence. Like the infant Hercules, it began to strangle serpents in its cradle. But this moral force met with an unexpected check. From universal peace Europe flamed suddenly into war. France and Austria almost simultaneously shook with revolution, and in the excitement of the time the prudent leaders of the Irish people lost sight of prudence and "moral suasion." If ever there was a time to strike for Ireland, it would seem to have come then! If ever the Irish people were to be free, then did Freedom appear to hover nearest them! All was arranged, all planned. France and America both gave hopes of assistance; the people, famished and despairing, called out to be led against their oppressors. The "rising" was fixed for September, and had it occurred then it would have in all probability succeeded. But the Irish camp swarmed with traitors, and the minutest intelligence concerning the projects of the Confederation was borne to the English Cabinet. On all sides the enthusiasts were cheated and betrayed— their most trusted agents were in reality spies, hired with English bank-notes.

Having made itself master of the designs of the "rebels," the English Parliament determined to force the Revolution to a premature birth, and so abort it without further trouble. The instrument used was a Treason and Felony Bill, which, passed through both Houses in one night, was transmitted to Ireland by the next packet. The arrest of the conspirators was resolved upon. The tallest poppies were cropped the first, and the Confederation saw with dismay its best men plucked from its midst and lodged in gaol. A hurried council of war was held in the cell of the Enjolras of this Irish Rue St. Denis, and it was resolved to strike at once. Better to perish with arms in hands than to be silently and ignominiously handcuffed. War was declared, and the "rising" took place. But English policy had been successful. The people were unprepared, foreign assistance was withheld; the stores, dependent on the harvest of September, were not yet arrived; the very leader was a makeshift. Mr. Smith O'Brien, a country gentleman of moderate fortune and high social standing, was forced into the position of general of these ragged forces. He was brave and enthusiastic, but utterly unfitted for the position in which the turn of fortune had placed him. It was necessary, however, to have a *name* at the head of the movement, and "O'Brien" was a watchword as dear to Irish hearts as had been "Stewart" or "Montrose" to the Highlanders of Scotland. Thus the "revolution" began—we know how it ended amid a savage horse-laugh from all in England.

There is to me something most pathetic in this Irish rebellion stifled in its birth. If the patriots—for no man will I trust deny them that title—had been shot down in the heat of battle, or executed on the scaffold, the world would have accorded to them the respect they merited; but to raise an insurrection, which is put down by a corporal's guard, to light the torch of revolution only to see it extinguished by a bucket of water, to be captured in a gooseberry garden and put in a Tasmanian corner like a naughty boy—most miserable! Poor Ireland's poverty has ever made her ridiculous, and to the sensitive, the torture of merited ridicule is of all tortures the greatest. In the day of defeat there was not a writer of any note in England who had the manliness to refrain from a sneer at the defeated. Even Thackeray—whose genius should have restrained him—rhymed in stinging couplets about "Meagher of the swoord," and "Shmith O'Brine." Everything connected with the brave and foolish Irishmen which should have been respected was cruelly sneered at, and held up to laughter. Their names, their accent, their patriotism, their ancestors, their affections, and their nationality—all were assailed in turn. The high aspirations, earnest labours, patriotic enthusiasm, and unhappy fate of these men seemed to the English press the best joke in the world. The jokers did not scruple to invent lies even, and to this hour the malignant fiction of poor Smith O'Brien's cabbage-bed is devoutly believed by a variety of respectable Philistines.

But to return. John Mitchel, originally an attorney practising in the north of Ireland, had, by some writings of his, attracted the attention of the editor of the *Nation*, who invited him to Dublin, and placed him on the staff of that journal. The reckless impetuosity of the man—unable to recognise that moderation when used as means to an end is always more damaging to an enemy than ill-judged outbursts of futile anger—could not understand the apparent sloth of the *Nation's* movements. He quarrelled with the editor, and set up for himself an opposition paper, the *United Irishman*, which became the recognised organ of the head-strong, and which, I am afraid, assisted by its senseless kicking against the pricks, to exhaust the strength of the Young Ireland party. When the blow fell, he was among the first of the captured, and was sent to Bermuda, where he was treated with respect and consideration, but put into solitary confinement. A man of ardour, taste, and education, his soul sickened at this horrible seclusion from his kind, and he would have become as insane as one of the hermit-saints. His nature was fiery, impetuous, and kind; his abilities were imitative and acute. His *Prison Journal* (from which this narrative is in part compiled), though drenched with a perverse conceit, is a remarkable production. Though in style slavishly imitative of Carlyle, and overlaid with that tawdry ornamentation, which is at once the blot and the brilliancy of Irish eloquence, the book is marked by passages of extreme beauty of imagination and vigour of thought. The fact that it was evidently written with an eye to publication, and that the writer, in the midst of his most unreasoning outbursts of passion and savagest denunciation of British tyranny, has ever before him his own figure bowing in the character of a martyred man of genius to an admiring reader, tends to raise a doubt as to the trustworthiness of the information conveyed. In this *Journal* the slow torments he suffered at Bermuda are all set down. I take up the thread of the narrative with the landing in Van Diemen's Land.

The "political prisoners," as they were called, were permitted to reside at large in the police-districts, out of communication with each other, on condition of reporting themselves to the police-magistrate once a month. "This condition of existence," says Mitchel, "is, I find, called a ticket-of-leave. I may accept it or not, as I think proper, or having accepted I may resign it, but first of all I must give my promise that so long as I hold the said ticket I shall not escape from the colony." Smith O'Brien refused to give this promise, but

Martin, Meagher, and the rest did so. Mitchel being in ill-health did not think it necessary to emulate the self-denial of Smith O'Brien, and so was sent to Bothwell, a charming village on the Clyde, there to reside on parole. The reason of Mr. O'Brien's apparent quixotism was this. It was decided by the poor fellows that they would treat England as a hostile power, and instead of protesting against the severity of their *sentence*, exclaim with all power of body and breath against what they considered the injustice of their *trial*. "The whole of the proceedings are monstrous," was in effect their plea. "We are not traitors, for Ireland has been usurped. If you imprison us with convicts we will not tacitly acknowledge ourselves criminals by purchasing indulgence at the expense of submission. We regard ourselves illegally in duress, and we will escape when we think proper."

Plots to escape were numerous, and Smith O'Brien was twice nearly torn out of Maria Island. The treachery of those who should have befriended him, however, caused the failure of the best-laid scheme, and he was removed to Port Arthur, where a little hut was set apart for his reception. The story of this attempted escape makes a pendant to that of Mitchel himself. The friends of O'Brien in Hobart Town had bargained with a man named Ellis, the captain of a small schooner, to hover about the island till a fitting opportunity arose for the sending on shore a boat which should pick off the prisoner. O'Brien was at that time permitted to walk over the island attended by an armed constable, and his friends having succeeded in communicating to him their plans, it was decided that when the boat came ashore he should elude his warder and scramble aboard her, when Ellis would make all sail for San Francisco. Ellis, however, had sold the details of this desperate plot to the Government, and the gaolers at Maria Island were in full possession of every particular. Every step of O'Brien's daily walk was watched, and his eager glances towards the seaboard noted with grins and jerkings of elbows. At last the boat appeared, and O'Brien, having, as he thought, seen the warder safely into the bush, ran down to the beach, and, plunging into the water, waded towards his rescuers. The water was shallow, and thick with tangled weeds. He could not climb into the boat without assistance, and while leaning over the gunwale the constable appeared with his musket. "The moment he showed himself," says Mitchel, "the three boatmen cried out together, 'We surrender!' and invited him on board, where he instantly took up a hatchet—no doubt provided by the ship for that purpose—and stove the boat." O'Brien saw that he was betrayed, and on being ordered to move along with the constable and the boatmen towards the station refused to stir, hoping, in fact, by his resistance to provoke the constable to shoot him. However, he was seized, and carried to his cell. Removed to Port Arthur, he afterwards gave the required parole, and was set at liberty. Master Ellis was caught afterwards at San Francisco by some of the O'Brien party, and being brought out of his ship by night, was tried then and there by Lynch law, with a view to instant hanging, but was "acquitted for want of evidence."

John Mitchel having got over the first agonies of separation and contumely, found life in Van Diemen's Land pleasant enough. He had money and friends; liberated on parole, he rode, walked, fished, shot, and hunted. Around him were many of his old friends, Martin, Meagher, and Doherty were living within a journey of his house, and forbidden meetings were frequent. The squatters, and even constables and gaol officials, treated the "political prisoners" with respect. When passing a chain-gang of poor devils who, failing the dignity of revolution, had earned their misery by shooting a hare, or snaring a partridge, the overseers "touched their hats" to the well-mounted, well-dressed, exiles. Yet the fact that they *were* prisoners —that a slight deviation from the rules laid down for them, that a momentary outbreak of passion against a "man in authority," would condemn them to share the fate of the ruffianly hare-shooters and desperate snarers of pheasants, rendered the thinking hours of the Irishmen heavy with angry regrets. They were free and merry, but the fabled sword yet hung suspended, and a caprice might at any time give them over to the coal mines of Port Arthur, or the travelling sheds of the road gangs. That fortune had not cursed them with the companionship of those monsters among whom the poachers and rick-burners learnt to curse God and *live*, was much to be thankful for; but believing in their detention as infamous and unjust, nothing short of absolute freedom would content them. At every hour, in every place, the thought of their captivity embittered their pleasures. Did Mitchel ride afield, or read at home, gallop (in the company of the wife who had joined him) through the summer bush, or float with Meagher and Doherty on the bosom of the crater-lake Sorrell in the fastnesses of the mountains, the same thought was present—he was a prisoner. Every page of his *Journal* breathes the same sentiment.

"The spring day has been most lovely, and the mimosa is just bursting into bloom, loading the warm air with a rich fragrance which a European joyfully recognises at once as a well-remembered perfume. It is precisely the fragrance of the Queen of the Meadows 'spilling her spikenard.' At about ten miles distance we descend into a deep valley, and water our horses in the Jordan. Here, as it is the only practicable pass in this direction between Bothwell and the Oatlands districts, stands a police station. Two constables lounge before the door as we pass, and, as usual, the sight of them makes us feel once more that the whole wide and glorious forest is after all but an umbrageous and highly perfumed dungeon."

Again,—"We approach the brow of a deep glen, where trees of vast height wave their tops far beneath our feet, and the farther side of the glen is formed by a promontory that runs out into the bay, with steep and rocky sides worn into cliffs and caves—caves floored with silvery sand, shell-strewn, such as in European seas would have been consecrate of old to some Undine's love—caves whither Ligeia, if she had known the way, might have come to comb her hair; and over the soft swelling slope of the hill above, embowered so gracefully in trees, what building stands? Is that a temple crowning the promontory as the pillared portico crowns Sunium, or a villa carrying you back to Baiæ? Damnation! it is a convict barrack."

But help was nigh at hand. On the 3rd January, 1853 (three years out of the fourteen having passed), the following entry appears in the journal:—" A new personage has appeared amongst us, dropped down from the sky, or from New York. When I arrived in Hobart Town two or three days ago, I went first, of course, to St. Mary's Hospital, where I found St. Kevin in his laboratory. He opened his eyes wide when he saw me, drew me into a private room, and bid me guess *who* had come to Van Diemen's Land. Guessing was out of the question, so I waited his revelation.

"'Pat Smyth!'

"'Transported?'

"'No, my boy, commissioned by the Irish Director in New York to procure the escape of one or more of us, O'Brien especially, and with abundant means to secure a ship for San Francisco, and to provide for rescuing us if necessary out of the hands of the police magistrate after withdrawing the parole in due form.'"

Smyth was to meet O'Brien and Kevin at Bridgewater that evening to arrange plans. Thither went John Mitchel; but some mischance delayed the coach, and the hour approaching when O'Brien and Kevin must return to their "registered lodgings," Mitchel was left alone. By-and-by the coach arrived, and amongst others a young man alighted. Mitchel guessed that the stranger must be the Smyth of whom he had heard, so walking round the coach he abruptly accosted him. Smyth at first took him for a spy, but soon was convinced that he was one of the men he had been sent to seek. The next evening, at O'Brien's lodgings at New Norfolk, the plot was unfolded. Smyth was hopeful and acute. He had himself passed through many perils, had agitated in Ireland, escaped in peasant guise to America, fulminated there with newspapers, raised friends and money, and now adventured his head a second time in the noose. He was well provided with letters of introduction, and with current coin. The sudden "gold fields" excitement had brought to Australia many bold spirits ready to venture a ship in such a cause, and by dint of bribery and stratagem it would be easy to get the exiles aboard her. But Smith O'Brien would hear of but one mode of escape,—to resign the parole, and *then* trust to fortune. Mitchel suggests that the four should place themselves in such a position as to be arrested all together, and then rescue themselves by force of arms, or that the parole should be simultaneously withdrawn at all the police-offices; but this notion is overruled. O'Brien's sentence being for "life," it was pressed upon him to avail himself first of the services of Smyth, but he refused. "I have had my chance," he said, "and it has failed; the expenses incurred have been borne by public money, this is *your* chance. Take it." It was then decided that Smyth, or "Nicaragua," as he was termed among the conspirators, should lend his best aid to rescue Mitchel, on condition that Mitchel gave up his parole, and did not make use of the liberty it afforded him to assist his escape.

All being decided upon, Smyth departed for Melbourne, there to obtain a ship and crew. John Mitchel began also to make his preparations. Mr. Davis, the police-magistrate of the district, owned a white horse, "half Arab, full of game, and of great endurance." Mitchel, hearing that this horse might be bought, purchased him. "I don't know the *precise work you want him to do*," says Davis, "but you may depend upon his courage." Mitchel, with an inward smile, stables his new purchase at Nant, and waits for news. On the 18th of March came a letter from Melbourne, and on the 24th "Nicaragua" himself arrived at Lake Sorell. All was prepared. The brigantine "Waterlily," owned by John Macnamara, of Sydney, was to come to Hobart Town, clear thence for New Zealand, and then coast to Spring Bay (on the east side of the island, about seventy miles from Bothwell), and lie there for two days. Mitchel was to go to the police-office at Bothwell, accompanied by "Nicaragua," and five others, *all armed*, and, having delivered up his parole, gallop on his new horse midway to Spring Bay, where a relay would be provided, and reach the shore by midnight. A boat sent by Macnamara would pick him up, and if the police at the Spring Bay Station attempted a rescue, so much the worse for them.

On Sunday evening, however, a friendly resident at Bothwell informed the six that "all was known." "Nicaragua's" intentions had been known to the Governor for a fortnight, the "Waterlily" was purposely allowed to clear out of Hobart Town, the police force at Spring Bay had been doubled, and two constables were on watch at Mitchel's cottage. In Mitchel's own language, "the plot was blown to the moon!" and the party dispersed with heavy hearts.

On the 12th of April an incident occurred, which, appearing at the time unfortunate, proved ultimately the aid to escape. "Nicaragua" going to Spring Bay to send off the "Waterlily," was arrested as John Mitchel. He was carried to Hobart Town and there lay sick. Mitchel went to see him, and the two determined to seize upon the first opportunity to escape together. It was not, however, until the 6th of June that such opportunity offered itself. Then Smyth found a ship about to sail for Sydney, the captain of which would receive his friend on board. A week after this Mitchel and Smyth started from Nant Cottage to make their desperate venture. "Nicaragua" rode "Donald the Arab," and Mitchel, a half-bred mare named "Fleur-de-lis."

A quarter of a mile from the house Mitchel's boy coming at full gallop from Bothwell met them. He bore a note from the shipping agent. The ship had gone—it was impossible to keep her longer without exciting suspicion. Nevertheless, it was resolved to give up the parole as agreed, and to hide in the mountains until a means of escape presented itself. With this last hope, then, the two galloped to Bothwell. They overtook a Mr. Denniston, who chatted agreeably about agricultural matters, and asked Mitchel if he meant to put any of his land in crop for the ensuing season. Mitchel answered truly enough that he "did not know." At Bothwell their companion left them, and the pair rode leisurely down the main street. At the police barracks on the hill were eight or nine constables armed, "undergoing a sort of drill," while at the door was as usual a constable on guard. A Mr. Barr, "a worthy Scotch gentleman and magistrate of the district," was standing close to the gate. The two boys had by this time reached the township, and flinging the reins to them as agreed upon, Mitchel and Smyth walked into the police-office. Mr. Davis, the magistrate, was sitting at a table in the court-room. His clerk was with him, and a constable was in the police-office itself.

"Mr. Davis," says Mitchel, "here is a copy of a note which I have sent to the Governor."

Davis cast his eye over the note and looked up at Mitchel. "Nicaragua" planted himself at his friend's side with a menacing gesture, one hand thrust into his breast feeling the butt of his revolver. Mitchel held in his hand a heavy riding-whip, and had two pistols in his breast-pocket.

The note ran as follows:—

"Bothwell, 8th June, 1853.
"To the Lieut.-Gov., &c.

"Sir,—I hereby resign the ticket-of-leave and withdraw my parole. I shall forthwith present myself before the police-magistrate of Bothwell, at his office, show him a copy of this note, and offer myself to be taken into custody.

"Your obedient servant,
"JOHN MITCHEL."

Mr. Davis, feeling doubtless pretty certain that if he accepted Mr. Mitchel's offer he would be shot dead upon the spot, stared speechless.

"You see," says Mitchel, "my parole is at an end. I offer myself to be taken into custody."

Still the magistrate and clerk gaped.

"Good morning!" says Mitchel, putting on his hat and moving to the door.

The movement, which probably brought the *hands out of those dangerous breast-pockets*, broke the spell.

"No, no, stop!" cried Davis, "stay here! Rainsford! Constables!"

But it was too late. The constables had heard nothing, and knew nothing, saw only the "ticket-of-leave prisoner, Mitchel," accompanied by his friend, walk out into the Court, and—any suspicions they may have had silenced by Smyth's "judicious bribery,"—only ran against each other in confusion. The pair leaped into their saddles, and nodding to a few "grinning residents of Bothwell," who "knew the meaning of the performance in a moment," dashed down the street at full gallop. A mile deep in the forest the fugitives changed horses. Smyth riding due north to Nant Cottage on "Fleur-de-lis," intending to make for Oatlands, and thence by coach to Launceston. Mitchel, a mile further, met a friend, T.— H.—, who undertook to guide him to Lake Sorrell through the mountains. All night they rode, only to lose their way in the thick darkness, and camp on the edge of a precipice in the wildest part of the ranges. In the morning they reach the hut of "old Job Sims," the friendly shepherd of Mr. Russell (he had assisted already at the escape of Meagher), and there Mitchel wrote to his wife telling her of his fortune. The next day he fell in with friends, and received the hospitality of a gentleman who had a "large and handsome house at the base of the Western Tier." Mitchel calls him "Wood," and says in a foot-note that "Wood is a fictitious name." At the farmhouse of a Mr. Burke, six miles from "Wood's," he lay concealed, waiting for news of "Nicaragua" and a chance of escape.

In the meantime "Nicaragua" had done well. Galloping furiously to Oatlands, he inquired eagerly for "horses to Spring Bay," slipped out of the hotel, climbed the wall, got round to the road, met the coach, and went to it by Launceston, lying hid there duly shaved and disguised. Seven mounted police dispatched by Davis to "scour the country," find Mitchel's "Fleur-de-lis" reeking with sweat in the stable at Oatlands, and hearing that a gentleman had been asking for horses to Spring Bay, make desperately in that direction. The Westbury police are patrolling day and night, though bets are freely made in Hobart Town that Mitchel has left the island; Davis is laughed at a good deal; Sir William Denison repudiates all notion of the prisoner's letter; the constable who was on duty at Davis's door is dismissed for having been "bribed," and getting amazingly drunk that evening, and loudly expressing his hope that Mitchel is safely out of the island. In the meantime a strict watch is kept upon all "suspected persons."

So matters shape themselves until the 20th, when a friend, riding to Burke's farmhouse by night, brings a letter from "Nicaragua." That indefatigable conspirator is at Hobart Town, openly walking about unarrested, and is negotiating with Macnamara, of the "Don Juan" brigantine. Two days after this another message arrives. The "Don Juan" is secured, and will call at Emu Bay on the 27th. Mitchel must by hook or by crook be there to meet her. The floods are up, and to cross to Emu Bay by land is impossible. All the river mouths, moreover, are watched by police-constables, furnished with written descriptions of the prisoner Mitchel. In this dilemma a new arrangement is effected. A trusty messenger hurries to Launceston, there to tell the captain of the "Don Juan" to lie off a "solitary beach" to the west of the mouth of the Tamar, somewhere between West Head and Badger Head. To this place Mitchel can get without crossing any river but the Meander.

On the night of the 24th a start was made. The weather was gloomy and foreboding, the flooded meres and marshes now sheets of thin ice. Mitchel having despatched two letters—one to his wife, one to his mother in New York—gives himself into the hands of his guides and body-guard. This last is of considerable number, consisting of the two Burkes, Mr. "Wood" and his brother O'K——, O'Mara, Burke's brother-in-law, and Foley, a gigantic "Tipperary boy." All day long prudent Mrs. Burke occupies herself with preparations for the journey, and "amongst other things, the good creature gets some lead, and judiciously casts bullets."

After two days and nights of the flooded bush, scrambling up mountain-sides, fording swollen creeks, and shivering benighted among winter woods, the party reached Badger Head, only to find the brigantine departed. Wearily waiting, at length another brigantine appeared, but, despite all signal fire and smoke, held on her course. Something was wrong, and Mitchel's escort determined to place him for safety in the hands of a Mr. Miller, who owned a station on the shores of Port Sorrell. Miller—a hater of Sir William Denison —promised to do his best for the fugitive, and with him Mitchel stopped four days, waiting for the "Don Juan." Sick to death of this hand-to-mouth liberty, he urges upon Miller a variety of desperate schemes, and at last hits upon one that seems to have in it some gleam of sense. Four miles down the river lies the "Wave," about to sail for Melbourne with a cargo of sawn timber, and Mitchel shall sail in her as Miller's brother. All is arranged, the Chief Constable who "clears" the vessel unsuspicious, when a message arrives that changes all their plans. Mr. Dease, a merchant of Launceston, has secured for Father Macnamara a passage in the steamer to Melbourne. So Father Macnamara, in the person of Mitchel, bids farewell to the Millers, and in the dress of a Catholic priest gets to Launceston through pouring rain. Mr. Miller's brother will not sail this trip.

But the haven is far from won. Rumours of the fugitive's midnight rides are afloat, and the Captain of the steamer says that the rigor of searching has been so much increased of late that he durst not take the holy father aboard. Macnamara must risk his cloth and life in an open boat to the mouth of the Tamar, there to lie until the steamer, in passing, can fling him some unseen rope. The night sets in wet and stormy, and drenched, weary, and despairing, Macnamara arrived, just before dawn, at a point of the river seventeen miles from George Town. There a man named Barrett was to take him aboard another boat, and get him to the steamer. Lying hid on the banks of the Tamar, the false priest saw the steamer pass, pause, then make direct for the Heads, and then pause again. Barrett had gone across to George Town to make some excuse for bringing out his boat, and did not return for an hour. The steamer could not wait, and, after fifteen minutes, got up steam again. Father Macnamara, sitting in the stern of Barrett's returned boat, and pulled by four strong men desperately down the bay, saw her suddenly sweep round the lighthouse and disappear. There was nothing for it but to get back to Launceston with all speed.

Lying hid in the well-bushed banks again until night, the hunted wretch made the passage up the river. The night was as black as pitch, the rain poured in torrents, the woods groaned and shrieked; nothing was visible but the glimmer of the white foam on the water. Four times was the boat driven ashore, and the fourth time, when sixteen miles from Launceston, the boatmen refused to proceed further, and, exhausted and disheartened, flung themselves on the wet banks, and slept under the pouring rain. Desperate, Mitchel now resolved to trust to his disguise, and go to Hobart Town by the public coach, so, getting into Launceston by midday, he walked coolly down the street to the house of a friend, and having eaten, took passage as Father Blake by the night coach. He accomplished his journey safely, notwithstanding that he had a fellow-passenger, the Hon. T. McDowell, then Attorney-General, who tried to get him into conversation about his "bishop." At Green Ponds, where every creature knew him by sight, he had a narrow escape. The chief-constable, on "special business," looked in upon him; but Father Blake, with one hand on the farthest door-handle, and the other grasping the butt of a pistol hidden beneath his cassock, met the inquiring gaze unflinchingly. At Bridgewater Father Blake alighted, feeling that to brave the "door of the 'Ship Inn' in Hobart Town, crowded with detectives" would be madness. He spent the day walking by the river bank, and took passage by the night coach to Hobart Town. In the centre of the town he made the coachman pull up, and walked to Conellan's house in Collins street. The door was opened by "Nicaragua" himself, the first time they had met since they changed horses on the banks of the Clyde five weeks before. Father Blake was among friends at last.

Half an hour sufficed to arrange their plans. Conellan's house was watched, and was unsafe, so Mitchel, as "Mr. Wright" was to lie for a week at the house of Mr. Manning (Macnamara's agent), and then take passage in the passenger brig "Emma" for Sydney; "Nicaragua" to start for Bothwell in the morning, and bring down Mrs. Mitchel and the children, who would go on board the "Emma" openly, "Mr. Wright" being picked up in the evening by a special boat.

On the 19th of July the "Emma" cleared out of Hobart Town, and the next day a Mr. Wright, who has appeared on board, makes casual acquaintance with "Nicaragua" and some of the other passengers, and sits down to smoke and chat. Mrs. Mitchel with her children—the object of compassion to many worthy souls aboard—watches Mr. Wright eagerly, but does not speak to him. On the 23rd of July Mr. Wright, under the name of "Warren," is domiciled at the house of James Macnamara, in Sydney, waiting for a vessel, and in the meantime lionises Sydney, "a seaport town of 80,000 inhabitants," says he, "and there's an end."

At length a cabin passage is secured for Mr. Warren in the "Orkney Lass," bound for Honolulu, and on the 2nd of August that good ship was cleared at Sydney Heads, and John Mitchel, at five o'clock in the evening, saw the "coast of New South Wales a hazy line upon the purple sea, fading into a dream."

Of his further adventures, until he landed on the 29th of November, 1853, in Brooklyn, it is not my province here to relate. His family followed him, and in America his faculties found scope for expansion. Among the Confederates his name is almost famous.

A word, however, about the manner of escape. It is hard to say that Mitchel *broke* his parole, but I am afraid that at best his escape was due to a melodramatic quibble. He certainly gave up his "ticket-of-leave" before he attempted escape, but he made all the *arrangements* for escape by virtue of the liberty which that ticket-of-leave afforded him. His parole obtained him interviews with Smyth, freedom to plot, money, horses, and arms. To march like a stage hero into a police-office, and with hand on pistol (purchased by virtue of the parole) disdainfully ask an unarmed police-magistrate to take him into custody, was not an honest withdrawal of his plighted word. To fulfil the terms of his contract with the Government, he should have placed himself in the hands of the constable in the condition he had been in when the parole was granted him—namely, unarmed, a prisoner, with bars and stone walls around him, and no fleet horse waiting at the door to carry him to safety, or bold companion at his side ready to withstand attempt at capture. Poor Smith O'Brien, eating his heart in his cell at Maria Island, better understood the nature of the promise of a gentleman. I am willing to believe, however, that Mitchel,—perpetually *posing* as a hero—was blinded by the melodramatic heroics of the proceeding to a true comprehension of its merits.

# THE "NELSON" GOLD ROBBERY.

ON the evening of Friday, 2nd April, 1852, the barque "Nelson," Captain Wright, bound from Geelong to London, with 8183 ounces of gold aboard, was lying off the Williamstown Lighthouse. All was quiet; the captain had gone ashore, and with a carelessness that has never been satisfactorily accounted for, only seven men were left on the vessel. These seven men were Draper, the chief officer; Carr Dudley, the second officer; Davis, the second mate of the "Royal George," who was spending the evening; and the ship's carpenter; with two men and a boy in the forecastle. No watch was set, and at about eleven o'clock everybody went to their bunks, Davis sleeping in the cuddy. Between 1 and 2 in the morning two boats, containing twenty masked men, pulled with muffled oars alongside the gold-ship. Some half-dozen got into the forecastle without alarming the sleepers, and in a few minutes the gold-ship was their own. Dudley, the second mate, was the first man disturbed, and he was confronted by a loaded pistol. "Go down and send the chief officers here," said the voice which belonged to the pistol hand. Dudley obeyed, and roused Draper, saying, "Come on deck, there are robbers on the ship." Draper went on to the quarter-deck, and was there met by seven men, variously dressed, but all having handkerchiefs over the lower part of their faces. "We've come for the —— gold," said one of these men, "and the —— gold we'll have." Draper, somewhat staggered at the number of the robbers, asked to be allowed to go and put his trousers on. This was permitted, a masked man standing over him with a loaded pistol, levelled at his head while he dressed. "We've not come here to be played with," said this gentleman; "so make haste!" In the meantime, the men in the forecastle were brought down into the cuddy, and Davis, roused from his slumbers, asked "What the row was about?" "Only a lark," said a man in a cabbage-tree hat; presently adding, "You'll find this no lark—lie down!" and the argument being enforced by the production of a revolver, the unfortunate guest yielded. Draper was then brought out and backed against the capstan, "Show us the lazaret," said his captor, "or I'll blow a hole through you!" Draper pointed it out, and the hatches were taken off. "Come down and point out the gold," was the next order. Draper refused, but one of the men pricked him with a cutlass, and threatened to run him through the body. Thus persuaded he went down, but—according to his own account—positively refused to take part in handing up the boxes. The men in the cabin were then bound with strips of the tablecloth, and the twenty-three boxes containing the bullion were handed up, passed over the side, and so lowered into the boats. During this proceeding the robbers appeared to forget their caution. The leader repeatedly allowed the handkerchief to fall from his face, and the light of the candle was allowed to shine on the features of all below. Nor were the party in the cuddy less free. The boy, a half-witted lad, named Jasman, began to cry, and the men roughly jested with him. As the last box was going up, the leader said to Draper, "You'd better have some, nobody will be the wiser." "No," said Draper, "I have lived honestly until now." "Well, if you won't, we will," said the robber; and the box was handed up with the rest. The arm chest was opened, and the ship's muskets handed out, and the successful pirates prepared for departure. Draper looked over the side as the men were going down, but was ordered back, and one of the party turning, shot him in the thigh. The shot was almost instantly apologized for, and the shooter rebuked, but by orders of the chief, the prisoners were securely tied up and stowed in the cuddy. The sailor, however (I do not know his name), had hidden himself, and as soon as he dared, came out of his retreat and released his mates. The robbers had foolishly yielded to Draper's entreaties, and left the quarter-boat. This was lowered, and the water-police at Williamstown informed of the occurrence. Pursuit was at once begun, and when morning dawned the pursuers found two boats, one on the beach at Williamstown, and one, bottom upwards, at St. Kilda, near the track of dray wheels, which speedily lost themselves in the thick scrub which at that time covered the site of the now pretty and populous suburb.

Let us pause here and take a brief glance at the condition of social life in Australia at this period of its history. I think that the following advertisement, published in the same newspaper which contained the first news of the robbery, will save some description of the state of Melbourne :—

"NOTICE.—The person who accidentally found a pocket-book in a gentleman's pocket this evening at Noble's Circus is requested to send the same to the *Argus* Office. The papers are valuable to the owner only. Such trifles as the £1-note and the four or five small nuggets of gold are of course not worth mentioning. Melbourne, March 31st, 1852."

For the rest, two columns of advertisements from gold-buyers and seven columns of the same from the owners of stolen horses, show that the amenities of civilization had already ameliorated the roughness of the bush. It is remarkable to find the *Argus* newspaper, even at that early period of its life, engaged in the congenial occupation of Governor-hunting. It speaks of the Queen's representative, Mr. La Trobe, as having "reduced Royalty to its lowest denomination," and ridicules the notion of the citizens going to a *levée* to "bow to a hat and feathers." Its proclivities, however, are more congenially shown by a vigorous article on the benefits of Free Trade, as enunciated by a gentleman bearing the somewhat suggestive name of "Walker!" Nor had the *Sydney Morning Herald* occasion to chronicle items of very much more importance. The then vexed question of the cessation of transportation is dealt with in a "leader" concerning Mr. King's mission to Earl Grey. Governor Fitzroy prorogues the Legislative Council. A parochial meeting is held at St. Mark's, Alexandria, and in the parish school-room at Ryde, concerning circulars affecting Church government, submitted by the Bishop. Mr. Mort advertises the sale by auction of a station on the Barney Downs, New England, and also a "block of land" on the west side of George Street, adjoining the "Currency Lass" and "Eagle" public-houses. The Victoria Theatre and Malcolm's Royal Australian Circus both offer inducements to the playgoer. At the former Mr. Rogers plays "Dominie Sampson" in *Guy Mannering*, Mr. Howson playing "Bertram," Mrs. Guerin, "Lucy," Sara Flower, "Julia," and Madame Carandini, "Flora." At the circus the principal attraction seems to be Miss Howard's "daring equestrian act," followed by "the Pearl of Andalusia on the Rotatory Cask."

The first discovery made in connection with the daring act at Williamstown, was made by a compositor in the *Argus* office, Mr. Masters, who, taking a walk at St. Kilda on Sunday morning, the 4th April, stumbled over a broken gold-box. More of these boxes were found in the scrub, also the stock of a gun, a pipe, and a blue shirt. Some gold-dust and a few small nuggets were scattered on the sand. Masters gave information to the police, and the articles were removed to the Melbourne watch-house, where someone had already brought a bag of gold dust, found in Latrobe Street.

On that same Sunday night suspicion was excited in Geelong by the conduct of five well dressed men, who, having with them a chaise-cart and two or three saddle horses, seemed unable, or unwilling, to explain their business. On Monday two "suspicious-looking characters" demanded drafts on Sydney from the Geelong branch of the Union Bank in exchange for gold and notes. These two were arrested summarily by the police. They gave the names of Barnes and Ball. Barnes had on him a draft on Sydney for £500, £64 7s. 6d. in money, a nugget, two watches, and a pocket-pistol loaded to the muzzle. Ball had a draft for £500, £21 15s. 3d. in money, a nugget of gold, a gold watch, and a loaded pistol. The prisoners stated that their five friends were to call for the chaise-cart and horse, and that the rendezvous was at the "Ocean Child," a public-house at Cowie's Creek, about three miles from the city. Chief-constable Carmen and Sergeant Grant started for Cowie's Creek, and succeeded in arresting four men, whom they brought in a cart to Geelong. When they arrived they found a seventh man in custody. This man when taken had £10 10s. in money, and was riding a grey mare, with a new saddle and bridle. The four men taken at the "Ocean Child," gave their names as Hutchinson, Grimes, Morgan, and Duncan. On Hutchinson was found a draft on Sydney for £500, £330 3s. 6d. in money, a watch, a nugget, and a loaded pistol. Grimes had only £20 13s. 4d. in cash; and Morgan only £32 6s. 4d.; but Duncan had two drafts, one for £415, and another for £585, £58 in money, and a loaded pistol. Another arrest was made at Williamstown on Tuesday, the 6th. The water-police took out of the "Thomas and Henry," bound for Sydney, a man who was possessed of twenty sovereigns and a carpet-bag containing a suit of black clothes. He gave his name as John James, but was recognised as having been in the police at Hobart Town under the name of William Johnson. They dressed him in the black clothes found in his bag, and Davis swore to his identity. Both Draper and Davis recognised Duncan and Morgan as being on board on the night of the piracy, and they were committed for trial. After some delay, Barnes, Ball, Jones, Hutchinson, and Grimes were also committed. But the prisoners were not without friends. James retained Mr. Pearson Thompson, and the others—apparently at the suggestion of Duncan—employed Mr. Wrixon, afterwards County Court Judge. It was soon resolved to abandon the charge against all but Duncan, Morgan, and James. They should have been tried on the 19th of April, but Mr. Wrixon applied for a writ of habeas to bring up Barnes, Hutchinson, and Ball, still detained in Geelong gaol, as witnesses in favour of Duncan and Morgan. The Attorney-General, who prosecuted, opposed the application as being "tantamount to a postponement of trial." Judge Barry, reviewing the argument of the counsel in an eloquent and weighty speech, concluded by granting the writs, and postponed the trial until the 21st of May.

In the meantime the detectives arrested another man, John Roberts. He was brought before Dr. Greaves, at the District Court, on the 10th of May, and the boy Jasman swore that he was one of the men who threatened him in the cabin. He, too, was sent for trial, and on the 21st of May made his appearance in the dock with the three others.

Anything more contemptibly feeble than the conduct of the prosecution at this juncture can scarcely be conceived. The four prisoners were charged with feloniously assaulting the person of Henry Draper, on the 2nd of April, on board the ship "Nelson," then lying in Hobson's Bay, and stealing from the said ship 8,000 ounces of gold, value £24,000; twenty-four boxes, value £6; three muskets, value £9; and nine cutlasses, value £9. A second count termed the gold the property of Walter Wright. To support this charge, the Crown had secured Draper, Davis, and the boy Jasman. None of the sailors or passengers of the vessel (for there were passengers, as we shall see by-and-by) had been detained, and Captain Wright, who so curiously had left his ship, without watch, to make a night of it in town, had been suffered to take himself off, "Nelson" and all, without being even required to make an affidavit or sign a statement of any kind! The evidence against James, Duncan, and Morgan, was the simple oath of Davis and Draper. "Those are the men!" they said. "We had opportunity to see their faces, and we swear to them." Against Roberts was only the word of the lad Jasman, a half-witted Belgian, who, when asked the nature of an oath, said, "I know what will become of me if I tell a lie, but I can't say it in English." This boy admitted that he was so terrified that he thought more of his own safety than of remembering faces. Carman, the constable, said that Duncan and Morgan told him, when they were arrested, that "they should get a heavy sentence, but they would have a thousand apiece for it," but nothing was alleged against James except that Davis had recognised his voice at the theatre. The defence was that so loved by Mr. Weller—an *alibi*. "There is no evidence," said, in effect, the learned counsel, "that Morgan and James were on board the ship, except the belief of two men, one of whom declines to swear to the accuracy of his eyesight, while I have evidence to prove that Duncan and Roberts were miles away on the night of the crime." The first witness called was Dr. Ford, who said that he had been for some time attending a man named Ashton in Little Bourke Street, who, though living in a poor house, appeared to have plenty of money. This man died some days before the robbery, and Duncan, who was his brother-in-law, produced a large bundle of notes to pay the fees. Mary Ashton, the widow, deposed that her late husband had given Duncan all his money, and that he had paid the funeral expenses and other matters. She, and the servant Mary Doolan, swore that on the night of the robbery, Duncan was in the house, drunk, and locked into a room, and that he did not stir until morning, when the chimney was discovered to be on fire, and he was roused to extinguish it. Andrews, a publican living opposite to Ashton's house, asserted that he saw Duncan the following morning on the roof of the house with a bag, trying to smother the flames. On behalf of Roberts appeared quite a cloud of witnesses. Constable Everton, of the City police, swore that he saw Roberts at Kyneton on the 1st of April, and at Fryer's Creek on the 2nd (the day of the robbery). John Hennessy, a digger, saw him at "Starkie's Tent" on the 2nd, at four in the afternoon. John Smith, a butcher working for Hoffman, of Elizabeth Street, said that he went with Roberts to Fryer's Creek, and was with him there on the night of the 2nd; and Sanders, a shoemaker in Lonsdale Street, saw the pair start on the 29th of March. All this would not do. The Chief Justice evidently did not believe the witnesses, who were openly accused of conspiracy to commit perjury, and charged dead against the prisoners. The jury, after a retirement of ten minutes, brought in a verdict of guilty on the first count, and the Court adjourned, sentence being deferred. On the 28th of May the sentence was passed. It was fifteen years on the roads, three years in irons, and, I suppose, was perforce undergone.

So far the story of the robbery as given in the official records. But there are circumstances connected with business, which, though well-known to Melbourne residents at the time, and remembered by many folks who are now residing there, were never published in Court. For instance, there were two female passengers in the "Nelson" at the time of her seizure. These ladies were named Kidd———, one is the sister of———, the editor of a leading medical journal in London, and the other, married to Mr. Robert Evans, the brother of the City Inspector in Melbourne. When the robbers broke open the cabin doors, a masked man, "who had the air of a gentleman," begged the ladies not to be afraid, and handed them politely into the cuddy where champagne was waiting! After the transhipment of the gold was made everybody had a glass of champagne, even the bound men, to whose lips the courteous robber held the glass. A curious story concerning the enrichment of numerous influential citizens was mooted at the time, but for obvious reasons it is unwise to repeat it here. The remarks of Duncan and Morgan that they would "get a thousand a piece for the job" was held to confirm the opinion that they were but the agents of scoundrels less daring in action, but more ingenious in contrivance. The "gentleman" who conducted the proceedings of the robbers was said to be identical with a well-known and respected colonist. It was whispered that more than one financial concern profited by the £20,000 which remained to the "firm" which paid £5000 to its agents for the forced loan. So many years have passed that it is now unlikely that the true story of the "Nelson" gold robbery will ever be told. That which I know I am constrained to conceal. Readers can but weigh and surmise.

Let me close this by briefly recording the fate of the vessel. She never reached London. Leaky and unsound she put into Rio for repairs, and her passengers were transhipped from that port. Curious Mystery of the Sea, if ever there was one!

# PORT ARTHUR VISITED, 1870.

"YOU will find it difficult to get down to Port Arthur unless you've friends there!" said the genial but imperative landlady of the "Ark Hotel." "Of course, I mean friends in the *Government*," she added, seeing that I looked askance.

We had friends in the Government, for Hacker, my companion, was a man of mark at the office of the *Peacock*, and had hinted vaguely of columns of leaded minion to be supplied by my eminent hand, while I had artfully expressed profound interest in the admirable structure of Castray's Parade. "If you'll be at the wharf at six in the morning," said the Comptroller-General; "you can go down in the schooner, and I'll send word to the Commandant to be ready to receive you. There's a young fellow from the barracks who wants to go; so you can make a little party." Arrived at the schooner in the misty dawn, we saw the "young fellow from the barracks." He was a slightly made, gentlemanly young fellow, who wore an eye-glass. "How do you do?" said he. "Fellow-travellers? My name's Cool. Have a touch of this rum!" He produced from under his pea-jacket a black bottle containing some "regulation," and affably handed it round. "Dear me, it's very strong, sir!" coughed the skipper, who had taken a pull of some vigour. "Remarkably strong!" spluttered I, accustomed to thinner potations. "Decidedly strong, but d——d *good*!" said Hacker of the *Peacock*. So we were all on a friendly footing without further ceremony.

I have often wished that my squeamish stomach had suffered me to take more extended notes of our short voyage. There were some four women—warder's wives, I think—and three ironed convicts aboard. These latter poor devils roosted to leeward, like captive canaries, and sometimes gave a haul on a rope and a melancholy Yo-ho. I had a sort of indistinct hope that they might do something romantic in the way of seizing the schooner, and carrying Hacker and myself off to bondage, or putting Cool, minus his rum bottle, ashore upon a desolate rock. But they did nothing of the sort, being apparently but too glad to be allowed to take dog-sleep in the little forecastle. The passage which we were now making must in former days have been fraught with terror to many a poor soul. The same cliffs, the same green slopes, the same dull and dirty waves upon which I, the holiday maker, was gazing, had met the glances of many despairing wretches, had been yearned over or blasphemed at by men who bore with them I knew not what weight of sad and evil experience. The very bluff and jovial captain, who, swathed in multiplicity of coats, pointed out to us the beauties of the harbour, had a store of strange learning, and talked as familiarly of murderers transported for life as "maids of thirteen do of puppy-dogs." The little craft seemed to bear about with her an atmosphere of villainy, to be saturated with convictism, and though I knew full well that the only occupant of the cabin was a warder's wife, with a sick baby at her breast, I glanced towards the hatchway almost expecting to see emerge from it the savage visage of Captain Swallow, the heads of the mutineers of the "Cyprus," or to be thrilled by the appearance in the flesh of one of those miscreants whose fictional history I was then engaged in writing.

The approach to Port Arthur has been often described, and always with rapturous enthusiasm. Doubtless upon a sunny morning, when the leaping waves flash into showers of glittering spray, or during some peaceful summer evening, when the sinking sun floods all the tender heavens with crimsoned gold, the rugged wilderness of the rocky settlement may be called beautiful. To me, brooding over stories of misery and crime, sitting beside the ironed convicts, and shivering at the chill breeze which whitened the angry waters of the bay, there was no beauty in those desolate cliffs, no cheering picturesqueness in that frowning shore. I saw Port Arthur for the first time beneath a leaden and sullen sky; and as we sailed inwards past the ruins of Point Puer, and beheld barring our passage to the prison the low grey hummocks of the Island of the Dead, I felt that there was a grim propriety in the melancholy of nature.

The jetty at the settlement is a fine structure, built with that surprising excellence which distinguishes the public works of Tasmania. It would be hard indeed if the roads, bridges, and breakwaters of the lovely island were not of admirable workmanship, considering how many able-bodied men have given their best blood and sweat to the building of them. The long white line of the pier was spotted with groups of prisoners. Some wore grey—these were good-conduct men. Some wore a parti-colour costume of yellow and black; these were prisoners for life. Some were dressed all in yellow, these were the irreclaimables. We walked up the pier amid respectful salutes and a sort of stolid curiosity. A gentleman named Dale (I hope that there is no one at P.A. of that name) met us. He was affable and easy. "The Commandant sent his compliments, and regretted that a fit of the gout prevented him from attending personally to our comforts. Government Cottage, however, was at our disposal, and he (Mr. Dale) had instructions to show us over the settlement." We bowed and followed our guide to Government Cottage, a charming little wooden, wide-verandahed building, overlooking the bay. Some half-dozen superannuated convicts were making a pretence of gardening, and took advantage of our arrival to suspend work altogether. These old fellows were the jetsam of the great transportation wave. Transported years ago, they had run the dismal round of prison discipline—had been insubordinate and been flogged, had lost their "tickets," and been exiled to Norfolk Island, had perhaps joined with Jacky-Jacky in the mutiny of the copper kettles, or endured the ingenious punishments of the bridle and the stone, which were found so efficacious by that noted disciplinarian Captain John Price. "They don't seem to do much work," said Hacker, nodding at an old fellow who was sitting on a fountain-basin, and rubbing it tenderly with his hand. "No," returned Mr. Dale, "they do not do much work, for they are all cripples, don't you see; but they've no home but this, and the Commandant makes them do *something*." In the helpless old age of these crippled criminals, the prison which had made such excellent use of them, gave them generous shelter!

The housekeeper of Government Cottage was profuse in her apologies for lack of accommodation. "If she had only known! His Excellency had been there last week! Only to think of three gentlemen! And the Commandant ill, too!" Lieutenant Cool, who had been painfully uneasy, as with a sense of duty unfulfilled, since we landed, having made a hurried toilet, produced the familiar bottle, and said, screwing in his eyeglass with a fashionable air, "Mr. Dale, have a touch at this rum, and then, if you please, we'll call on the Commandant." We had a touch of rum, and we called on the Commandant. The Commandant received us with courtesy, apologized for his gout, informed us that he had ordered boats'-crews innumerable to take us round the settlement, and that if to-day we would visit the workshops and the barracks, we could start to-morrow overland for Eaglehawk Neck, cross the bay in a whaleboat, and so to Kangaroo Point and Hobart Town. He showed us his curiosities, explained a map of the settlement made by a prisoner, and permitted us to examine the canoes of attempted absconders. "I am afraid that you will find but little to interest you," he said mournfully. "The place is not like it used to be." This regretful allusion to past glories is common to Tasmanian settlers; and naturally so. But then they all pretend that they are so delighted to have ruined themselves by the abolition of transportation!

The Commandant's house is a most picturesque and comfortable residence, overlooking the town. The approach to it is contrived not without an eye to the resistance of assault, and beyond the entering arch, upon a terrace, paces (more as a sign of authority than a threat) a sentry with loaded musket. On the brow of the hill stands the convict barracks, like a factory, and above all shoots into the air the gigantic semaphore. Voluble Mr. Dale took us into the signal-house, and we looked through the glasses, despatched and received useless messages, and generally conducted ourselves after the intrusive and objectless manner of men out upon a holiday. The signalman was a fine handsome fellow—a sailor of course—and, upon the conclusion of our vagaries, Cool produced his pocket flask, and blandly suggested a touch of the inevitable rum. The swallowing of ardent spirits was against convict regulations, but Mr. Dale suggested that the Commandant did not object to a small present of tobacco. So we all tobaccoed our friend, and departed into the township. "We will first visit the workshops, gentlemen," said Mr. Dale, "and then the gaol; then we will see the church, and the quarters of the stipendiaries." "Of the which?" asked Hacker. "The stipendiaries, sir," said Mr. Harris; "I am a stipendiary." He said this with an air of such dignity that a stipendiary might have been an archbishop.

I am afraid that my memory will not serve me sufficiently to enable me to accurately detail all the arrangements of the prison. I know that the saws in the workshops made a great noise, and that the tanpits had a very strong odour about them—an odour, by the way, which Mr. Dale (who incontinently fell into one during some enthusiastic explanation of the doings of the Commandant), persisted in carrying about with us, despite all hints. I know that the prisoners seemed all alike in feature, and that I could no more distinguish them the one from the other than I could swear to a Chinaman or a twotoothed wether. I know that a general scowl of depression seemed to be on the fellow's faces, and that the noise of the irons made my unaccustomed ears tingle. I know that I thought to myself that I should go mad were I condemned to such a life, and that I caught one of the men looking at me with a broad grin as I thought it. I know that there seemed to me to hang over the whole place a sort of horrible gloom, as though the sunlight had been withdrawn from it, and that I should have been ashamed to have suddenly met some high-minded friend, inasmuch as it seemed that in coming down to stare at these chained and degraded beings, we had all been guilty of an act of unmanly curiosity. Then turning from the almost empty workshops to the huge barracks, and hearing the stipendiary's glib stories of escapes, and murders and suicides to avoid the agony of living, I pictured the many windows of that hideously square and practical structure crowded with heads; saw the open ground before us once more dotted over with chain-gangs, heard the cat hiss and swing, and caught the echoes of the awful mirth with which the doomed wretches cheered their lingering hours. How many sighs had gone up to Heaven from among those trim trees, how many tears had moistened those neatly chiselled flagstones? The scene upon which we gazed had been the loathed life-long prospect of many a poor scoundrel, who perhaps was not so much worse than I. I do not think that I have any maudlin sympathy for convicts, but as I looked round upon the seamed and sullen faces, I thought of the saying of the enthusiast, "There, but for the grace of God goes John Newton!" and seemed for the first time to realise how thin is the planking of "favourable circumstances" which is between the best of us and such a fate.

We made progress through the gaol. We saw the kitchens, and tasted the "skilly," and replied to the enquiry, "is not that remarkably good, sir? Many an honest poor man would be glad to get that, eh?" by a proper "yes, indeed," as is the etiquette to do on such occasions. The mess-room was admirably ordered. At one given signal, somebody says an orthodox grace, at another the 150 men who comprise the available force of able-bodied criminals sit down and eat, at another they rise up and return thanks for their daily bread, at a third they clank away to their dormitories. The dormitory was like nothing so much as the 'tween decks of some huge ship. The bunks were railed off, and the convicts lay with their heads to the ship's side. Lamps were kept burning all night and a watchman patrolled the space between the berths. We viewed the baths where each day each man has five minutes' washing, and looked into the "old prison," where are the cells for the refractory. This old prison is a frightfully gloomy spot. The walls are like those of a bastille, the air is damp and heavy, and the one unlucky man who was undergoing confinement crouched in a sort of yellow darkness, and came to his barred window to stare at us, like a wild beast in a cage. We saw the "punishment yard," where men had in old times received their 200 lashes, and regarded it with the same curious awe with which we peeped into the torture chamber at the Tower on some school holiday, or watched the genial beefeater imprison in the "gaoler's daughter" the dainty wrist of our pretty cousin from the country. Grass grew now in the interstices of the stones, and the turnkey shut the door with an air of relief—as though he was shutting up a haunted room. "We will now see the 'solitary' prison," said Mr. Dale, and so we perforce visited that ingenious contrivance for making madmen. The prison is like others of its kind. A central hall has radiating corridors, on each side of these corridors are cells. The prisoner sentenced to "solitary confinement" is placed in one of these chambers, and from the moment the door closes upon him until his term of sentence expires is left alone with whitewash. His exercise is taken in a little yard into which his cell opens. The consolations of religion are administered to him in a box which is so constructed as to shut out from his view all other "miserable sinners" (save the officiating clergyman). His head is muffled in a helmet of cloth pierced with eye-holes, so that he is irrecognisable, and, his mind thus distracted from earthly things, his intellect is fed with tracts, for the most part expressions of sectarian opinion upon theological dogmas, or cheering promises of an eternity of future torment. An absolute silence reigns in this monument of official stupidity. The warders wear list slippers, and from time to time the convict, meditating on the "worm that dieth not and the fire that is not quenched," sees the peep-hole of his door slide noiselessly back, and meets the cold gaze of his gaoler's eye. "We find that a man who does more than twelve months' solitary," said Mr. Dale, in a whisper, "becomes weak in his mind."

When at Hobart Town I had asked an official of position to allow me to see the records, and—in consideration of the *Peacock*— he was obliging enough to do so. There I found set down, in various handwritings, the history of some strange lives—"John Doe, Marpelia, poaching, ten years, York Assizes, 1832; assigned, 1833, to Richard Roe, Esq., of Green Ponds; May 4, 1833, insubordination, fifty lashes; August 18, 1833, refusing to work, fifty lashes; September 7, 1833, absconding from his hired service, ten years' penal servitude; June 12, 1835, attempt at murder," &c.—and glancing down the list, spotted with red ink for floggings, like a well-printed prayer-book, had asked, "Who is the worst man you have alive now?" The obliging official considered. "I think that Mooney is the worst. Let me see. *M.*, *Mac*, *Mic*, *Moo*. Here we are. Transported at thirteen years of age for poaching, flogged—but there, you can read it yourself. He was in the Jacky-Jacky business at Norfolk Island. He has drawn lots with another man for murder; he has been a bushranger—oh, a terrible fellow!" "And where is he now?" I asked. "Oh," said the genial official, with a calm self-satisfaction (so it seemed to me) at the excellence of the system which he administered, "He's all right now; we've got him all right *now!* He's a lunatic at Port Arthur *now!*"

I requested to be shown this fortunate example of convict discipline, and Mr. Dale obligingly directed his steps towards the asylum.

The asylum was chiefly remarkable for the number of old men which it contained. Port Arthur, in the year in which we visited it, was a hospital for cripples, and decrepid, blear-eyed convicts basked in the sunshine of the yard, or warmed their maimed limbs at the fire in the keeping-room, with a senile complacency that was almost as affecting as is the helplessness of an infant.

Having passed Smith O'Brien's cottage—pointed out to us with a reverence which spoke much for the gentle breeding of that rash but patriotic Irishman—we were conducted into the asylum. Visitors to Bedlam will remember Cibber's statues, "Melancholy and Madness." The living statues whom we saw were mere reproductions of the hideous stone. Some leant listlessly against the walls, some raved locked in cells. In ordinary lunatic asylums one sees in one's melancholy progress a variety of character—the mad folks sing, laugh, relate anecdotes, imagine themselves to be endowed with good fortune, or to possess claims to reverence. Here were no such pleasurable emotions. The criminal lunatics were of but two dispositions—they cowered and crawled like whipped fox-hounds to the feet of their keepers, or they raged, howling blasphemous and hideous imprecations upon their gaolers. I was eager to see my poacher of thirteen years. The warder drew aside a peep-hole in the barred door, and I saw a grizzled, gaunt, and half-naked old man coiled in a corner. The peculiar wild beast smell which belongs to some forms of furious madness exhaled from the cell. The gibbering animal within turned, and his malignant eyes met mine. "Take care," said the gaoler; "he has a habit of sticking his finger through the peep-hole to try and poke someone's eye out!" I drew back, and a nail-bitten, hairy finger, like the toe of an ape, was thrust with rapid and simian neatness through the aperture. "That is how he amuses himself," said the good warder, forcing-to the iron slote; "he'd best be dead, I'm thinking."

From the asylum we visited the quarters of the stipendiaries, saw the neat theatre erected for the edification of those gentlemen, and examined the books in the library. "I will take you round by the church and the chaplain's house," said Mr. Dale, "and it will be then time for you to return to Government Cottage." We saw the church, a handsome building, built in 1836, and heard the legend of the stolen money which was supposed to have been built into the wall of it. "A curious place!" cried Cool, when we reached our cottage. "Very curious. ("Have a touch of this rum, Mr. Dale.")

Pray how many prisoners have you here now?" "Mrs. Glamorgan," says Dale, "oblige me with a pen. By-the-way, there are goats in the garden, Mrs. Glamorgan; you know the Commandant's objection to goats. Here is the list, sir, as forwarded to Hobart Town by the schooner. Gentlemen, my compliments." And with a bow (and a touch of rum) he departed. The list was as follows:—

|  |  |  |
|---|---|---|
| Convicts | ... | 301 |
| Do., invalids | ... | 13 |
| Do., insane | ... | 8 |
|  |  | — 322 |
| Paupers not under sentence | ... | 166 |
| Lunatics do. | ... | 86 |
|  |  | — 252 |
| 26th Jan., 1870. |  | 574 |

How shorn of its glories was Babylon! How ill had the world wagged with it since the days of the settlement of Port Phillip in 1835, when the prison owned 911 men and 270 boys, their labour for the year being valued at £16,000! As we slept beneath the hospitable roof of Government Cottage, we, travellers from despised Port Phillip, were cognisant that over the doorway of our shelter was even then written the melancholy "Ichabod. Thy glory hath departed."

Next morning came the whale-boat to take us to Dead Man's Island, and we embarked under the noses of a guard. Cockney travellers, anxious to find foreign similes for their local conveniences, have long persisted in calling gondolas the hackney-cabs of Venice. Following the same humour, I may say that the whale-boats are the omnibuses of Port Arthur. Six convicts of good character represent the horses, while a free coxswain, having loaded revolver in his belt and carbine ready to his hand, sits in the stern-sheets and represents the mild cad who is so careful of his sixpences from the Marble Arch to Bayswater.

Dead Man's Isle, or *L'Isle des Morts*, as the maps term it, is a foolish little sand island hummocked with graves. There many scoundrels mingle their dust with that of more fortunate men. May (the murderer of the Italian image-boy) is rotting there; so also is Robert Young, 51st Regiment, accidentally drowned; so also are three seamen of the schooner "Echo," together with many of the 21st, 51st, and 63rd Regiments. I trampled over the graves in full humour to be orthodox, and to look with abhorrence upon the clay that suffered in life beneath a yellow jacket, but decided upon the exercise of Christian charity when I found myself gazing with virtuous indignation at the headstone of one, the wife of Private Gibbons, 21st Regiment, and who (poor woman) died virtuously in childbed.

From the Island of the Dead our whaleboat took us to Long Bay, and landed us there at the wooden pier. In the "good times" before mentioned, the isthmus between Long Bay and Norfolk Bay was bridged by the railroad of clever Captain Booth, and travellers like ourselves were dragged in waggons by harnessed murderers or

burglars. In the decadence of convict discipline, however, this
gratification was denied us, and we walked over sandy soil and
through prickly scrub, while a taciturn convict of unprepossessing
appearance drove a cart containing our baggage. In this happy
manner we reached the corresponding pier at Norfolk Bay, where,
tossing in the chill waves, lay another whaleboat with another convict
crew and another armed coxswain. So embarking—not without a
touch of the inevitable rum—we passed Woody Island, and made for
the famed Eaglehawk Neck.

Eaglehawk Neck is a strip of sand some 500 yards across. On
the western side of this isthmus lies Eaglehawk Bay, opening out
into Port Bunche, and guarded by the signal station of Woody
Island and the peninsula of One-tree Point ; on the eastern side the
Southern Ocean breaks unchecked upon the rocky point of Cape
Surville, rages in white wrath upon the long length of Descent Beach,
or burrows in treacherous silence beneath the honeycomb rocks that
guard the southern horn of Pirate's Bay. Across the isthmus is built
a plank-road, in the midst of which is a guard-house. Sentinels
patrol night and day, while the eye of the new-comer is startled by
the sight of dogs set out upon stages extending far into the shallows
on either side. To reach the further shore the escaping convict
must—like the adventurous Cash and his companions—dare the
sharks and swim the rapids of Pirate's Bay, but to land upon the
barren sand of Forrestier's Peninsula, blocked by another isthmus,
which leads to civilisation and recapture.

Our boat, beached upon the further shore, was met by the
sergeant in charge, who received us with military honours, turned
out the guard in respect to Cool's forage cap, and conducted us to
his house. In old days a commissioned officer, with a subaltern's
guard (and a rationed shark, as legends go), looked after this
important spot, and the line of neat white huts upon the sand
testified to the presence of troops. At the time of our visit,
Hezekiah Macklewain was judged sufficient protection. To describe
Sergeant Macklewain is not my intention. Suffice it to say that he
was an "old soldier," and that he fulfilled the promise of hospitality,
artfulness, and discipline, which those two words imply. It is my
fortune to have many friends who hold the Queen's commission, and
Macklewain seemed to have relatives in every regiment in the
service. "The Fighting Onety-oneth ? Me cousin Tim was colour-
sergeant at Badajos !" "Did ye say the Princess's Plungers ? Me
brother was bâtman to the ould divil of a colonel, and me wife's
father knew your uncle well. Och—"

"Have a touch of rum," says Cool. "What's the motto of the
Tearing Tenty-tenth—*Risky, frisky, whiskey*, eh ? "

" By the wooden man, sir, but Sally's great uncle, Corney
O'Keefe, was——"

" Oh, have a touch of rum," cries Hacker.

"And so you're a grandson of General Barry, are ye ? Roaring
Harry Barry, of Barry Oge—him they called Barry Lyndon.
Och—"

"Have another touch of rum," said Cool.

I trust that I shall not be misunderstood when I say that we spent a merry night—within the limits of becoming mirth, of course. We related anecdotes of moving accident, we told camp-stories—of a Shandean order, not unfrequently; we sang military songs, and that jolly sergeant and his wife danced a reel, or I am much mistaken, to the music of Cool's melodious whistle. Then, having been all bedded down, in the sergeant's best bedroom you may be sure, with all the good-wife's blankets heaped above us, we slept the sleep of the just, lulled by the music of the murmuring waves, as they ran in upon the ocean beach.

At daylight the sergeant roused us. "To the Blow-hole!" The Blow-hole is a curious freak of nature. At the southern horn of Pirate's Bay the sea has bored an enormous cavern, and having—in remote ages—forced its way upwards through the roof of this tunnel, there now remains an arch of rock, called by the first discoverers of it "Tasman's Arch." To this spot, by a rough track, did our jovial sergeant lead us. We advanced through the scrub, and saw suddenly open at our feet an immense chasm, at the bottom of which the sea was lazily lapping. Beyond this chasm the scrub continued apparently unbroken, but upon skirting the enormous hole we felt the salt breeze lick our faces, and a few steps further placed us at the brink of the cliff. The morning was an exquisitely calm and bright one, and the tide was low. We looked down through a funnel nearly 200ft. deep, and saw at the bottom but wet and weed-girt rocks. Our sergeant informed us that in times of violent storm the water, driven in with the full violence of the wave which breaks upon the cliff, is spouted up through the funnel into air! I was long inclined to doubt this statement, until I found it confirmed by Dr. Ross, who records that, visiting the place on a comparatively calm day, he saw, "between me and the light, little sparkles of spray rising up several feet into the air;" and, after stating that the impression of terror produced upon his mind by the "awful depths of the 'boilers of Buchan'" was many degrees inferior to that induced by the Blow-hole, he says that "the spectator could observe, at a depth of 150ft. or 200ft., the waters rolling in by a subterraneous channel, and *dashing the spray in his face.*" The aspect of this spot during a gale must be as marvellous as that of the Douvres. The Blow-hole, in fact, repeats at the antipodes the marvels of the Channel Islands, for, descending by a narrow pathway to the foot of the precipice, we found ourselves on a ledge of rock which at high-water is covered by furious surf, and the huge cavern, intersected and bored into by several smaller ones, bore an aspect sufficiently romantic to have warranted its selection as the scene of a drama of the sea scarcely less wonderful than that one played at the order of Victor Hugo by Gilliatt and the *pieuvre* on the Man-rock of Guernsey.

Cool and I bathed in a pool of water some ten feet wide, and heaven knows how deep, left by the retired sea at the base of the cliff. The sides of this natural bath were covered with sea-weeds,

and its depths were inhabited by a variety of oceanic life, which the
clearness of the water allowed to be distinctly seen. It was as
though we had plunged into an aquarium. Refreshed by our bath,
and a walk over the beach to the guard-house, we breakfasted
heartily, and took leave of our hospitable entertainers to embark in
the ready whaleboat which was to convey us back to civilisation.
The boat voyage was not remarkable for aught save weariness. The
wind had freshened, and for some hours we laboured against the
tide, beguiling the time with anecdote and story. The coxswain
related to us the history of Cash and Cavanagh, told of the exploits
of the "Jaguar," the acuteness of Mr. John Evenden, chief constable,
and the unfortunate death of one "Hangman Thompson," who,
being recognised at the diggings by some of his old prison mates,
was dragged to pieces with bullocks. At these tales we laughed and
shuddered by turns; but no expression of merriment or of disgust
moved our stolid crew. They did not seem to listen, or, listening,
did not appear to heed. We free men talked in the presence of
these prisoners as if they had been dogs. "You bathe in sight of
your slaves," said someone to the Empress Theodora. "Well, they
are but slaves," was the reply. When we landed at Ralph's Bay,
waiting for our cart to jog towards Kangaroo Point, I said to Cool,
busy in distributing tobacco to the boat's crew, "What do you think
of it?" Cool looked at the prisoners, at the sea, at the sky, and at
Hacker. "I respect the power of the press," said he; "have a
touch of rum." "See," said I, reversing the flask, "it is empty!"
"Ay, only the smell of it left, your honour!" said a prisoner,
breaking silence for the first time.

\* \* \* \* \* \*

This exclamation of our prisoner's—rude, but true—is, in fact,
an admirable summing up of the convict system. When, safely
seated after supper in the comfortable coffee-room of the "Ark," we
began to compare ideas and impressions of our recent experiences,
the remark of the convict oarsman recurred to me again and again.
The frightful blunder had become a thing of the past—the victims of
it were dead or insane. Everybody admitted that "mistakes had
been made in the old times," and begged that the loathly corpse of
this dead wickedness, called "Transportation," might be comfortably
buried away and ignored of men and journalists. But "the smell of
it" remained—remains. Cripples, self-maimed, lest worse might
have befallen them, walk the streets of Hobart Town. In out-
of-the-way corners, in shepherds' huts or roadside taverns, one
meets "old hands" who relate terrible and true histories. In the
folio reports of the House of Commons can be read statements
which make one turn sick with disgust, and flush hot with indignation. Officialdom, with its crew of parasites and lickspittles, may
try to palliate the enormities committed in the years gone by;
may revile, with such powers of abuse as are given to it, the writers
who record the facts which it blushes for. But the sad, grim
truth remains. For half a century the law allowed the vagabonds

www.ingramcontent.com/pod-product-compliance
Lightning Source LLC
Chambersburg PA
CBHW021836230426
43669CB00008B/987